HARVARD STUDIES IN URBAN HISTORY

SERIES EDITORS   Stephan Thernstrom
                      Charles Tilly

THE INDUSTRIAL REVOLUTION IN LYNN

CAMBRIDGE, MASSACHUSETTS LONDON, ENGLAND

CLASS AND COMMUNITY

ALAN DAWLEY

HARVARD UNIVERSITY PRESS   1976

Frontispiece: Strike Demonstration of Men and Women Shoemakers in Lynn on March 7, 1860. *Culver Pictures, Inc.*

Library of Congress Cataloging in Publication Data
Dawley, Alan, 1943–
  Class and community.

  (Harvard studies in urban history)
  Bibliography: p.
  Includes index.
    1. Shoemakers—Lynn, Mass. 2. Social classes—Lynn, Mass. 3. Boots and shoes—Trade and manufacture—Lynn, Mass. I. Title. II. Series.
  HD8039.B72U618   331'.045'3097445   75–29049
  ISBN 0–674–13390–0

FOR THE LYNN SHOEMAKERS

ACKNOWLEDGMENTS

Without the early involvement of Katy Dawley this project probably would not have been conceived; she also made important contributions to the planning and execution of the statistical study of shoemaker mobility. Steve Watt contributed his programming skills and labor time, without which computer techniques would have been inaccessible. Oscar Handlin's thorough critical reading of the first version of the manuscript caused me to make substantial changes in both style and content that considerably improved the work at numerous points throughout the text. David Montgomery confirmed his reputation as an unusually astute and generous historian by giving an earlier version of the manuscript such a searching reading that it seemed well worth the effort to push on to completion. Edwin Moser's example of intellectual and moral courage raised the level of critical historical analysis. Others who read sections of the manuscript or offered valuable suggestions also have my gratitude.

The staffs of the Harvard and Trenton State College libraries and the Massachusetts State Archives were very helpful in facilitating access to certain materials. Katherine Little of the Lynn Public Library assisted with essential sources, and Harold Walker and others at the Lynn Historical Society not only made available the Society's invaluable collection but also made convivial company during my research visits there.

Finally, this study has benefited immeasurably from the work of Paul Faler.[1] A creative labor historian and a sympathetic student of the Lynn shoemakers, his research and writing on the culture of working people during the Industrial Revolution have set a standard I have tried to emulate. From our first conversations to our recent collaboration on a joint article, his insights into the cultural values and beliefs of Lynn workers invariably deepened my understanding and broadened the scope of my own inquiry. The result that appears here is a truer picture of historical reality than would have emerged if he and I had not hit upon the subject at the same time.

Alan Dawley

CONTENTS

TABLES

CLASS AND COMMUNITY
THE INDUSTRIAL REVOLUTION IN LYNN

INTRODUCTION
A MICROCOSM OF THE
INDUSTRIAL REVOLUTION

This book is about the shoemakers of Lynn, Massachusetts, and their search for social equality. The author has attempted to recapture their world by an effort of the imagination that took him into the homes they lived in, the factories they worked in, and the city streets in which they marched and protested. Like the peoples of all times and places, they yearned for both security and adventure, needed both independence and dependence on others, and tried as best they could to fulfill their images of manhood and womanhood. But they also had a distinctive concern that set them off from people of other eras, a special goal they would have called "equal rights."

They defined equal rights according to their interests in society: a general elevation in the moral and material condition of labor and an equalization of the upper and lower ranks of the social order. This definition also set them apart from others of the same period who pursued their own versions of equality—Women's Rights advocates, Abolitionists, and antimonopoly entrepreneurs. The issue of equality confronted all sectors of American society, and apart from its reactionary opponents—commercial nabobs of the Northeast and planter aristocrats of the Southeast—most groups embraced some form of the idea. Because it was so pervasive, the "Age of Egalitarianism" has become a favorite label among historians; however, the label blots out the vital differences in the definitions of equality and obscures the social conflicts behind the differences. To a frontier planter or farmer, equality meant free access to land. To the rising entrepreneur, it meant open competition in the race for wealth. But to the worker, whose central interests were bound up with wage payments—not property, ownership, or capital accumulation—equality did not mean an opportunity to win a fortune but a chance to live in comfort and dignity.

To capture the meaning the labor movement imparted to the idea of equality, and to become familiar with the main theme of the chapters to come, we might imagine ourselves in Lynn, Massachusetts, in the spring of 1844 at a meeting of the Journeymen Cordwainer's Society. Apart from resolutions, speechmaking, and votes, there is musical entertainment, and one song seems to have a special appeal to the audience:

> Now EQUAL RIGHTS the motto,
> *Wax* your *threads* as true *souls* ought to;
> Though the run-*round* bosses *bristle,*
> We'll raise a *peg* and let them *whistle.*
> *Stick* to the *last,* brave cordwainers!
> In the *end* you'll *awl* be gainers![1]

Such rollicking evening entertainment in the mold of music hall comedy was good for their souls because it lightened the drudgery of the day's toil and enlivened their complaints about the boss. With hearts warmed and spirits uplifted, cordwainers left the meeting feeling that manual laborers were the true lords of creation and the equals of any person on earth.

A person who feels this way is not likely to take economic oppressions or offences to dignity lying down, and, accordingly, when shoemakers were subjected to several years of unrelieved hardship in the 1850s, they responded by organizing the greatest strike in American history before the Civil War. During the strike of 1860 a Lynn poet wrote the "Cordwainers' Song," calling upon strikers to "stand for your rights" in the face of police and militia mobilized to break their spirit.

> The workman is worthy his hire,
> No tyrant shall hold us in thrall;
> They may order their soldiers to fire,
> But we'll stick to the hammer and awl.[2]

Only fiercely independent individuals would defy authority in this manner, daring would-be tyrants to make them into martyrs. A third of the strikers were women, indicating that resistance to tyranny and the willingness to risk martyrdom were not male virtues alone.

The tradition of Equal Rights passed over the great historical divides of the century—Civil War and Industrial Revolution—and arrived intact in the Gilded Age. The folkways of antebellum, pre-industrial communities survived long enough to give birth to new versions of the old refrain, as in this anthem of high-spirited defiance popular in the 1880s:

> Storm the fort, ye Knights of Labor,
> Battle for your cause;
> Equal rights to every neighbor,
> Down with tyrant laws.[3]

In the half-dozen decades before the twisting passageways of time absorbed the last echoes of this refrain, Equal Rights had become a powerful mode of action and belief. Each new generation between 1830 and 1890 recreated the legacy of the previous generation, making the past available to the future in a cohesive form, and thereby transforming the everyday experience of "one damn thing after another" into a living historical tradition.

However, history does not afford the luxury of writing about equality as if *in*equality did not exist. It may be reasonable to argue that the average white man had it better in preindustrial America than in Europe, but to conclude that the American social order was, therefore, egalitarian is to engage in the kind of self-serving myth-making that privileged interests habitually perform. Myths about equality have always overblown its true extent and have always over-looked the larger context of inequality. But the context is just as important: white workingmen won equal political rights by assuming the position of a privileged caste vis-à-vis black workingmen; the pioneer's frontier of free land was the Indian's virtual extinction; the businessman's equality of opportunity for success was the misfortune of failure for his fallen competitors; the factory owner's grand estate was the misery of the operatives. In this setting, shoemakers' songs about equality were but the substance of things hoped for and the evidence of things unseen.

If inequality is taken seriously, then a class analysis of its causal foundations also merits serious consideration. Because of the intimate connection between class analysis and political radicalism, it has not always been possible, and apparently in certain circles will never be possible, to get an open hearing on this method of inquiry. Unfortunately, each generation of American scholars has to waste considerable energy working its way back to the points of valid insight originally propounded by Marx, when they should be standing on those insights as vantage points from which to view other matters. In the last decade, the pathway to the vantage points has been widened considerably by the work of such scholars as William A. Williams, C. Wright Mills, Eugene Genovese, Barrington Moore, and David Montgomery.[4]

The concept of class is the analytical foundation of the present work. It appears in the following pages in the form of basic questions about the nature of social relations in the Industrial Revolution. Who owns what? Who is in charge of production? Who receives the fruits of industrialization? What are the links between economic and political power? What is the interplay between cultural values and the social hierarchy? These questions assume an underlying unity in the study of economics, politics, society, and culture, an assumption of considerable utility to the study of industrialization, because its character was revolutionary and its origin lay in the simultaneous occurrence of sweeping changes in all spheres of life.

If it is to be effective, class analysis must provide an accurate explanatory framework for subduing the chaos of individual experience and making it intelligible as the social experience of groups of people over time. As E. P. Thompson reminds us, if we stop history at any particular moment, there is no social context at all, only a multitude of unconnected individuals. But as soon as individuals acquire a past and a future, it becomes clear from the recurrent patterns in their relationships that they interact through group processes.[5] Therefore, a strong attraction of class analysis is its capacity to encompass such a rich variety of materials from such a broad range of human experiences—social, economic, political, and cultural. If the various materials are thought of as the flakes of brightly colored stone in the barrel of a kaleidoscope, then class relations are the mirrors that impart patterns to the stone flakes. The task of the researcher is to joint the kaliedoscope at the light and gaze at the brilliant display within.

No event in history has had a more massive impact than the Industrial Revolution. Like the upward thrust of a mountain range, it formed a great continental divide across the streams of history, causing the past and the future to flow away from one another down the opposite slopes. In the process, existing class systems (master/ slave) were cut off from the future, and new class systems (wage worker/industrial capitalist) emerged from the steep slopes of the peaks that faced forward. Old forms of inequality (master and servant) were destroyed, and new forms (employer and employee) were created. Old institutions, like the producer's household and the guilds, were eliminated as the new institutions of factory and trade union took their places. The sexes came into new relations as women left the hearthside to take jobs outside the home. New communities were founded which gathered together people from all parts of the globe.

To explore these generalizations about the Industrial Revolution at close range, one must take up the study of particular industries. For economists, sociologists, and historians interested in the factory system, the textile industry has often served this purpose, and other investigations are yet to be made of such industries as garment making, meat-packing, farm implements, and iron fabrication that converted from household to factory organization.[6] The present work focuses on the shoe industry, a field well suited to serve as a case study of the industrialization process, because its history during the century and a half after 1750 reproduced on a smaller scale the major developments of the Industrial Revolution. Originally an artisan occupation carried on in a multitude of single households, shoemaking became increasingly oriented toward the impersonal marketplace in the late eighteenth century as merchants arranged to have ever larger lots of shoes made for wholesale trade. Beginning in the second decade of the nineteenth century, merchants embarked on a course that would transform them into manufacturers and would replace merchant capitalism with industrial capitalism. The climax of this transformation was the shoe factory, which came to the industry during the Civil War. The reader will find these events related in detail in the chapters on "Entrepreneurs" and "Factories."

Because the shoe industry was a model of industrialization, it attracted the attention of an important American economist and dean of labor studies in this country, John Commons, a seminal scholar who was to labor history what Frederick Jackson Turner was to the history of the farmer. Through a multivolume history, another multivolume compendium of documents, and the writings of his students, Commons dominated the field for almost a half century. He worked out many of his major themes in a long article published in 1906, and still influential today, which described a series of evolutionary stages in the development of the shoe industry in the United States.[7] The enduring contribution of the article was its convincing demonstration that capitalism had thoroughly undermined the position of the skilled artisan several decades before the factory system. For other matters, however, it can no longer be taken as a useful point of departure. Commons' contention that the labor movement in the industry was a hopeless rearguard action of nonfactory workers trying to fend off the effects of industrialization will not stand the test of quantitative analysis. As will be shown in the chapters on "Workers" and "Militants," most of the men and women who organized the Knights and Daughters of St. Crispin were modern industrial workers fighting for both social reform and improved wages and conditions.

More than a purely economic institution, the factory had a decisive impact on the overall shape of class relations in industrial society. The equations of class power were written into the deeds that conferred proprietary rights on the owner and gave the wage earner nothing but the right to sell his labor at the prevailing rate. Both owner and worker, of course, enjoyed freedom of contract, but one told the other when to start and stop work, when to eat his lunch, and when he was out of a job, leaving little doubt about who enjoyed more freedom after the contract was made. When the owner entered the factory he heard the busy hum of machinery, saw the swift, smooth flow of production, and felt a satisfaction akin to a magistrate in a well-regulated commonwealth. When the worker entered, he braced himself against mayhem, heard the cacophony of clattering machinery, saw only the same small segments of the finished product he had seen the day before, and felt a sense of order akin to a man being put behind bars.

When owner and worker left the factory in the evening, one walked home to a bungalow or boardinghouse, while the other climbed into a horsecarriage to be driven to his fine stone house in another part of town. One had a neighbor who had a niece who worked as a chambermaid in the home of the other. One sat down to a supper of cornbread and fish soup, while the other dined on roast lamb, rare wine, and rich pastries. One pinched pennies when he made rare purchases of clothing or home furnishings, while the other pinched five-hundred-dollar notes from the bank. Since both lived in a society where money talked, the one who had a tenth or a twentieth of the other's income talked softer and lived at a level so far below the other's that he could scarcely afford to buy the very shoes he manufactured. The unequal distribution of income, a fact resulting not from supply and demand but ultimately from the difference between owners and nonowners, assured both parties that the effects of class would follow them home at night. This subject is pursued in the chapter on "The Poor and the Less Poor."

The fact of unequal income is obvious to observers of living standards in nineteenth-century cities. Much more difficult to trace are the twisting paths that led from the factory to the cultural values, political opinions, and the organizational activities of these two classes. Just because wage earners and their employers stood firmly opposed to one another on certain ethical questions and perceived a fundamental conflict of interest in the wage bargain, it does not mean the two groups never voted for the same candidates and always regarded each other as enemies. How best to explore these pathways from the workplace to other parts of the community is a problem in itself. The study of an entire industry might lead to an overemphasis on purely economic matters, while studies of one group, one event, or one period of history present obvious limitations for someone concerned to discover the broad interrelations among groups, events, and historical epochs. One highly suitable solution is a community study. The method of community studies was developed by field researchers in anthropology and sociology and has been applied successfully by historians often enough to warrant continued attention. To be successful a community study must avoid an antiquarian preoccupation with purely local details and must strive instead to establish a larger context that, in the words of Herbert Gutman, "permits the careful examination of grand and sweeping hypotheses."[8]

The community chosen to be the subject of this investigation is Lynn, Massachusetts. Because it was once a slow-paced, agricultural village nestled along the New England coastline, and because it went through a dynamic period of growth and transformation that made it a factory city, Lynn was an ideal representative of the larger shift in America from an agricultural to an industrial way of life. Moreover, Lynn's part in revolutionizing the production of shoes was crucial: it was the first to manufacture large numbers of wholesale shoes, was usually ahead of its nearest rival, Philadelphia, as the world's largest producer of ladies shoes, and was the first to adopt the sewing machine and the factory system on a large scale. Lynn was, of course, unique as any community is unique, and it was unusual as any leader is unusual, but because it was the leader in one of the leading industries in the United States, it exemplified the larger processes of American economic development. It was, in short, a microcosm of the Industrial Revolution.

Throughout most of its history, Lynn was a burning coal of discontent. Although most of its fire is gone today—having been smothered by the decline of the shoe industry, the long-term depression common to the mill towns of New England, and the city's gradual absorption into the Boston metropolis—it was once the home of hosts of uplifters and reformers, including Quaker and Methodist dissenters, Garrisonian abolitionists (indeed, Garrison himself was briefly a resident cordwainer), temperance advocates, Free Soil organizers, militant electrical workers, and five generations of protesting shoeworkers. In the nineteenth century the community was notorious as a hotbed of radicalism. Observers agreed, whether friendly or not, "There is within its limits more radicalism, more genuine, unadulterated, red republicanism than could be found in any other place of the same size in our Commonwealth."[9]

Frederick Douglass thought the reputation well deserved. At a time when the railroads of the nation operated segregated passenger cars, Douglass, who lived in Lynn for a time, bought a first-class ticket in the Lynn depot and took a seat in the car reserved for whites. When the conductors came to eject him, Douglass held tight to his seat, and in the ensuing scuffle, the seat, along with two or three others, was torn away from its mountings. For this show of strength against racism, the railroad management decreed that trains would no longer stop in Lynn. However, as Douglass fondly recalled, "the people of Lynn stood bravely by me and denounced the railroad management in emphatic terms."[10] Eventually, the trains resumed their normal schedule, and Douglass had his way.

This same uncomprising temper infused all segments of the community and all ranks in its leading industry. Whatever the cause shoemakers, manufacturers, or shopkeepers pursued, they were sure to do it with great ardor, issuing vehement manifestoes against the status quo. This prompted one action-minded abolitionist to conclude that "radicalism went with the smell of leather."[11] But there was a point in the meaning of the term "radicalism" beyond which certain members of the community could not go. As the men with capital to invest took full command of production and took the lion's share of the bounty of distribution, they became bulwarks of the new status quo themselves. A shoe manufacturer could be radical on the question of slavery, but could scarcely be radical on questions of the rights of ownership, unionism, the use of police in strikes, or the distribution of wealth. Thus in the course of the Industrial Revolution, radicalism came to mean democratic opposition to the pervasive inequalities resulting from industrial capitalism, and it passed into the hands of the labor movement.

This brings us back to Equal Rights. Among the men and women who stitched and sewed leather or cloth, cut and shaped stone, poured and molded iron, or sawed and chiseled wood, nothing was more sacred than the prinicple, "He who does not work, neither shall he eat." This first axiom of labor actually had two possible interpretations. It could mean simply that anybody who put in some time on the job was entitled to receive at least a living wage, never mind the fact that a few owners and managers received stupendous incomes. But it also implied the more radical meaning that anyone who lived well off the labor of others who lived poorly was a vile social parasite whose privileged status derived not from moral right but from economic might. According to the tenets of Equal Rights, this was monopoly, whether it was supported by a public charter of incorporation from the state or not. And if those who labored with hands, backs, and brains wished to break the power of monopoly, they had to organize economically and politically. (Accounts of efforts along these lines follow in the chapters on "Artisans," "Militants," and "Politicians.") But at this point a trap was sprung on Equal Rights: seeking a way out through fair wages and honest elections, it found itself boxed in. Instead of opposing the status quo, it became its captive. Therefore, in the last decade of the nineteenth century, workers who saw pure-and-simple trade unions and the two main political parties as blind alleys reassessed their position. They decided to slough off the philosophy of Equal Rights and turned instead to socialism, the brand of radicalism most relevant to industrial society.

1

ENTREPRENEURS

The western world saw the United States of America in the eighteenth century as a place only slightly removed from the aboriginal state of nature. Europeans debated whether this environment produced degeneracy or enlightenment, but both sides in the debate agreed that America lay on the outer fringes of traditional civilization. A leading protagonist, J. Hector St. John de Crevecoeur, put forth this notion in one of his celebrated *Letters from an American Farmer*. "Europe contain hardly any other distinctions but Lords and tenants; this fair country alone is settled by freeholders, the possessors of the soil they cultivate, members of the government they obey, and the framers of their own laws, by means of their representatives."[1] The freeholder image was the common European stereotype of Americans; it dominates the most influential statement ever published on American character, de Tocqueville's *Democracy in America*. It was fashioned out of a comparison to the Old World by critics of the ancien régime, who deliberately distorted New World reality in order to make the Old look bad.

In reality, freeholders were not as numerous as the stereotype suggested. For every five freeholders, there were five adult males that fit some other description: two were slaves, two more were either servants or tenant farmers, and one held an urban occupation in trade or manufacturing.[2] The independent yeoman farmer occupied an important place in this roster, but he did not overwhelm the others. Indeed, he was crowded by those whose ties with the marketplace were stronger than their ties with the soil. In the cities, merchants, mariners, and manufacturers depended entirely on the flow of commerce, and in the countryside, many of the freeholders were market producers rather than the sturdy, self-sufficient proprietors of legend. Wheat farmers in Pennsylvania, owners of timber stands in New England, and planters in the South were all busy supplying the cities of Europe with the products of American soil. The New World was not so detached from the Old as the patrons of the yeoman liked to imagine.

The Market

The main link between the New World and the Old was the British trading empire. England was the vortex of a worldwide whirlpool of trade that sucked in raw materials from Eastern Europe, India, the Caribbean, and North and South America. The storied enterprise of the nation of shopkeepers, the mercantilist policies of Crown and Parliament, and the imperial conquests of the seventeenth and eighteenth centuries started the pool whirling. The onset of the Industrial Revolution multiplied the speed with which both older products— sugar, tea, and wheat—and newer products—cotton—flowed into the country to feed the growing urban population and to satisfy the cravings of industrial machinery. By 1800 England was well on its way toward becoming the fabled workshop of the world.[3]

England's progress was an obstacle to industrial devevolpment in the colonies. Basic goods like ironware and cloth were produced more cheaply in England, and, on top of this, Parliament superimposed a set of laws designed to thwart the rise of industry in its colonial possessions. Given the abundance of land in North America, labor and capital resources tended to wind up in agricultural production anyway. he obstacles encountered by early American ventures in manufacturing were illustrated by the Saugus Iron Works, a Massachusetts enterprise that produced small quantities of iron from the 1640s to the 1680s, but which never grew large enough to meet local needs and never turned a profit for the investors. The failure stemmed from the difficulty of finding skilled ironworkers, the conflict over land use with surrounding farmers, and the reluctance of the investors to recommit large sums of capital.[4]

Yet where the Saugus works failed, numerous other ventures in iron refining succeeded in overcoming the general obstacles to industrial development. At the time of the Revolution there were actually more facilities for producing iron in the colonies than in the metropolitan country. Likewise, one-third of the ships in the British merchant fleet had been constructed at dockworks in the colonies. And with the launching of the new Federal Constitution, shoes manufactured in the United States took a comfortable lead over English imports. Thus when Alexander Hamilton filed his famous report on manufactures in 1791, he pointed to these three industries as models of successful industrial development. The time when the United States replaced England as the world's industrial vortex was still more than a century in the future, but within the realm of agrarian America at the end of the eighteenth century there were significant outposts of industrial enterprise.[5]

Even rural America was home to capitalist business methods and to a modern bourgeois mentality. Much of the best arable land in the country was used to grow money, in the form of cash crops like tobacco; every state had a significant group of land speculators; and the yeomen farmers themselves were buying land in order to sell it at a profit. The larger commercial centers supported the leading businessmen of the age—full-time, sea-going merchants—plus a number of shopkeepers and other residents with small investments in shipping. The merchants and the commercial growers were the most dynamic groups in the economy; they filled the American environment with the things European middle classes still had to fight for: careers open to talent; individual civil and political liberties; fee simple land tenure; private enterprise. The classic analysis of this society was made by James Madison in *The Federalist*. He lauded the new Constitution as the frame of government which would best secure the general rights of property against the claims of people without property and against the competing demands of particular interests. "A landed interest, a manufacturing interest, a mercantile interest, a moneyed interest, with many lesser interests, grow up of necessity in civilized nations, and divide them into different classes, actuated by different sentiments and views. The regulation of these various and interfering interests forms the principal task of modern legislation, and involves the spirit of party and faction in the necessary and ordinary operations of the government."[6]

The preoccupation with economics was characteristic of the age of mercantilism, but America's backwardness added a special concern for material progress. Paradoxically, the wilderness environment opened the way for the most advanced techniques and the most modern attitudes. Labor and capital scarcity prevented full-scale industrialization until the late nineteenth century, but perhaps more than any other country including England, the United States was enmeshed in the capitalist relations of the marketplace and imbued with the acquisitive capitalist spirit.

This was the sea on which shoe manufacturing was launched, and it is time to trace the progress of the industry itself. The growth of the shoe industry was directly tied to the emergence of the new nation. Like a rowboat in tow behind a large sailing vessel, manufacturing surged ahead with every plunge the nation took toward independence. The colonial nonimportation agreements of the 1760s cut back the flow of imports from England and made the purchase of domestic goods a patriotic act. Retaliation against the unpopular Sugar and Stamp acts was expressed in terms of a rising demand for American-made shoes, and this was reflected in the rising output of Lynn's workshops. Before 1760 the town probably turned out only a few thousand pairs each year, whereas the town of less than 2000 people made 80,000 pairs in 1768.[7] Manufacturing in Lynn was also stimulated by the commercial dislocations of the War of Independence, and at the end of that conflict the manufacture of shoes had become the foundation of the town's economy. Thus the town was severely hit by the postwar depression when British and French imports glutted the east coast markets. According to one view, "The trade at Lynn was languishing and the most energetic were disheartened." The hardship engendered made it appear to another observer that the residents "were in an almost starving condition."[8]

To set the economy on an independent course, Americans sought tariff protection against British imports. There was state action in the mid-1780s, when Massachusetts enacted a broad tariff that included protection for shoes,[9] and more effective help arrived with the new Federal government. The architect of the Federal tariff policy was James Madison, and he put into practice what he preached in *The Federalist*. In 1789 he led a tariff bill through Congress aimed at promoting domestic industries. Before its passage, two Quaker merchants living in Philadelphia (though they were natives of Lynn and traded in Lynn shoes) held a dinner party for Madison and several

other congressmen at which they aired arguments in favor of protection. Boots and shoes emerged on the protected list in 1789, and
successive revisions of the duties pushed the rate up to about 20
percent of the price of shoes in 1794.[10]

The tariffs had a significant effect in reducing existing import competition and in preserving the future American market for domestic
firms. After the first Federal levies, Lynn's output rose in spectacular
fashion. George Washington visited Lynn on his journey through
New England in 1789 and jotted down in his diary that 175,000
pairs of shoes were made there. Seven years later another illustrious
visitor passed through the town, the Duc de La Rochefoucauld, and
he recorded 400,000 pairs.[11] Trench Coxe, an assistant secretary of
the Treasury under Hamilton, who assisted his superior in preparing
the report on manufactures, published his own *View of the United
States of America in 1794*. To counter arguments that the United
States would have to depend on British imports for her manufactured
goods, Coxe cited the shoe industry as proof that manufacturing
could be profitable in America. To drive home his point, he calculated that the value of shoes used in one year, nearly all of which
were fabricated domestically, was greater than the total expenditures
of the federal and state governments combined. He singled out Lynn
for special notice, praising the work there as "very expert."[12] Philadelphia merchants and Lynn craftsmen alike relied on the tariff to
protect their interests.

Most of the shoes made in the country at this time, however, were
not produced for the market but for individual customers. In rural
areas, itinerant shoemakers would go from farm to farm, stopping
for a few days to outfit the entire family. Small towns usually had a
shoemaker or two, and the larger population centers supported a
larger number. Nonetheless, shoemaking was being drawn more and
more deeply into the commercial market. Newspaper ads attest to
the existence of such a market for imported shoes, especially women's
wear, prior to the 1760s. Lynn broke into this market with women's
shoes that were a cut below luxury items and a cut above rough-
hewn, everyday footwear. Two Lynn historians reported that "working women . . . throughout the country had a pair of 'Lynn shoes'
for Sunday."[13] As time progressed, Lynn entrepreneurs deepened

the market by taking over the demand for everyday wear as well, thus pushing aside the independent shoemakers. The coming triumph of market manufacturing over custom shoemaking was clearly signaled by 1800, when Lynn itself was producing one pair of shoes for every five potential customers in the entire country.[14] The image of America as a land of self-sufficient yeomen and independent artisans living close to nature cherished by some eighteenth-century contemporaries and glorified by nineteenth-century Jacksonians was a mask covering the bourgeois character of the era. In much of its agriculture, in its commerce, in its land transactions, and, finally, in its growing manufacturing, America was the world's leading example of a society based on the ideals and practices of the marketplace.

The Master

Taking the highway from Boston to Salem, the eighteenth-century traveler saw little outward evidence of the presence of the market in Lynn. Perhaps a few fishing craft and a small sloop or two were anchored in the estuary of the Saugus River, and, out of sight from the highway, other sea-roughened rowboats dotted the shore as it arched eastward toward Marblehead. Continuing past the salt marshes near the river, the traveler followed the highway near the foot of rocky, inland hills and arrived at the western end of the town commons, where he was greeted by a cluster of little shops that looked as much like dwelling houses as hardware or food stores. Here and in the eastern end of town were some two dozen retail stores, blacksmith shops, and gristmills, humble outposts of trade and manufacturing. Houses and barns were scattered along the numerous lanes that ran helter-skelter across the western coastal plain and into the hilly sections inland and to the east. Cows grazed lazily in the larger fields, plow horses stood stolidly in the barns, and pigs were mired in yard pens. Few of the several hundred households were without one of these animals, and the number of beasts was larger than the human population.[15]

This was the town that received George Washington in the fall of 1789 on his grand tour of New England. Washington was fresh from Boston, where he had been regaled with a sumptuous parade in which the leading ranks of the Commonwealth lined up in order of eminence to pass his review. In the front rows were the military, town and state officers, professional men, merchants, traders, and sea captains. These were followed by rows of craftsmen, with sailors bringing up the rear.[16] What did Lynn have to match this display? No officialdom and no military orders; no lawyers or newspaper editors; no sea captains, international merchants, or sailors. Instead, Lynn had a few petty shopkeepers and a contingent of artisans, but otherwise it began where Boston's parade left off, among farmers and people who combined farming with shoemaking. From its outward appearance, Washington might have mistaken Lynn for any of the hundreds of other rural communities in New England and the Middle Atlantic states.

Yet there was one distinctive feature in Lynn's landscape that set it off from the other towns. That was a rash of little wooden outbuildings that stood close by every second or third dwelling. Larger than privies, smaller than barns, these were the workshops of the shoe industry. Accommmodating name to size, they were called "ten-footers," and to the travelers they were curiosity shops. One traveler who visited a few years ahead of Washington was Simeon Baldwin, a future Connecticut jurist and congressman, but a mere tutor at Yale when he wrote in his diary that he had "dined among the rocks and shoemaker shops of Lynn—went into one of the shops (of which there are 150) to see ye manufactory."[17] Ducking his head and squeezing inside the cramped quarters, Baldwin probably would have seen three men straddling low benches that served as worktables. Two of them were likely to be journeymen, who owned their own "kit" of awls, knives, and hammers, and the third, a master shoemaker, who owned the leather and also "ye manufactory," the ground it occupied, and a nearby house.

All of these elements in the production of shoes—masters, journeymen, ten-footers, tools of the trade, real property—were fused together in the household. As the basic unit of production, the household was also the basic link between the economy and the social structure of the community. To be the head of a household was to be an overseer of a small work team, to exercise moral and spiritual authority, and to represent the group as a taxpayer and voter to the community at large. In the master shoemaker's household the work team normally included nonrelated journeymen and apprentices, plus wives, daughters, and sons. By the end of the eighteenth century, women had completely taken over the branch of shoemaking called binding, in which the upper parts of the shoe were stitched together. Thus the household brought together children and apprentices assisting on minor tasks, women binding the uppers, and journeymen and masters cutting out the pieces of leather, tacking uppers and soles to a last, and sewing the uppers and soles together. It was common, therefore, for a half-dozen people or more to work under the direction of a single master.

The authority of the householder in production supplanted the authority of the guild. European immigrants to America abandoned forms of guild regulation soon after settling in the New World, despite the fact that in England, at any rate, shoemaking was one craft that maintained the old forms while other trades were taken over by merchants and converted to a putting-out basis. German shoemakers who settled at Philadelphia and built a thriving shoe trade there also chose not to reconstitute the traditional guild. There were short-lived attempts at public regulation in the seventeenth century, but such efforts soon were abandoned, and instead the household became a self-regulating mechanism.[18] Headship was determined by sex, marriage, and property ownership, meaning that a new unit was established when a man who owned property got married. Should he possess the requisite skill, the man who became the head was entitled to master status. The master's supervision was exercised through intertwining chains of command that combined the sex roles of husband and father with the economic role of property owner. As a husband and father, the master superintended his wife and children; as the owner of a workshop and raw materials, he set the tasks for the journeymen. In regard to dependent apprentices, the master's paternal and property authority were indistinguishable, and journeymen, too, especially those that boarded with the master, were subject to both forms of authority. Thus the organization of production under personal hierarchies in independent units tended to prevent the formation of solidarities among journeymen, among lady shoemakers, or among masters. Even though masters "hired" journeymen and were in some sense their employers, the conflict between employers and employees over the wage payment was barely perceptible, masked not only by the personal bond between master and journeyman but also by the common payment of wages in kind—clothing, firewood, room, and board.

Eighteenth-century account books reveal the features of these relationships. One master's accounts show he did custom work for his neighbors and entered charges in his books beside the names of individual customers. He also hired several journeymen to produce for unknown customers in some distant region. Another master hired a twenty-three-year-old journeyman named Nathaniel Tarbox, who moved into the master's house and soon thereafter married the boss's daughter Abigail. The year of his marriage was the year of the first battle of the Revolution, and Tarbox fought at Concord with his local militia company. During the years of the War of Independence, he continued to make shoes for his father-in-law, and on at least one occasion Abigail was paid by her father for binding. After the war he became a master, selling his products to local shopkeepers and to at least one distant retailer in Portsmouth, New Hampshire.[19]

Small masters like Nathaniel Tarbox flourished from the 1760s to the end of the century. Their mentor was a Welsh immigrant named John Adam Dagyr, regarded by local historians as the man who put shoemaking on a sure footing. He came to Lynn in 1750, when there were but three master shoemakers who employed journeymen, and began to initiate artisans and farmers in the mysteries of the craft. A half century later, the number of masters stood at 200.[20] Reflecting the fact that they purchased raw materials, owned the basic implements of production, and sold finished products, they were commonly called "manufacturers." Reflecting the fact that they did manual labor, they were called "mechanics." Sometimes they sold to Lynn shopkeepers who resold elsewhere, but they also made direct contact with retailers and consignment merchants, as in this description: "There were many who wrought their own stock and employed two or three journeymen and an apprentice or two. It was customary with some of the smaller manufacturers to trudge off to Boston with their bags on their shoulders, when they had made up a sufficient number of pairs to 'pay the way.' But sometimes neighbors would join forces and take a horse."[21] This practice developed in other towns as well, that became shoe manufacturing satellites around Boston. In the course of a long day a "bag boss" from Weymouth, Abington, or Lynn could walk or ride into Boston, hunt about for someone to take his goods, purchase raw materials, and return home late the same night. For Lynn masters, the trip to Salem was even shorter, and records from Salem in the 1790s showed that shoes consigned by shoemakers were frequently in cargoes clearing the port.[22]

Ambiguities abounded in the master's position. Like the merchant, he bought and sold, but, unlike the merchant, he used what he bought to make what he sold. Like the nineteenth-century manufacturer, he hired labor to make his products, but as an eighteenth-century "manufacturer," he and his family worked right alongside the people he hired. In sum, the master was *in* the marketplace, but he was not *of* it.

The Shopkeeper

The ten-footers were special monuments to Lynn's particular enterprise. Less numerous, but more commonplace, were the community's retail shops. Among the typical small-town complement of grocers, apothecaries, dry goods dealers, bakers, and undertakers were several shopkeepers who had a hand in the shoe trade. During the 1760s, shopkeepers began to include barrels of shoes in their daily round of shipping and receiving, thus opening new outlets for the town's special product through the colonial enterpôts of Salem and Boston. One such entrepreneur was Sylvanus Hussey, the owner of both a dry goods store and a twelve-acre farm. Hussey accepted the products of local shoemakers as payment for provisions, and when he had accumulated a sufficient store of their shoes, he set about finding a purchaser. In this vein he wrote to Nicholas Brown (one of the famous Browns of Providence, Rhode Island) in 1773 proposing an exchange of 100 pairs of shoes for 100 lbs. of tea.[23]

These two New Englanders operated in the context of the far-flung British trading empire, which enabled them to exchange goods made in New England with agricultural products of Asia. Shoes were just another commodity circulating in this complex network, causing no disturbance in the channels of trade. Certainly the shopkeepers who entered the new line experiencd no dislocation whatsoever. They continued to deal with the general public, supplying flour, cloth, thread, pots, and pans to shoemakers and nonshoemakers alike. Shopkeepers in other Massachusetts towns, notably Haverhill, saw the same opportunity and followed close on Lynn's heels. The role of the shopkeeper has been unfortuntely ignored in the standard history of shoemaking, *The Organization of the Boot and Shoe Industry in Massachusetts,* by Blanche Hazard. This generally reliable account describes the typical entrepreneur of this period as a "capitalist shoemaker," overlooking entirely the much more thoroughly capitalist shopkeeper. Exhibiting a restless entrepreneurial energy, and exploiting family and religious contacts, the shopkeepers ventured beyond Boston to New York, Philadelphia, Baltimore, and, before the century was out, they had ranged as far south as Savannah. They were not content to sit and wait for opportunity to knock at their door; as one observer recalled, "It was the custom for the manufacturer to travel a distance, for the purpose of soliciting orders, instead of waiting at home for the appearance of purchasers."[24]

The Lynn shopkeeper was one of a menagerie of merchandisers involved in the distribution of shoes. At the turn of the century, he shared space in the market with consignment merchants, wholesale jobbers, and retail distributors; even sea captains got into the act by loaning masters money and taking their pay in the form of shoes, which they would hawk in every port they visited. Such ambition to ferret out every possible customer was the mark of the Yankee trader, and what Richard Bushman writes of Connecticut was also true of Massachusetts, where the Puritan was losing his place to the sharp-dealing Yankee: "By 1765 the door was open for a release of the cupidity that was in time to bring him such notoriety."[25]

Ebenezer Breed was a Lynn entrepreneur who epitomized the Yankee trader. Cupidity gushed like a geyser from his Quaker soul. Born in a long line of Breeds that ran back to the original seventeenth-century settlers in Lynn, he moved to Philadelphia for his start in business. By 1792 he had formed a partnership with a Quaker shopkeeper in his native town, and while the shopkeeper acquired shoes locally, Breed visited various places in Europe and America to purchase raw materials for shoemaking and find customers for the finished products. He maintained a steady correspondence with his partner, and his letters reveal a personality whose inner state mirrored the state of the shoe business. When business was brisk, his letters exuded charm and warmth for his customers and friends, but when the market turned down, he grew irascible and abusive. In a letter from Philadelphia in 1793, he wrote about sea captains preying on the shoe trade and complained, "I can never do anything here while shoes are bought and sold in such a manner." He yearned to wipe out such competitors by cornering the entire output of Lynn's workshops, making shoes "difficult for so many hawkers to get." In another letter a short time later, he wrote about his troubles collecting debts and moaned, "I am perfectly sick of doing business in the shoe line here." He diagnosed the cause of his ailment as poor workmanship on the goods he sold on credit to Philadelphia retailers; if they could not sell a misshapen pair of shoes, he could not claim his money. "If I call for the money, they begin to show me the large number of small, unsaleable ones they have left, that they never can sell, and say I must not expect my pay, &c.&c. And what can I say to them? It is so, and so it will be, while the shoemakers in Lynn are a set of confounded fools."[26] Ebenezer Scrooge would have understood Breed's maladies.

No individual in the history of Lynn offers a more brilliant illumination of the quality of life in the American marketplace than Ebenezer Breed. The saga of Breed's rise and fall was told by Lynn's leading man of letters and town historian, Alonzo Lewis, in his *History of Lynn*. According to Lewis, young Ebenezer was quick to demonstrate his "talents, diligence, and correct deportment," all of which brought him to a position both "prosperous and influential." Breed used his influence to promote his business and his community in the nation at large. He arranged the dinner party in Philadelphia at which James Madison was persuaded to include boots and shoes on the list of protected items, and he persuaded Federal officials to locate a post office in Lynn, no doubt with an eye toward improving the handling of his own voluminous correspondence. But then, while still in the "vigor of manhood," calamity struck. Breed began a pre-cipitous decline. He abandoned business altogether, lost whatever economic security he had gained, and returned to Lynn to work as a common shoemaker. The geyser ceased to flow, as the inner energy that had supported his ambition and deportment drained away. He ceased to keep his body clean; his breath often reeked of liquor; his clothes were unkempt. And at the depth of his abasement, he became addicted to opium.[27] In his degraded condition Breed often shuffled about the streets of his community and was spurned by all but a handful who saw or knew him. Lewis wrote: "His person was gross and uncleanly; and those who met him on these excursions were compelled to pronounce him as miserable and forlorn a looking object as could well be presented to the eye of pity."[28] He lived alone for several years before retreating to the almshouse, where, still, he found no asylum as the superintendent taunted him for his habits and infirmities, and he died there in 1839.

This harmless old man was scorned and ostracized by his fellow townsmen because they were terrified that the same thing could happen to them. Perhaps at some turn near the peak of success, suddenly something within them would also snap, and all would collapse, just as Breed had given out under the weight of years of business anxiety. They feared him because he simultaneously at-tracted and repulsed them. He was the symbol of what they wanted to become—at least those with business aspirations—yet he was also the embodiment of what they strove to avoid. And they were right to see themselves in him, for as a rising entrepreneur and as a fallen outcast he represented the dual nature of American individualism: its success and its failure.

Individuals fell by the wayside, but their places were quickly taken by other eager entrepreneurs who spread the network of busi-ness contacts ever further throughout the Middle Atlantic states and the South. At the tips of the network were the final customers—wives of small planters in the Georgia upcountry, domestic slaves on the great estates of South Carolina, daughters of Baltimore carpenters and Philadelphia hatters. They normally purchased on credit at local stores, and the retailers, in turn, bought on credit from the agents and shopkeepers of Lynn. Increasingly after 1789, Lynn businessmen solicited orders for large lots of shoes—500 or 1000 pairs in a single order—and these, too, were arranged on a credit basis. Thus the marketing practices in the industry put great pressure on capital resources in Lynn, with the result that by 1804 leading citizens of the town petitioned the Massachusetts General Court for a charter of incorporation for a bank. Although the initial effort failed in the legislature, a second try in 1814 led to the establishment of the Lynn Mechanics Bank. The same people and the same pressures were behind both attempts; the 1814 petition stated that the forty-one "gentlemen" signers had interests in the manufacture of shoes and leather which were hurt by the absence of local credit facilities. They were obliged to give credit lasting from three to twelve months to buyers in the middle and southern states, but lacking large reserves of capital themselves, they had to borrow to meet their current expenses. This subjected them to considerable sacrifices because they had to "pay extensively" for the short-term loans they used to buy materials and pay their labor costs.[29]

Creating the bank was a communitywide action, not simply an expression of the private interest of a few citizens. Though the original thirteen incorporators were drawn from the town's register of prosperous merchants and landowners, and though the forty-one petitioners were styled "gentlemen," ninety residents from all walks of life also supported the new institution by their official attendance at the corporation's first meeting, and when the time came to select a name for the bank, "Lynn Mechanics" was the obvious choice.[30] This deference in reverse was a token of the ability of small-propertied masters to command the respect of the more substantial property owners. In a larger context, it reflected the persistence of the older mechanism of community integration around the property-owning household. Given household organization, no group of townspeople could consolidate instruments of power to be used against other social groups. As long as the household was the basic unit of production, class ties among journeymen were indistinct. As long as propertied artisans sold commodities and performed manual labor in a day's work, the class position of the artisan was ill-defined. And as long as the scale of production and the size of the individual firm remained small, the power of capital in the hands of the shopkeeper was held in check. Thus the origin of manufacturing under the auspices of merchant capitalism took place without major dislocations in the older social relationships that bound the community together.

The Manufacturer

The founding of the bank marked a final moment of the economic and social synthesis of the eighteenth century. After 1814 the dynamics of capitalist development broke apart the old links between household and marketplace. The search for profits drove the Yankee traders ever deeper into the realm of production, causing the emergence of groups who bought labor as a commodity and groups who sold their ability to work to the highest bidder. The half century after 1814 produced an economic transformation that eventuated in the industrial revolution based on the factory system; concurrently, it generated rising social conflict in the community, which culminated in the Great Strike of 1860.

The first incident of dislocation was the total elimination of the master from the structure of manufacturing, a process that occurred everywhere in Europe and the United States as industrialization advanced. Account books from the early nineteenth century in Lynn reveal a clear picture of the independent master in decline; more and more the accounts showed the skilled shoemakers doing contract work for the shopkeepers.[31] In losing their direct link to the market and in relinquishing ownership of the basic raw materials, the 200 shoemakers with master status in 1800 gradually ceased to operate on the old basis, and no new generation replaced them. The term "master" became an anachronism and was replaced by the universal "journeyman."

The master did not simply wither away; he was done in. The agents of the master's demise were the shopkeepers. Their weapons were the standard implements of business warfare—a wily cunning for a favorable price, personal credit with a set of business allies, the possession of wealth. The call of battle was the small talk of the marketplace heard daily in the shops of Boston, Salem, and Lynn: "I need six barrels of satinet rand shoes; at what price can thee have them made?" "I have steady employment for thirty or forty hands to make spring heel pumps." The pages of history do not echo with conversation the likes of this; the voices of these petty tradesmen could barely be heard above the reverberating phrases of Jefferson or Napoleon. But hanging on every breath was a minute turn in the wheels of social change. Each turn by itself was imperceptible, but together they worked a revolution greater than Jefferson's and produced a power more profound than Napoleon's. Virtually everyone who has lived in any part of the globe since the middle of the nineteenth century has been directly and deeply affected by industrial capitalism. So it was no small matter for the shopkeeper to hire thirty or forty people to make six barrels of shoes; week after week, month after month, the shopkeeper was extending the control of capital over industry, pushing aside the traditional limits to increased output. One of these limits was the master. His property holdings were meager collateral for loans to purchase raw materials or pay journey wages, and since everyone waited on someone else's promise to pay, credit was essential. Unable to command large amounts of credit, the master boxed up production inside the ten-footer. The shopkeepers were in a far better position; with more ample property holdings, they occupied the strategic high ground overlooking the future development of the industry. The Mechanics Bank became a mausoleum in the graveyard of the master mechanics.

The contest between the master and the shopkeeper was a Madisonian conflict of economic interest groups, and Madison's own work helped shape the outcome. The Federal Constitution and the tariff legislation of the new government created a large protected market that favored large-scale production. Masters and shopkeepers alike apparently supported the Constitution (Lynn remained Federalist until Jefferson's second term), and certainly both groups were equally enthusiastic about the tariff. But only the shopkeepers were able to convert to large-scale production and extend the market to eliminate custom made shoes and to take in new customers who appeared as population grew and spread south and west. In 1837 Lynn sold one pair of shoes for every 2.5 white females (the great bulk of the customers were white) in the United States, a considerable improvement over 1790 when the ratio stood at 1 to 10, and over 1800 when it was about 1 to 5.[32]

In financing this expansion, the shopkeepers took sole command of production, casting away the eighteenth-century system where they shared control with masters, coastal merchants, and sea captains. First, they put the most critical step in the process of making shoes —cutting the soles and uppers—directly under their control by hiring expert shoemakers to work in their shops. They also made room for finishing and packing the finished product and hired a couple more people for these tasks. They made these changes without letting go of their old lines of business, and the appearance of their shops reflected their multiple lines: "On one side of the front was the cutting of shoes and stuffs; on the other, a counter with a few dry goods. In the rear was the grocery department, and in the center, back of an entry way, was the shoe room, about six by ten feet."[33] However, the success of the new plan enabled shopkeepers to slough off their retail activities and concentrate solely on the wholesale production of shoes. They cleared out the other rooms, hired more cutters and finishers, and made their stores into "central shops," a useful term devised by Hazard. Once this was accomplished, they were no longer shopkeepers: they were manufacturers. A local newspaper offered a definition of the term "shoe manufacturer" in an 1837 article prompted by the publication of Harriet Martineau's views of Lynn in her book on society in America: ". . . a wholesale dealer, who owns an establishment, purchases the various kinds of stock, in large quantities; employs many individuals in the various branches of making and superintends the whole. This requires a considerable capital."[34]

One entrepreneur who fit this description perfectly was Micajah Pratt, a member of Lynn's robust Quaker business community. He was born in 1791 into the family of a well-to-do landowner and shoe dealer who took a leading role in establishing the Lynn Mechanics Bank. Micajah followed closely in his father's footsteps, embarking on his own shoe business in 1812 and becoming an officer in the bank within a decade. He built his fortunes on southern and western sales of cheap, strong, durable shoes, and his success enabled him to expand from a two-story, wooden, central shop into a larger brick building in 1850, worth in the neighborhood of $80,000. The building was converted to a steampowered, mechanized factory around the time of his death in 1866. For a generation prior to this, he was the largest manufacturer in town, employing as many as 500 men and women in peak seasons to make about a quarter of a million pairs annually[35] The two generations of the Pratt family embodied the evolution of industrial roles from retail shopkeeper through central shop manufacturer to factory owner. Born in the world of eighteenth-century merchant capitalism, Micajah Pratt took his father's money and principles and helped create the new world of nineteenth-century industrial capitalism.

Pratt's ability to survive two major depressions and a series of radical changes in productive organization and technique was not unique; he represented a nucleus of hardy, well-established manufacturers whose careers spanned several decades and whose business practices set the pace for the industry as a whole. Since most of them marketed a cheap grade of shoes, they exerted a general downward pressure on wages, both in the form of cash payments and in the form of orders for consumer goods at local stores. For this they were excoriated by their employees as bloodsucking beasts and tyrants grinding the face of the poor. They also took the lead in introducing new techniques of production, such as standardized patterns and sole-cutting machines.[36] Within the group of successful manufacturers was a smaller cluster of Quaker capitalists who were linked together in a complex matrix of religious, neighborhood, family, and business ties. Micajah Pratt was closely allied in business with his neighbors and coreligionists Nathan and Isaiah Breed. Together Pratt, the Breeds, and a few other Quaker businessmen took control of the Mechanics Bank in the late 1820s, and from 1830 until 1864 Micajah and Isaiah took turns in the office of president. The same allies founded the Lynn Institution for Savings in 1826 and bent the first railroad line through their section of town, rather than along the existing turnpike route further west. The location of the railroad paid off handsomely for the perspicacious Breed brothers, who owned the tract of low-lying, coastal swampland called Black Marsh Field that became the site of the main station.[37]

The rise of these maufacturers rested on their capacity to expand. "Grow or Die!" was common business wisdom of the age, as fundamental an article of faith as the law of supply and demand, or the commandment to buy cheap and sell dear. To stand still while competitors rushed by was to risk a brush with failure, and so they grew. The leading central shop in 1832 turned out ten times more shoes than the leading shopkeeper sold in 1789.[38] The size of the central shops increased accordingly; in 1837, when Nathan Breed built a new shop, "visitors flocked to see a three story building which was to be devoted to the manufacture of shoes," and in the next decade, the first of several "brick blocks" was erected. The length of the payrolls increased, too, from an average of 50-100 people for the largest firms in 1830 to an average of 300-400 in 1850.[39] Spurred by the growth of its main industry, the community swelled in size. After 1800 population doubled every twenty years, a rate considerably faster than Massachusetts and slightly faster than the United States as a whole. Lynn experienced its largest decennial increase of the century in the 1830s, when it registered a 50 percent gain, and the growth of the next decade was nearly as great.[40]

Yet in spite of this phenomenal expansion, shoemakers were not flooding the town fast enough to meet the industry's labor needs, and the manufacturers began to send out their cut stock to nearby fishing villages and more distant country hamlets. Using primitive mass production techniques, the manufacturers hired thousands of semiskilled farmers and fishermen to complete the work begun in the central shops by the highly skilled cutters. Each cycle of production included two trips for the raw materials out and back from the central shop—once to be bound by women and girls in Marblehead or Maine, and once again to be lasted and bottomed by men and boys in rural Massachusetts or New Hampshire. The amount of work thus sent out reached 60 percent or more of the total output of Lynn firms.[41] Other Massachusetts centers of shoe manufacturing, such as Haverhill and Natick, followed the same practice, with the result that from the 1830s until after the Civil War, the boot and shoe industry was the largest single industrial employer in the state, exceeding the nearest rival—textiles—by several thousand people.[42]

These labor intensive methods made the industry the most significant example of manufacturing on a domestic, or putting-out basis in American history. While carriages, cabinets, bricks, houses, and a host of other items continued to be made on the old custom basis by local artisans, and while certain other products like cloth and munitions were made by modern mass production methods, most shoes made in this period came out of a transitional mode of organization that combined both artisan and factory techniques. In New England the system resembled the pattern of old English textiles prior to the factories. In Philadelphia manufacturers did not send their stock into the surrounding countryside, but instead accomplished the same end—production of cheap, wholesale goods—through another labor intensive method, the sweat shop. Philadelphia merchants who owned the raw materials contracted with "garrett bosses," who, in turn, hired semiskilled shoemakers to do the work.[43] The exploitation of the urban poor by wholesale manufacturers was more devastating than the hiring of hard-pressed farmers, but both features of shoe manufacturing marked the increasing dominance of capitalist organization.

Increased output and increased sales were two sides of the same coin. Lynn's manufacturers regarded output and sales, production and distribution, as parts of the same economic task. They hired added workers to fill their growing orders, and they solicited additional orders to be able to hire more workers. And so they were as aggressive in pursuing new sales opportunities in the South and West as they were in scouting New England for shoemakers. Although they sold some lots to wholesale jobbers in Boston, New York, and Philadelphia, they preferred to deal directly with retail distributors and sometimes underwrote their own branch outlets in places as far away as Augusta and St. Louis. Micajah Pratt and Nathan Breed, for example, jointly supplied $1000 worth of shoes to two young residents of Lynn who had little of their own besides reputations for being "very capable, enterprising men, of undoubted integrity." The two traveled to St. Louis in 1829, where they made out well enough to open another store in Natchez, and when they returned to Lynn a few years later they each had modest fortunes to invest in real estate and banking. (One of them, George Hood, also absorbed the Jacksonian passions of the frontier and became a staunch Democrat and the first mayor when Lynn became a city in 1850.)[44]

Given the unity of purpose with which the manufacturers pursued profits, it is difficult to accept the scheme of analysis developed by

John Commons to explain changes in the organization of the shoe industry. Commons must be credited with vital, pathbreaking work in economic history, and accordingly his influence has been widespread. His view of the antebellum economy provided the conceptual foundation for George Rogers Taylor's *Transportation Revolution,* which in turn influenced more recent works, such as Lee Benson's *Concept of Jacksonian Democracy.*[45] Commons argued, first of all, that changes in the mode of production result from the "historical extension of markets." Second, production passes through a series of stages, corresponding to the extent of the market at any given time. The stages passed in America by the end of the eighteenth century were "itinerant," "custom order," and "retail." Beginning in the 1790s, increased use of natural waterways and canals introduced the "wholesale order" stage, which was followed by a "wholesale speculative" stage under turnpike and rail use (this is the period under discussion by Taylor and Benson), and, finally, the evolutionary scheme culminated in a "factory order" stage in the context of a worldwide market. Commons analyzed each stage in terms of three main economic tasks he called the "merchant function" (selling the product), the "master function" (employing labor to make the product), and the "journeyman function" (making it). Thus the colonial cobbler combined all three functions in himself, whereas the introduction of a middleman between producer and consumer in the "wholesale order" stage separated the "journeyman function" from both the "master function" and the "merchant function."[46]

Commons' scheme can be criticized on two counts. First, it is a type of monistic economic determinism that abstracts the "historical extension of markets" from historical reality and ascribes to this factor enormous powers of causation in political and social as well as economic affairs. Second, it is a form of mechanistic functionalism, subject to all the faults of this philosophy. In retort to the functionalist view that human actions are the result of behavioral functions, one may ask, does the merchant sell goods because it is his function to do so, or because he sees the possibility of gain? And if gain is his real desire, what is the use of "function" to explain his motivation? Commons' conviction that the "merchant function" is the "determining factor" in the course of industrial evolution does not explain the realities of the rise of manufacturing. In Lynn, manufacturers did not simply respond to the market; they also created it. They did not simply hire labor to meet consumer demand; they also stalked their customers as a hunter stalks game and relished the business-man's unique pleasure of making a killing in the market. How else could they make profits? How else could they compete? How else could they grow?

A quarter of a century before the factory system, the relations of production essential to industrial capitalism were already present in Lynn. In fact, the existence of a group of entrepreneurs who competed in the market, owned the raw materials and the critical means of production, and hired wage labor as a commodity was a necessary precondition for the successful conversion to mechanized, factory methods of production. Extending the work of the eighteenth-century masters and shopkeepers, the central shop manufacturers stretched the mass market for standardized goods to the point that every consumer in every town and village throughout the country could be linked directly to the hives of industry in Lynn. The factories increased the number of products flowing in these channels but did not alter the market structure itself. Moreover, the prefactory shoe manufacturers also assembled the largest labor force of any industry in New England, bequeathing to the factory owners a great reservoir for use in making up the crews that ran the factories. Furthermore, the prefactory entrepreneurs drew upon their own profits for the major source of capital expansion, and the profits resulting from this expansion, in turn, became the major source of investment in machines and factories. Thus the Industrial Revolution in shoe manufacturing built up momentum for half a century before it began the final, irrevocable turn to the factory system.

The Spirit of Capitalism

The historical extension of markets in the eighteenth and nineteenth centuries was the result of the prodigious energies of thousands of individuals impelled by class interests to cross and recross the Atlantic, coast the Eastern seaboard from port to port, trek inland over turnpikes and footpaths, ride river steamers and canal barges, and travel hundreds of miles in stage and rail coaches. While these legions were in the field, added thousands stayed close to their homes and shops and hired labor to manufacture things for the roving traders to sell. Each individual was caught in the contradictory predicament of being a competitor and a dependent of all the others; a seller of goods required a buyer, yet in their bargaining, the advantage of one was the disadvantage of the other. Even as they contested with one another, these bourgeois multitudes collectively created the marketplace. Their experience was a cacophony of individual rivalries but a harmony of class interests.

Industrial capitalism resulted from the application of the values and practices of the marketplace to the production of commodities. The manufacturer bought labor and raw materials as cheaply as he could and sold finished products as dearly as he could, just as the merchant bought and sold nails or barrels of flour. So it is not surprising that nineteenth-century manufacturers talked the same language and followed the same code of conduct as their eighteenth-century predecessors. To accumulate capital, it was necessary to practice industry and frugality, to eschew spiritous liquors, and to imbibe only the spirits of capitalism.

These beliefs penetrated deep into the heart of Benjamin Franklin Newhall, a self-made man who described his initial success in business as "the beginning of life with me." Newhall wrote an autobiography, long segments of which are preserved in the published history of Lynn. Such revelations of the inner lives of unknown, ordinary people are rare and valuable documents. They are found buried beneath layers of more prosaic annals of local events and the more commonplace registers of births, deaths, and marriages. The birth records of Lynn dryly noted the birth of Newhall, Benjamin Franklin, on 29 April 1802. His marriage on 25 April 1825 occasioned another entry in another set of record books, and at six points in the course of the marriage, the records were opened, and the names of the offspring—Benjamin, Jr., Charles, J., Ellen M. . . . —were duly inscribed. His death occasioned greater notice in the community than his birth, since he had gained some reputation in the town as a successful manufacturer and amateur litterateur, but still the record books said only that he died on 13 October 1863.[47]

Such records are graveyards of departed facts; their contents are as lifeless as interred bones. In reconstituting the past, the application of demographic and statistical techniques to records of this type is essential to a full reconstruction, but vital statistics by themselves are never vital. Thus the value of a memoir like Newhall's: it is an extraordinary illumination of the experience of an ordinary nineteenth-century businessman. It is a golden object among the bones.

In his early childhood, Newhall developed an intense attachment to his mother and a strong dislike for his father. Assisting his father in the ten-footer, he came to detest even the occupation of shoemaking, and he also blamed his father's drinking for family sufferings. But his mother was his prize; feelings for her reached levels of intense romantic rapture, and he yearned to grow up so he could find work to support her. "I hated shoemaking," he recalled, "and was yet determined to earn something for my mother." His recollections overflowed with sentimentalism:

How well do I remember in the late hours of night, when my father and her dear ones were sleeping, that she would come to my bedside, and kneeling with overflowing heart pour out her soul in prayer that God would preserve her darling boy from the snares so thick around him. . . .
How many times I wished that I were older, and had some good work so that I could support her.[48]

Here in this midnight setting young Benjamin tapped the wellsprings of ambition.

Newhall's family lacked the capital to start him off in business, and so he pursued various manual occupations in his youth. At thirteen he implored his mother to find an opening for him, and she persuaded Amariah Childs, a local manufacturer of chocolate and head of the Lynn Institution for Savings, to hire the boy. The work was excruciating: "From the beginning to the end of a week I did not get into a bed." But he remembered his silent vow:

Sometimes she [his mother] would say that the work was too hard, and I had better quit it; but I could not think of it; work I must, and work I would. Mr. Childs would stand and look with astonishment to see me paper the chocolate so much faster than was ever done before.

. . . But with all the hard work and suffering, I got through my first winter at the mill; how I bore the fatigue God only knows; some unseen hand supported me; and when I was just on the point of giving up, several times, some impulse of mind forbade it. God helped me.[49]

Self-sacrifice was inherent in such an occupation; even under modern, twentieth-century conditions with child labor laws and minimum hours, self-sacrifice is built into the system of industrial regimentation. However, Newhall subjected himself to more stress than was absolutely necessary, as if to justify himself through his sufferings before his God and his mother. Later in life he ventured a mild criticism of this youthful glutton for punishment: "I now think that such labor for a boy was too much; but I was ambitious."

The fusion of worldly ambition and religious duty is the essence of the Protestant ethic. Newhall grew to maturity in a community seething with Protestantism, and it was natural for his personal strivings to take a religious form. He joined the Methodist connection and for a brief period in the 1820s became a lay preacher. The Methodist church in Lynn was the pioneer church in the state; it had been settled in 1791 when a group of residents inspired by the evangelical preaching of Jesse Lee broke away from the orthodox Congregational church. Methodism rapidly advanced to become the largest denomination in the community, but the Congregationalists retaliated in 1818 with a large dose of "undiluted Calvinism" in the form of a new minister who preached the total and utter depravity of man. That left more liberal Congregationalists out in the cold, and they began a search for a new home that took them through a brief encounter with Episcopalianism to the formation of a Unitarian society in 1822. Not content to sit quietly by, the Quakers had their own schism in 1821 that separated new lights from old and occasioned a trial of four Friends on charges of "having committed riots in the Quaker meeting house." With all this turmoil swirling about him, it would have been difficult for a young man like Newhall to remain aloof.[50]

Young people unsettled in a calling were the target of new methods of social control developed in the 1820s as the old forms weakened. Most important, the household was losing its position as the primary link between economy and society. As the central shop eliminated the master's role in production, the authority of the artisan head of the household was diminished, rendering the household less effective in maintaining social discipline. Other institutions that might have filled the gap were also in disarray; the denominational squabbles and internecine struggles in the churches made them a source of confusion and disorder, rather than a force of coherent social leadership.[51]

The Society for the Promotion of Industry, Frugality, and Temperance epitomized the search for new forms of control. Organized in Lynn during the winter of 1826, the Society combined religious and secular messages, just as its officers were drawn from both the clerical and business leadership of the community. The three main denominations found something to unite behind; the Methodists contributed a lay preacher, the Quakers sent their religious leader, and the First Congregational Church added their undiluted Calvinist. Most of the other officers were businessmen from the shoe industry, and most were also officers of the Lynn Institution for Savings, established about the same time with the avowed moral purpose of promoting frugality among the young men of the community. Economic self-interest and religious ethics fused into one substance in the mind of these businessmen, as in the following exhortation against liquor: "Let us not keep it in our houses, and neither give it to, nor receive it from, our friends; nor provide it under any considerations for our workmen; and let us give employment to such men as use no ardent spirits in preference to others."[52] Like industry and frugality, temperance was an old virtue, but in contrast to the former meaning of the term as "moderate drinking," it was now defined as "total abstinence." The rising manufacturers of the early nineteenth century saw sobriety both as a manifestation of their own success (recall the treatment accorded to the inebriated failure, Ebenezer Breed) and as a means of asserting control over the production of shoes. The loose eighteenth-century system of industrial discipline infuriated the shopkeepers, but they were unable to do anything about it until the central shop gave them the reins of control and, therefore, some influence over their employees' daily work habits. Once, shopkeepers had customarily supplied grog to the shoemakers as wages in kind; now, the manufacturers denied them strong drink, hoping sobriety would be an incentive to productivity.

At the time these new organizations were founded, Benjamin Franklin Newhall was still casting about in search of a calling. The 1820s were a period of tribulation in which he experienced a series of disheartening "trials, successes, and mishaps," the most serious of which was a business reversal in a Canadian retail enterprise that left him with numerous debts. At the end of the decade he returned from Canada, and, like an insect caught in a spider web, he struggled to free himself from the snares of failure:

By the assistance of my uncle Makepeace I paid up the small debts, and got one or two of the largest creditors to wait. The next step was to get into some business, that I might support my family. The shoe business presented the fairest prospect, as I thought; so I hired a small room in the upper part of what is now the Henry Nichols house, got trusted for one bundle of leather from Isaac Bassett and a dozen of kid from John Lovejoy, and hired of John Emerton fifty dollars, giving him a mortgage on my horse and wagon for security.[53]

The fashion in which Newhall became a manufacturer was not unusual for the time; the low capital requirements of the central shop era permitted petty entrepreneurs with nothing more than a horse and buggy and a little real estate to try their luck in the industry. The turnover among firms was correspondingly high; at any point up to 1860 a majority of the manufacturers had not been in business ten years earlier.[54] One year's new businesses were the next year's business failures; opportunity struck with a double-edged sword. A commercial crisis like the panic of 1837 had devastating consequences on these marginal manufacturers. Caught in the web of credit, the cash they needed to continue operations was tied up in the hands of their customers, and if their customers could not pay, the web held them tight while their own creditors and competitors closed in for the kill. This nightmare of failure disturbed the secret thoughts of the manufacturers; the specter was personified by Ebenezer Breed, stalking the dusty streets of their community, a walking prophet of doom.

Newhall fortified himself against inner weakness through a strict regimen of Protestant self-discipline, and at the same time he strengthened his outer position in the marketplace through the weapons of rational capitalism. Inner and outer self became one; Methodist became manufacturer. Not the "economic man" but the whole man made a fetish of precise cost calculation, double-entry bookkeeping, and turning a profit.

I kept an exact account of all I bought and sold, so that I might at any time know whether I was making a profit. Everything in business was as dull as could be and workmen were hard to be got. But perseverance and prudence were my motto. After three months of close application, I found a little had been made. This was to me encouraging, and I labored on. Never shall I forget how hard it was to sell shoes in Boston. The seller had to beg, and be insulted besides. But no discouragement deterred me; and I now look back and see a kind and over-ruling Providence in all.
I considered this the beginning of life with me, and felt determined to succeed, if prudence and economy would ensure success.[55]

Newhall was rebaptised in the religion of business. In beginning life anew, the moral virtue of "prudence" became essential to business success, and the business virtue of "economy" became an integral part of his character. Here was a vivid demonstration of the interplay between the way a person made a living and the way he interpreted himself and his world. His code of personal conduct grew out of the conduct itself, and, in turn, gave motivation and direction to his actions in the material environment.

Newhall's personal behavior, then, was a manifestation of the behavior of his class (though it goes without saying that no one else lived in quite the same fashion as he). He absorbed his code of conduct through the culture about him, and he continuously tested the code in his daily business activities. The larger contours of the culture corresponded to the larger contours of behavior in the American marketplace. The institution of the market was developed by private merchants and manufacturers, shopkeepers and sea captains, acting in conjunction with state governments. As they extended the market, as they invaded handicraft production with capitalist techniques, as they developed methods of rational accounting, they also laid down rules of behavior, standards of taste, and concepts of reality that were consonant with their business preoccupations. It is not so much that ethics, aesthetics, and ideology were branches of business behavior, but that all facets of bourgeois life were interrelated parts of the same process of class development. The main lines of development originated in material relationships (the particular organization of production, the level of technology, the methods of exchange), but material relationships themselves were influenced by cultural traditions. Culture unified the outlook and general aims of individual businessmen and thereby channeled raw, subjective experiences into forms that were available to the class as a whole. The Spirit of Capitalism pooled the disparate energies of innumerable individuals, so that whether they thought about the general interests of their class or not they pursued those interests in fact. They identified personal fulfillment with success in the marketplace, and they sacrified parts of themselves and certain vital ties with other members of humanity in order to live out the commitment to prudence and economy.[56] And since some self-sacrifice was involved, who could tell where rational calculation left off and irrational faith began? To wound one's self for the sake of sheer survival has a clear logic, but what is the sense in making self-punishment a virtue?

The cultural forms that guided Newhall and his fellow manufacturers had long flourished in America. A century prior to his venture in shoe manufacturing, Benjamin Franklin had penned a series of essays and sayings that constituted the classic statement of the acquisitive spirit of capitalism. Born in 1706 the son of a master artisan, Franklin grew up in three of the most active mercantile centers in the world—Boston, London, and Philadelphia. Thus Max Weber is hardly convincing when he uses Franklin as evidence that the ethos of modern rational capitalism existed before the capitalist order itself;[57] the eighteenth-century Anglo-American trading network in which Franklin thrived was an impossibility without widespread capitalist business practices. Franklin condensed the commonplace wisdom of the marketplace into various commentaries on the way to wealth. The most famous of these was *Poor Richard's Almanac;* in another, *The Instructor, or Young Man's Best Companion,* Franklin added his thoughts to a text originally published in England, and his message struck home in the hearts of generations of struggling young entrepreneurs. "In short," Franklin wrote, "the Way to Wealth, if you desire it, is plain as the Way to Market. It depends chiefly on two words, INDUSTRY and FRUGALITY; i.e. Waste neither Time nor Money, but make the best Use of both. He that gets all he can honestly, and saves all he gets (necessary Expences excepted) will certainly become RICH: If that Being who governs the World, to whom all should look for a Blessing on their honest Endeavors, doth not in his wise Providence otherwise determine."[58]

The basic concepts were the same when Benjamin Franklin Newhall explained his way to wealth a century later. Newhall and his namesake learned their rules of conduct in a cultural environment conditioned by the same principles of the competitive marketplace. Both businessmen experienced the entrepreneurial war of all against all. Both saw merchants sometimes pursue interests different from manufacturers. And both stood committed to the underlying system of private property in the means of production owned and controlled by individuals and small firms who bought and sold commodities (including the time and skills of human labor) and competed with one another for sales and, ultimately, profits. This common ground underlaid the experience of the two Benjamin Franklins, though they were born a century apart, and it accounted for the strength of individualism, the intensity of their inclination to accumulate, and the definition of virtue as hard work and self-denial.

One further example will help make the point; Franklin instructed young men on the wise use of other people's money, counseling them to bear in mind that "money is of a prolific generating Nature," which, like a breeding sow, multiplies in each succeeding generation. Furthermore, since credit is money, one must be careful to establish good credit. "Remember this Saying, *That the good Paymaster is Lord of another Man's Purse.* He that is known to pay punctually and exactly to the Time he promises, may at any Time, and on any Occasion, raise all the Money his Friends can spare."[59] Newhall may not have read this passage, but he took the advice. Through a friend he was introduced to the president of a bank in Salem, "and thus I obtained the advantage of getting a discount as often as I wanted one. This was everything to me, as money matters were then situated.

I was very punctual in all my payments, and so my credit grew
better and better."[60] With this kind of financial backing, he survived
the Panic of 1837 and became one of the larger manufacturers in
town. The insect caught in the web of debt had metamorphosed into
a spider.

2

ARTISANS

It was not much past sunrise when Hiram Breed or Jacob Graves or Pelatiah Purington rolled over on his straw mattress for the last time and rose up out of bed. Exchanging his nightshirt for work boots and a set of clothes, each of these journeymen leaders in the shoemakers' societies of the 1830s and 1840s began his daily round of labor, after a pause for breakfast, by heading for his workshop—a corner inside the house or a ten-footer out back. If a ten-footer, each of these journeymen or any of the hundreds of other anonymous shoemakers who shared the same round of labor ducked his head beneath the low transom and stepped inside to begin work. The grey, early morning dampness clung to his clothes and made the tinder too soggy to catch the sparks flying from flint and steel, so he leaned back out the door and called up to the house for his son to run to a neighbor's and fetch a shovelful of coals. Ducking under the transom again, his eyes sorted out the pieces of kit he would have to arrange for the day's labor: a lap-stone and a hammer (for beating the leather to make it pliable); a stirrup (a leather strap that tucked under his heel and held the shoe stock securely in place at his knee); an awl (for piercing the leather); hog bristles and waxed thread; and also a shoulder-stick, pincers, fenders, scrapers, knives of different descriptions, such as skiver, paring-off knife, heel knife, tacks, a piece of sponge, paste-horn, blacking bottles, chalk, grease, channel opener, and dogfish skin (in the days before sandpaper).[1]

Journeymen and Binders

Whether a journeyman owned a ten-footer or worked in rented rooms, he invariably acquired a kit of his own. A good, sharp knife was the difference between a clean cut and a botched job, and when a man was fortunate enough to own such a well-tempered blade, "it was not considered a marketable commodity." A lap-stone could acquire the value of a precious gem: "It may have been brought by a near relative from the coast of Java, or from some of the beaches washed by the Pacific Ocean. It was so perfect in shape, so smooth upon its face, and so completely adapted to its purpose, that it was the envy of the whole neighborhood. Nobody had any clear idea of the wealth of the man that owned such a lap-stone." Other treasures of inestimable wealth were found in the journeyman's kit; perhaps an awl on loan from a cousin who had shipped out on a South Sea whaler; or a shoulder-stick carved from an Indian tomahawk picked up as a souvenir of the Colonial wars.[2]

These tools were the artifacts of artisan life. Like the archeological remnants of a bygone culture, they identified the technology of the central shop period as preindustrial, and they were emblems of the importance of human skill and industry. There was no mistaking the

Shoemakers at Work in an Old-Time Ten-footer Shop

fact that individual craftsmen transformed unusable raw materials into goods for human benefit. It was but a short step from observing the shoemaker plying the tools of his or her trade to the idea that labor was the source of all wealth. Shoes did not grow on trees; grain did not harvest itself; nor did iron come out of the ground as nails. The basic material necessities of civilization and its more complex goods like wooden ships and stone buildings were all fruits of human labor.

How unfair it seemed to the mechanic and the farmer that these goods were often owned by people who did nothing to produce them and who were nothing but parasites on the "producing classes." Lynn shoemakers were quite explicit about the parasitism of nonproducers, describing them as "bloodsuckers" and "leeches." In a typical denunciation of "those who have grown fat upon the earnings of the toil worn laborer," one journeyman depicted owners of real estate sticking "leech-like" onto the laborer "until the fountain of life is dried up."[3] The view of society as a dichotomy of producers and parasites was developed in the eighteenth century and was used by master shoemakers and other mechanics in Lynn to contrast their simple manufacturing community with the more opulent commercial centers of Boston and Salem. Paul Faler, a most perceptive student of the mechanics' ideology, has captured their view of the nonproducers: "The merchant princes of the North Shore, with their fine mansions on Chestnut Street, their contingents of retainers and retinues of slaves and servants, a haughty propensity toward ostentatious display in their life style, and their contempt for the producers whom they employed, sat abreast the social structure of their communities." In contrast to the cities inhabited by such "purse-proud aristocrats," Lynn was pictured as a town of republican petty producers. On the eve of the central shop era, the town's petition to the General Court for the Mechanics Bank stated: "It is a fact that there are but few Capitalists in Town. Fortune seems to have destined us to move in the sphere of Equality."[4]

Virtually as soon as these words were penned they became outdated; with the rise of the central shop after 1814, fortune turned toward Capital and away from Equality. A new dichotomy between Labor and Capital grew up *within* the community, and as the master was wiped out, it became increasingly rare for a shoemaker to cross from the realm of Labor into the realm of Capital. Although journeymen continued to speak of "prices" (reflecting the time when shoemakers sold goods and not just their labor), no one but the manufacturer actually bought and sold commodities. Whereas the central shops were stationed alongside the Bank within the realm of Capital, the old ten-footers were moved back so they rested wholly within the realm of Labor.

These long-range historical movements were not within the ken of the typical journeyman seating himself at the bench in the ten-footer. After arranging his kit for the morning's tasks, his attention was drawn to the boy helper returning to the ten-footer with the glowing charcoal embers to start the shop's fire. While the helper busied himself at the stove, the journeyman finished hammering out a pair of soles on the lap-stone and tacked them to wooden lasts to prepare for the next step. If the date was before 1815 or 1820, the journeyman might have turned to his helper and said, "Come John, go and see if your mother has got a shoe bound; I'm all ready to last it." And off the boy would go to get the uppers for the first pair of shoes of the day. However, such teamwork involving the whole family became increasingly rare as central shop manufacturers hired journeymen and binders on an individual basis, so that by 1830 the young helper was probably dispatched to a central shop instead of his mother's house to fetch the uppers.[5]

Taking advantage of the freedom of the streets, a boy often joined his friends in a game of marbles or some other youthful amusement. If a boy took too long on his errand, and his father's patience wore out, strong paternal discipline was forthcoming, often in the form of a stirrup used as a whip. Both as a style of child rearing and as a method of work discipline, the use of the lash has been condemned by later ages of history as a barbarous instrument; industrial societies have substituted psychological manipulation and material punishment for the whip. But it is doubtful that a suffocating love, an authoritarian regimentation, or a fear of being fired assure the individual any greater freedom. At any rate, the novice shoemaker certainly had a wide latitude for exerting his own will. This was partly the result of the weakness of bond servitude in the journeyman's household. Just as a guild system never took hold, so apprenticeship was weak in the eighteenth century and was fatally affected by the rise of the central shop in the nineteenth. There was no record of a formal apprentice bond after 1840.[6]

In asserting their independence, the young were following the lead of their elders. The work pattern of the household allowed each member considerable scope for individual decision-making. Women decided when to boil tallow for candles, when to darn socks, and when to bind shoes. Men chose when to repair the front stoop, when to manure the garden, and when to bottom shoes. Their control extended into the character and quality of the product, since they determined when the leather had been hammered long enough, whether to make the instep snug or full, how much stiffening to put in the heel. This is where the cliché about the "independent artisan" rings true—in the control artisans exercised over their own daily rhythms of work and in their influence over the final product. In these regards, artisans who did not own property were as independent as those who did.

The life style of artisan families resembled life on the farms from which they had sprung. Until the middle of the eighteenth century nearly all the people in Lynn were farmers, and for the next half century farmers converted their homes to shoemaking with no more dislocation in the underlying structure of their lives than the shopkeepers experienced going into the shoe business. At first, shoemaking was a rural by-industry, as farm owners and hired hands alike took advantage of the natural seasonal layoff in New England agriculture to add a bit to their income. In the early 1760s Nehemiah Collins earned money for plowing, carting wood, making cider, "six day's work in the marsh," and, in addition, making shoes. Wills from the revolutionary period commonly listed the occupation of Lynn inhabitants as "yeoman and cordwainer" (the ancient term for shoemaker). Even in the early nineteenth century, as the relative importance of farming and shoemaking reversed and farming became the by-industry, some residents still combined the two occupations. Joseph Lye rented a working farm from his stepmother in 1822, but at the same time steadily plied the shoemaker's craft and taught his younger brother the trade. Lye was active in community affairs, performing militia duty, attending town meetings, and serving as clerk of the new Unitarian church in 1822. He had a full intellectual life, as well, reading such works as Plutarch's *Lives* and a history of Napoleon's Russian campaign. Truly, Lye was one of those favored representatives of mankind who grew crops in the morning, read great literature at midday, practiced a craft in the afternoon, and in the evening discussed philosophy.[7]

The location of manufacturing centers emphasized the significance of the agricultural background. Lynn was the first of several villages scattered around Boston that converted from agriculture to shoe manufacturing at the end of the eighteenth century. By the 1830s more than thirty communities in Massachusetts each produced at least 100,000 pairs of boots and shoes annually, and all but three or four of these once had been farm communities. Moreover, by the 1850s dozens of villages scattered throughout rural Massachusetts, New Hampshire, and Maine were doing work put out to them by Lynn and other cities.[8]

Besides farm families, men and women in coastal fishing villages also bound and bottomed for Lynn entrepreneurs. One Marblehead woman was described in a poem by Lucy Larcom, "Hannah Binding Shoes," in which the aging Hannah sat at her window and pined for the love of her youth, a fisherman who had left on a voyage twenty years earlier never to return.

> Twenty winters
> Bleach and tear the ragged shore she views.
> Twenty seasons:
> Never one has brought her any news.
> Still her dim eyes silently
> Chase the white sails o'er the sea:
> Hopeless, faithful,
> Hannah's at the window binding shoes.

Leaving aside its overwrought romanticism, the poem portrays a common experience of long years spent binding shoes in the home. If the lost suitor had ever returned, the chances are good that he would have begun bottoming shoes between his fishing trips; a sizable portion of the Marblehead fishermen were wintertime shoemakers. The preindustrial culture of the sea infused the shoe industry at Lynn; the conversation of many workshops was highlighted by such "salt notes" as the description of shoebenches as "berths," references to snuffing the candle as "dousing the glim," and the use of "grog," the shipboard term for watered rum.[9]

The fullest development of the outwork system occurred in a cluster of towns in an arc from the New Hampshire seacoast to a point forty or fifty miles inland. Pittsfield and Northwood, both in New Hampshire, were among the most significant rural outposts of Lynn enterprise. Pittsfield's initial contact with Lynn was made in 1838 after a small cotton mill that had been operating for ten years closed down. Feeling the pinch of business depression, a local custom bootmaker decided to try his hand at making shoes for sale in the market and "went prospecting" in Lynn. He returned with a wagon-load of cut stock, and for the next two generations Pittsfield made shoes for Lynn. The relationship between Northwood and Lynn also dated from about the same time.[10]

The diaries of New Hampshire farmer shoemakers like Ivory Hill of Northwood are especially rich in the details of an outworker's life.[11] Hill's diary from the 1850s shows clearly the farmer shoe-maker's seasonal work pattern. He worked hardest at shoemaking in January and March, while in August and September he made almost no shoes. Instead, in these harvest months he recorded hoeing and haying in his own fields. The diary also shows how completely the farmer shoemaker controlled his own labor; when he didn't feel like working, he didn't work. On January 16, 1857, he wrote, "Ben loafing—out of work and happy as a clam." When he had a headache or felt "stewey" his daily output fell from six or eight pairs to two or three, and when he wanted to take a day off to witness twenty-four people baptized at Harvey's Pond, he went right ahead and did it. Not that he lacked the work ethic—often he chided himself for not doing better, as on February 11: "Have not made any. Just sick or lasy." But he made his own decisions about when to start and stop working.

At the beginning of February, 1857, with nothing to be done on the farm, Hill decided to take a few days and visit Lynn and Boston to investigate the shoe business and find some amusement. He wrapped himself in layers of wool clothing and set out on foot to meet

the "freighter," the wagon that ferried materials between manufacturers and outworkers. He rode the slow-moving freighter to a rail
connection at Hampton, Massachusetts, arriving well past sundown.
In the time he had to wait for the next train he found enough light to
write the following entry in the pocket-size diary he carried with him.

> Feb. 3   Started for Lynn this morning with the
>   Freighters got down to Hampton 9
>   o clock pm cold. I am going to camp
>   down in the depot until 12 o clock
>   tonight then start on the Freight
>   trane for Lynn.

The train was late or slow and Hill did not arrive until sunrise. Sometime after he left Lynn the same afternoon, he wrote again in his
diary.

> Feb. 4   Arrived at Lynn 6 o clock this morning.
>   Business light. Recd 23.94 from Lucian
>   Newhall Started for Boston 2 o clock pm
>   at uncle George's.

Hill stretched the $23.94 a long way. On the fifth he wrote from
Boston that he had been "running around the city;" on the sixth he
bought a watch and had a daguerreotype taken. With most of the
remaining money he apparently purchased raw and cut shoe stock
from wholesale leather dealers in Boston, because on February 7 he
was back in New Hampshire, stopping on the way to his farm to sell
sixteen pairs of soles to one neighbor and to leave small amounts of
upper leather with Vienna Chapman and to pay her $4.80 for bind-
ing. Two weeks later, in hopes of finding more work, Hill set out on
another journey, this time going only as far as Haverhill. But in this
depression year things were no better there than they had been in
Lynn, and Hill complained, *"Business hard."* The shoe trade improved
somewhat in March, but in April and May he turned almost all his
energy to the farm, ploughing, spreading manure, and mending his
fences, and it was not until early June that he visited Lynn and
Boston again.
    Hill's journeys in 1857 follow the route taken by thousands of

farmer shoemakers like him who hitched a ride with the freighter or rode in a neighbor's wagon to a coastal market town where they could catch a ride on the Eastern Railway as far as Lynn. When a short-term visit of this nature turned into a long-term sojourn, individual travel became population migration. Though people flowed in both directions between rural and urban areas, the net accumulation went to the cities as folks like Ivory Hill became neighbors to the Breeds, Graveses, and Puringtons.

The Community

Since the great revolutions of the eighteenth century, equality has been perceived as an essential foundation of a just society. At the times when historical events pursued justice, the cry for equality was a whip urging events forward. In the nineteenth century the whip was applied to inequalities based on class, race, and sex. Sometimes there appeared a radical thinker of special insight, like Susan B. Anthony or Wendell Phillips, who saw these three areas as a common ground of oppression. More often, however, American egalitarians wielded separate whips and sometimes fell to beating one another. Thus the popular movement for political democracy in the 1820s and 1830s pursued equal rights for white men, but stood firmly behind the civil and political nullification of women and vetoed the civil and political rights of "free" Blacks. "Jacksonian egalitarianism" was an ideology of equal rights among those who enjoyed special privileges. Clearly, it is necessary to sharpen the definition of "egalitarianism" and pinpoint the social basis of the claim to equality.

Different definitions emerged from different social experiences. The artisan's view of equality as a fair distribution of wealth, power, and status differed from the lawyer's "careers open to talent," and the businessman's "unfettered opportunity for trade and investment." Lynn offers an excellent opportunity to test the social meaning of the artisan claim, since it was an overwhelmingly artisan community: shoemakers alone equaled the total of all other occupations combined, outnumbering laborers 6 to 1, and businessmen 5 to 1.[12] Computations on the distribution of wealth have been made for several rural and urban communities from 1830 to 1860, including separate studies of

Trempleau County, Wisconsin, Philadelphia, and the Massachusetts communities of Boston, Newburyport, and Northampton.[13] But none of the studies published so far has dealt with a community as heavily artisan in makeup as Lynn.

The first thing that leaps out from the available statistical evidence on the possession of wealth in Lynn is that a decisive *majority* of journeymen owned *no real property*. This finding is contrary to most of the literary evidence on the topic. The prime source on artisan shoemakers is David N. Johnson's *Sketches of Lynn,* a highly engaging and well-crafted study of Lynn from 1830 to 1880. Historians have made frequent use of Johnson, sometimes incorporating whole sections of his work; for example, Norman Ware's study of the industrial worker cited Johnson's categorical declaration that around 1830 "nearly all the workmen owned the houses they lived in, with considerable land adjoining."[14]

These two authors were dealing in the most popular coin of the Republic when they recast the stereotyped image of the property-owning, independent artisan. Although it is true that independence characterized the life style of the artisan, it did not rest on the social base of universal, or even very widespread, proptery ownership. At no time in the second quarter of the nineteenth century did a majority of Lynn's adult males hold real property. Using the local tax records, Paul Faler has found that in 1832, 61 percent of the ratable polls did *not* possess real property, and at no time through midcentury did the proportion of propertyless fall below a majority.[15] Sifting the records somewhat more finely, about *four in every five shoemakers did not own real property*. Sifting more finely still, the propertyless majority extended to shoemakers who were heads of households; 68 percent were without real property.[16] It seems likely that in the vanished days of the master shoemaker a larger proportion owned real property, but records listing occupation did not go back beyond 1832, the date of the first city directory. Moreover, it is also likely that in the early phases of the central shop era up to about 1830 a larger proportion owned property than in 1850, since the data for the latter year apply to the end of two decades of soaring expansion when many younger shoemakers with no financial resources poured into the community. Still, after this bow to the sagacity of David Johnson, it remains a fact that propertyless shoemakers throughout the central shop era were in a clear majority.

To find the classical egalitarian community of small property owners, it is necessary to leave the rapidly urbanizing environment of Lynn and travel through the channels of the outwork system to the farming villages of New Hampshire and Maine. Coming to rest in Ivory Hill's hometown, a clear majority of the heads of households in Northwood were property owners: 72 percent of the farmers and 57 percent of the shoemakers. A check in the census records of two other rural outwork communities confirmed that property ownership was more widespread among outworkers than among Lynn craftsmen.[17] If the migration of shoemakers back and forth between Lynn and its industrial outposts in the country helped even out the attachment to property, still the urban artisan's claim to equality based on ownership of urban real estate rested on quite narrow foundations.

Prior to industrialization, land and buildings in almost any form were means of production. The occupant of a house possessed a workshop for the making of such articles as soap, candles, clothes, or shoes; the owner, or renter, of a plot of ground was a farmer, or at least a gardener, who raised vegetables, pigs, and chickens. Even those who simply hired a room or two benefited from being in a community where their neighbors raised fresh vegetables and sold cheaply or gave away their surplus. Johnson asserted that access to the land was survival insurance for the shoemakers during the depression of 1837, a time when there were "more potatoes, more beans, more corn, more squashes, and other vegetables, as well as more hogs raised, than for several years before." Pigs were especially valuable assets; as they matured they were looked upon as a kind of savings bank. When it came time to withdraw the savings, slaughtering the pig was an important community ritual, presided over by the neighborhood hog-butcher and attended by several men and boys. While the barrel of water was heating, the men drank rum supplied by the pig's owner, and the boys conjured up visions of future feasts of spareribs and ham, doughnuts and baked beans, which made up "so large a part of a boy's Elysium."[18]

This vision of abundance should not obscure the reality of hard times. The meat and vegetables raised locally were only a supplement to the shoemaker's diet, most of which was composed of flour, beans, pork, and salt fish bought at the store. In the depression, residents were forced to eat "miserable trash," such as the "rattlesnake pork" raised in the West and packed in barrels for shipment. With an eye toward dietary reform movements, Johnson observed, "It is not surprising that Grahamism flourished a few years after this. One look into a barrel of this pork would make more Grahamites than a whole course of lectures."[19] Moreover, since land ownership was so constricted in the central shop era, access to the means of providing subsistence was limited, and, therefore, Johnson's assertion that almost every family kept a pig and tended a substantial garden must be considerably discounted. In fact, most of the shoemakers relied solely on wages for the source of their livelihood.

Statistical information on wages and income is fragmentary and often unreliable. However, a few points stand out; first, a shoemaker's income was seasonal, with peaks in spring and fall, and valleys in summer and winter. The November-December layoff in production was the most trying season, since it coincided with the decline in the availability of local food supplements. Seasonal income was dictated by seasonal production cycles that developed with the rise of the central shop and the expansion of the market; manufacturers took orders for light spring wear and heavier fall goods, hired a large number of people to get the job done, and then laid off most of the employees when the orders were filled.[20] Second, they were wage earners wholly dependent on their industrial income, except for the small supplements in kind they raised themselves. Thus when the shoe industry expanded, new job opportunities attracted migrants to the city, and when it retrenched the inflow stopped. The boom of the 1830s came to an abrupt halt in 1837; for the next several years Lynn experienced an outright decline in population; then business revival in the mid-1840s brought renewed population growth. (See Appendix A.) Third, the outwork system tended to depress wages in the industry; in the absence of payroll records, a survey of literary references on piece rates in the 1840s showed work could be done in Pittsfield for about 20 percent less than in Lynn. Another source, the industrial survey incorporated in the census of 1850, used $20/month as the average income of male shoemakers in Lynn; in Northwood the figure ranged downward to $15/month. Outworkers were paid less for the same grades of work and also tended to make cheaper grades than Lynn artisans.[21] Since their position on the land was marginal, their ownership of property did not prevent them from having to work at low wages.

Since the days of Frederick Jackson Turner, historians have debated the effect of rural land ownership on industrial wages. The original argument that cheap land on the frontier drew eastern laborers west and drove up the wages of those who remained has been discredited, but the safety valve idea is an eel that has squirmed away from its detractors again and again. In the last dozen years revised versions have come forth which focus on frontier expansion as a mechanism that generated labor scarcity, which, in turn, insured high wages and capital intensive methods in American industry relative to European. One defender of the revised thesis, who describes this condition as a "truism" (though admitting "there is little statistical evidence") says that until the condition is disproved, "it alone indicates either that labor was relatively dearer than capital or that American entrepreneurs were mad."[22]

On the assumption that Lynn entrepreneurs were not mad, their use of labor intensive methods certainly challenges the "truism." The experience of one industry alone cannot disprove the condition, but since shoe manufacturing was the second most important industry in the union and wherever it was conducted on a large scale in the first half of the nineteenth century it was labor intensive, the datum of this one industry at least calls the revised thesis into question. It may have been that American wages were higher than European, but that did not automatically lead to capital intensive manufacturing, and it did not prevent large numbers of *relatively poor Americans* from being hired by labor-hungry shoe manufacturers.

Expanding opportunity west of the Appalachians spelled declining opportunity for New England's small farmers; as the more fertile soil of the Old Northwest was opened and linked to the urban markets of the East by riverboats, canals, and railroads, the Yankees were not able to compete. The new American breadbasket generated labor redundancy on less productive land in America, just as it did in

England; hardship (though not starvation) was the lot of New England families who sent their young women into the textile mills and set their other members to work making shoes in a last ditch effort to keep afloat. The fishing towns of the Massachusetts coast went through a similar decline at the same time, and hard-pressed families of Marblehead, Beverly, and Salem also turned to textiles and shoes.[23] In New York and Philadelphia, entrepreneurs found a comparable source of cheap labor among poor urban residents—casual laborers, common seamen, dispossessed immigrants. The rise of manufacturing during the age of Jackson, especially in the labor intensive shoe industry, demonstrated that America, too, was a society of rich and poor. Even if the poor were better off than their European counterparts—and their American counterparts at the end of the century— de Tocqueville's America was a society of unequals in which some lived well by the labor of others who lived poorly.

Where there is inequality of condition, the egalitarian claim may well rest on equality of opportunity. For preindustrial society, upward mobility is commonly seen as rising in wealth and status through different occupational ranks, or, especially, within the ranks of a given trade. The central shop era gave a few shoemakers the opportunity to rise from the bench to become manufacturers, but this experience was hardly typical, and is better described as uncommon. In a check of 100 shoemakers drawn from the city directories, Faler found that none of those listed in 1832 had become a manufacturer in the next nine years (though by 1851 there were three manufacturers among the sixty-eight who were still listed as Lynn residents— 5 percent). A separate sample beginning with every fourth shoemaker listed in the directory of 1841 showed 5 of the 145 individuals remaining in 1851 had become manufacturers (4 percent). Such data is not intended to give a full picture of mobility, but it is useful in defining the limits to the proposition that all shoemakers were given the same chance to rise to the top of their trade. In fact the few who did rise most likely were either cutters or sons of businessmen whose fathers had given them experience in the shop before establishing them as manufacturers in their own right. Again using city directories, Faler found that of the thirty-seven new manufacturers in 1851 who had been listed ten years earlier, fourteen had been cutters (38 per-

cent); and most of the fathers of the new manufacturers were themselves manufacturers or merchants.[24] Another facet in the pattern of
mobility was the experience of the masters; their eclipse had already
taken place by the time the first city directory was published so statistical measurement is virtually impossible, but it seems likely that a
portion of those who remained in the trade were able to become small
manufacturers, while others with equal skill but less capital became
cutters. To sum up, the picture of prefactory occupational mobility
suggests that the shoe industry could reasonably have been perceived
as a continuum from journeyman to boss, but that opportunity was
not diffused equally to all ranks in the industry, and, therefore, any
claim for social equality based on equality of opportunity stood on
weak foundations.

So where was the strength in the artisan claim? If equality was not
supported by a wide distribution of property, secure and stable income, or wide vistas on upward mobility, then what remained? The
strength of equality rested on independence within the household and
mutual dependence among households. Something has already been
said about the independence that resulted from the artisan's control
over daily decisions of production. Turning to the subject of mutual
dependence, artisans reached out from their own households to grasp
ties of fraternity and sorority in their neighborhoods, in the community, and among laboring people as a whole. Even as manufacturers were taking over the central command of production, artisans
successfully asserted control over vital folkways. Neighborhood storekeepers, for example, fell under the artisan influence, since the bulk
of their customers were shoemakers who kept personal accounts at
the store. The personalized, decentralized way of doing business gave
real substance to the retailer's adage that the customer is always right.
The sheer numerical preponderance of shoemakers added to their
weight in the community; during the central shop era roughly half
the males employed in Lynn were shoemakers, and, in addition, perhaps half of the women in the community were binders. Their purchasing power was demonstrated through the wide use of order slips
as local currency; manufacturers would often pay their journeymen
in orders on local stores instead of cash, and this scrip was accepted
as payment by the entire community including physicians, school

teachers, and clergymen. The dignity of the ministry did not seem to be impaired by acceptance of the shoemakers' currency, and local preachers could be seen emulating the shoemakers in pulling a little cart through the streets laden with provisions purchased with the order slips. Such behavior was regarded by artisans as a demonstration of equality in status.[25]

The *interdependence* of artisan households gave shoemakers a certain degree of independence from the forces of commerce. A string of household workers was commonly employed to outfit a family with clothes; after purchasing cloth at a dry goods store, a woman would often carry it to a tailor to be cut, and then later to a seamstress to be sewn into dresses, pants, or coats. (This was for the adults; the mother normally made children's wear herself.) As in farm communities, labor was often exchanged directly between households; the raising of a house and the slaughter of a hog were neighborhood events in which those who assisted were treated to grog and victuals, with the assumption that their labor would be repaid at some future event of a similar nature. Thus clothing, food, and shelter —the necessaries of life—were acquired, at least in part, through the cooperative work of many laboring families. Mutual assistance in times of extreme need—loans for burials, rooms for homeless friends or relatives, board for someone out of work—was a communal survival network before it was incorporated into the labor movement in the form of mutual benefit societies.

Equality became problematic, however, in the relations between artisans and manufacturers. On the one hand, men and women in the household made the day-to-day decisions about production and exercised a set of skills that no manufacturer could get along without. Smaller manufacturers who gave employment to 10 or 20 people were especially dependent on personal contacts with particular individuals and were subject to the same pressures from the artisans as the storekeepers and professionals. On the other hand, the extent of household authority shrank with the rise of the central shop, and the longer production rhythms and larger industrial decisions increasingly fell under the authority of the manufacturers. Manufacturers who gave employment to 200 or more people could replace one with another as if individuals were only names on a payroll ledger. In the dual context of the remaining household prerogatives and the experience of becoming an expendable wage earner, shoemakers pressed their claim for equality in the 1830s and 1840s through the collective agency of the labor movement. Their motto, the rallying cry of shoeworkers for the next half century, was Equal Rights.

Equal Rights

On a warm night in June in the year Karl Marx was writing his *Economic and Philosophic Manuscripts* and Freidrich Engels was immersed in research for his forthcoming *Condition of the Working Class in England,* members of the Mutual Benefit Society of Journeymen Cordwainers gathered in Lynn to consider means of raising their wages and defending the honor of manual labor. In high spirits that flashed between good humor and bitter defiance, they listened to the nationally renowned Hutchinson family sing a piece written by Jesse Hutchinson titled the "Cordwainers' Rallying Song," part of which has been quoted in the Introduction. Verse upon verse praising honest labor and condemning low wages rolled over the delighted audience. The last verse ended on a mingled chord of humor and defiance:

> Now EQUAL RIGHTS the motto,
> *Wax* your *threads* as true *souls* ought to;
> Though the run-*round* bosses *bristle,*
> We'll raise a *peg,* and let them *whistle.*
> > *Stick* to the *last,* brave cordwainers!
> > In the *end* you'll *awl* be gainers.[26]

The shoemaker's kit was a cornucopia for the culture of Equal Rights. Out of it tumbled a plethora of puns on souls, lasts, and awls that bejeweled the rich outpouring of songs, poems, anecdotes, and tales about the shoemakers. Satiric verse was accompanied by scathing prose rhetoric that excoriated manufacturers as parasites and "beasts of many horns" (the Biblical Behemoth).

More than just sharp literary flourishes, these were expressions of the shoemaker's profound sense of social dislocation in the central shop era. The encroachment of industrial capitalism into their community steadily narrowed the ground on which the old egalitarianism stood, and the shoemakers defended the remaining ground with a vehement counterattack against the manufacturers. They saw men like Micajah Pratt and the Breed brothers as representatives of the same forces of privilege and monopoly that were once incarnated at a relatively safe distance in the merchants of Salem and Boston. Unlike the princes of commerce, the captains of industry assembled their forces only a few minutes' walk from the shoemakers' homes, and every Saturday afternoon when the journeymen carted the week's shoes into the central shop, they came into contact with overweening privilege. Well-established, property-owning journeymen and propertyless recent arrivals wondered about the nature of a system that required them to labor for a week and then hand over everything they had done to someone else. The poorer journeymen carted in their work fearful of being told there was no more work; "to men never rising above poverty, and standing always on the brink of want, these tidings brought deprivation and suffering before their face." When the poor entered the bosses' shops, "it was with fear and trembling."[27]

Other more accomplished, more secure workmen may not have trembled in the presence of the manufacturers, but they equally feared and resented their power. A journeyman shoemaker assailed the economic might of the manufacturers in a letter to a local newspaper in 1830:

We see by the public prints that workingmen in many parts of the union are beginning to assert their rights, and are coming boldly forward to assume that respectable station in society, to which they are so justly entitled—but from which they have been debarred by that monopolizing class, whose works consist only in contrivance to build up their own popularity and aggrandizement, at the expense of the honest part of the community.

To this journeyman, as to the mechanics of New York, Philadelphia, and numerous other cities who were organizing Workingmen's parties at this time, the independence of the artisan work process and the interdependence of artisan households was the true basis of a just social order. Justice was undone when capitalists invested in large urban construction projects, in textile factories, in large daily newspapers, in canals and turnpikes, as well as in shoe manufacturing and took a large measure of control over production out of the hands of the master carpenters, hand spinners, printers, stonemasons, and household shoemakers. This structural change was the economic background to the artisan agitation of the 1830s; it gave social meaning to the accusations of the rise of a monopolizing class interested only in its own aggrandizement. The journeyman letter writer continued his attack:

We know of no place in this Union that stands in more need of a reformation, than the town of Lynn, and with a little exertion we feel assured that the object can be effectually and speedily accomplished. At present, the Mechanics in this Town scarcely have a voice in their own concerns. There are probably 1500 journeymen shoemakers in Lynn, and how is the price of their labor regulated? By no other rule than the necessities of their employers.

Employers! What did the old artisan community know of employers? A master might have employed a journeyman in his household, or a laborer might have found casual employment loading and hauling for a shopkeeper, but the emergence of a whole group in the community that purchased other people's ability to work was unprecedented. In his letter, the journeyman proposed to assemble the community on the old basis of republican equality in a town meeting so that "the shoemakers of Lynn may give ample evidence of their respectability, and evince a determination that they will not suffer under such gross impositions any longer."[28]

The assertion of Equal Rights involved a dilemma for the shoemakers. Sometimes they spoke as if inequality was an innovation, a gross imposition on a formerly egalitarian way of life. But they also spoke as if inequality was a legacy from the past, which would have to be rooted out by bold action of the common people. This dilemma permeates the rhetoric of the Jacksonian period and has led to confusion among contemporaries and historians alike. If the 1830s and 1840s were the "Age of the Common Man," why were common people forever complaining of their subordination to "purse-proud aristocrats"? The way out of this dilemma is to see the struggles of the period not as a contest between past equality and recent privilege but between an old and a new social structure involving different patterns of inequality.

Formerly, inequality was rooted in the household relations between the head and his dependents, between master and servant, between husband and wife. The houshold hierarchy was the social base of deference in the prescribed ranks of society. The lower ranks frequently did not pay the respect demanded of them by their nominal superiors, but their defiance occurred in the context of this hierarchy. The household structure incorporated class divisions between those who owned property and those who did not, because most propertyless people were dependents in a propertied household—wives, children, slaves, servants, apprentices, journeymen, hired laborers. Apart from these groups, a smaller number of tenant farmers, common seamen and casual laborers set up independent households without a property owner as the head. But for the most part, inequality between the property owners and the propertyless was a domestic affair. Inequality *among property owners,* of course, occurred outside the household, with a range of wealth from the petty holdings of the New England dirt farmers to the great estates of the tidewater planters, from the house and barn of the village artisan to the warehouses, domestic chambers, and multiple real estate holdings of the urban merchants. But in the eighteenth century the small scale of production and the common patterns of household organization minimized the consequences of these gaps among property owners.

The character of inequality changed in both kind and degree during the nineteenth century. First, the degree of separation *among* property owners increased as great fortunes appeared in American cities.[29] Second, the class system of industrial capitalism undercut the household as a buffer between property owners and the propertyless and tended to make those who owned productive property and those who did not into two separate social groups. In Lynn, the emergence of central shop owners to a position of command and the subordination of journeymen as wage earners introduced a new inequality into the lives of artisans who remembered the former importance of the master and who experienced every day a continuity with the household order of the past. When they confronted the manufacturers, they tended to ignore the old patterns of hierarchical social ranking and instead reasserted the old patterns of household independence.

The most visible reassertion of the old tradition against the new inequalities of industrial capitalism was the organization of trade associations by both binders and journeymen. The first of these was the Mutual Benefit Society of Journeymen Cordwainers, established in the summer of 1830 with the purpose of raising the wages and status of the journeymen. At the same time the binders founded The Female Society of Lynn and Vicinity for the Protection and Promotion of Female Industry, and apparently the Society lasted through 1833 when a mass meeting of about 1000 binders convened at the Friends Meeting House and approved a wage schedule and a strike call on those manufacturers who refused to meet it. Within a month the journeymen called a similar meeting at the Town Hall and voted to support the binders; for several years the journeymen had been distressed over the price paid to their wives and daughters, complaining that the bosses had "reduced it down to almost nothing." The independent action of each sex reflected the fact that men and women were hired as individuals, rather than as families, and this change was another incident in the dislocation caused by the incursion of industrial capitalism.[30]

Apparently no strike occurred until 1835 when shoemakers turned out to demand higher prices, convinced that their own necessities, not just the manufacturers', should set wages. Though the strike must have been small (it barely got a mention in the papers), it was a token of the decay of the old order, where no such thing had ever occurred. The Panic of 1837 brought the labor movement to a temporary halt. It was followed by seven successive seasons of low wages, which made scavengers of many shoemakers who were compelled to dig clams from the beaches and harvest dandelion greens.[31] At the start of an upswing in the business cycle in the mid-1840s, shoemakers reorganized the defunct Mutual Benefit Society of Journeymen Cordwainers and began a new assault against monopoly privilege. As in the first effort, the shoemakers of Lynn were but one phalanx of a movement that roused working men and women in scores of communities in the United States and Europe. Because of the local artisan strength, Lynn partook of the movement with greater depth and intensity than perhaps most other communities, and its example was a beacon to working people elsewhere, particularly in the outwork catchment area. The emblem of artisan strength in the

1840s was the publication of a vibrant labor newspaper the *Awl,* which reached, in addition to the several hundred subscribers in Lynn, hundreds more in places like Marblehead, Georgetown, Beverly, Woburn, and Lowell. The *Awl* rivaled the more famous *Voice of Industry* (organ of the New England Workingmen's Association) in giving a vivid portrayal of the experience and consciousness of working people and their resistance to nascent industrial capitalism.[32]

The key to interpreting the *Awl* is the fact that it expressed the mentality of people who were household wage earners. As householders, they experienced social and economic independence; as wage earners, dependence. Their lives were intersected by contrary historical crosscurrents: small-scale household production and large-scale mass production, the personal ties of small-town life and the gnawing impersonality of the city. Despite the impact of industrial capitalism, preindustrial influences were still strong. Thus the consciousness of the artisans was shot through with contradictions: they proclaimed they were freemen who knew no master, but worried they were slaves to their employers. They spoke for a community of harmonious citizens, but organized themselves to strike. They were the lords of creation, but also the wretched of the earth.

The first editorial in the *Awl* expressed the yearning for harmony among the community's various interests:

The object of the paper is the benefit of *all* connected with the trade. We do not advocate the claims of the jour in opposition to those of the employer, nor seek to benefit one at the expense of the other.

This was more than good public relations; the labor editors believed that the whole industry would benefit by getting rid of cheap work and low wages. But they also knew that manufacturers, particularly the big Quaker bosses in a section of town named Pudding Hill (they dubbed it "extortion hill"), benefited at their expense. Did manufacturers acquire their property fairly? No, "The cordwainers earned it all, and they took it from them by their system of grinding." Such exploitation, the *Awl* believed, led to conflict in the community:

The division of society into the producing and the non-producing classes, and the fact of the unequal distribution of value between the two, introduces us at once to another distinction—that of capital and labor . . . Labor now becomes a commodity, wealth capital, and the natural order of things is entirely reversed. Antagonism and opposition of interest is introduced in the community; capital and labor stand opposed.[33]

The history of an abortive strike in the summer of 1844 demonstrated both sides of the artisan situation. A month after the Society of Journeymen Cordwainers was reconstituted the group resolved in favor of a strike, set a date in August, and canvassed the journeymen to find out how many would be willing to pack up their kit. Expecting a virtually unanimous, communitywide upsurge of support, the canvassers were apparently disappointed in the results, and the strike date passed without any disruption. Some journeymen then turned to producers' cooperatives as the best means for circumventing the antagonism between capital and labor and benefiting all connected with the trade. By November the Associated Labor Company, No. 1, was producing fine grades of ladies shoes, and within a few months the Mutual Industrial Association of Cordwainers was also in operation.[34] These attempts to return control over production to the producers enjoyed no better prospects for survival than did the master shoemakers and had no more security than the multiplicity of small manufacturing concerns started on a capitalist basis. But if their failure within two years demonstrated the power of the forces they were designed to overcome, their creation demonstrated an important facet of the artisan mentality.

The new inequalities of the Jacksonian era provoked radical critiques of American society and attempts to redirect the course of social change. The growing disparity in power and wealth between capitalist investors, on the one hand, and small independent artisans or individual wage-earning employees on the other, drove laboring people into one another's arms for collective assistance in the forms of strikes, mutual benefit societies, and cooperatives. In this context, the old idea that the labor of the "producing classes" is the source of all wealth took on new meaning. Since the idea held that capital was accumulated labor, it was a short step to conclude that capitalists grew rich by accumulating the fruits of the laborers' toil and that laborers were entitled to a fair or even the full share of the wealth they produced. These conclusions were the organizing principles of trade associations, with their demands for a fair wage, and producers' cooperatives, with their aim of an equal sharing of the proceeds. Trade unionism and cooperation were created in the same milieu by the same people who espoused the same philosophy of Equal Rights. The Wisconsin School of labor historians has usually posited a conflict between trade unionism and general social reform, seeing the former as forward looking and the latter as backward looking; from the actual point of view of laboring people through most of the nineteenth century, however, these were complementary, not conflicting, aspirations.[35]

Labor in Lynn consistently opposed the concentration of wealth and power in the hands of a few: monopoly was theft, whether it occurred in the shoe industry or in agriculture. Artisans worried that a few capitalist land speculators and paper money bankers were stealing the treasure of America's unused land. It is not so much that urban working people wished to reserve the land for themselves but that they wanted to prevent the spread of "aristocracy" on the land. This was the basis of the artisan opposition to slavery. They saw the expansion of the slave labor system as the expansion of monopoly over the soil. Whereas few artisans voted for the Liberty party in 1840 or 1844, great numbers voted for Free Soil in 1848. Although white workers feared the competition of nonwhite laborers and shared the racism of a white-Anglo-Saxon-Protestant culture, they hated the institution of slavery, identified with the slave, and grouped overbearing Lynn manufacturers together with slavemasters as "a set of lordly tyrants."[36]

After the attack on the engrossment of proprietary power in real estate, chattel slaves, and manufacturing establishments, the onward rush of radicalism slowed to a crawl. Only a few were prepared to extend the antimonopoly critique of the manufacturers to the point of denying the legitimacy of all private rights in the means of production (the position of Thomas Skidmore, Arthur Brisbane, Robert Owen, and other utopian socialists), and virtually no one in Lynn went beyond this to call for the elimination of all proprietary rights accumulated from the past (the position of Marx and Engels). Still, the radical core of artisan consciousness was an attack on capitalism as it presented itself to America in the 1830s and 1840s. Artisans watched the manufacturers race one another to increase their sales and contemptuously referred to such behavior as "making a dash in trade."

They were appalled at the "dishonest competition" among business competitors and creditors, who preyed on one another like predatory insects. They measured the extension of the boss's command by the shrinkage of the houshold. They calculated the profits of the manufacturers by mentally deducting a sum from their own wages. From these observations they concluded that harmony between capital and labor and justice in the community at large may have once prevailed but was now all but destroyed by the grasping ambition of self-aggrandizing shoe bosses.

The Tree of Liberty

Equal Rights was the fruit of the Tree of Liberty. With roots running deep into the Anglo-American past, the Tree pushed up through the dead weight of Imperial tax collectors, overbearing Royal governors, and aristocratic corruption during the American Revolution. The successful defense of domestic liberty against Imperial power raised the problem of reconciling power with liberty under new forms of government at home. State and federal constitutions sought a synthesis of power and liberty through a separation of powers into different branches of representative governments that were based ultimately on popular sovereignty. Defenders of the new forms argued that republicanism made power dependent upon liberty, since republican rulers depended on the suffrage of those they governed. Suffrage itself was limited to property owners, who were presumed to represent the interests of everyone in their households. In disfranchising household dependents and other adults without property, republicanism incorporated the inequalities of eighteenth-century society. Among freeholders, however, republicanism posited the equality of rights, duties, and privileges, which is how a wealthy slaveowner named Thomas Jefferson could become a popular symbol among yeomen and mechanics.

In the early nineteenth century these Jeffersonian sentinels stood guard against attack, prepared to water the Tree of Liberty with their own blood and the blood of tyrants, if need be. Under this care the Tree branched out and grew democratic in form: the right of suffrage expanded to embrace men without a freehold; political parties, once suspect as seditious factions in the republic, became regular features of state and national politics; the exclusiveness of the Washington community was challenged by rough outsiders; the assumption that the rich, well-born, and the able should govern (an assumption that underwrote the Federal Constitution and underlay the selection of its officers) was overwhelmed by the assumption that the people were well able to represent their own interests.

Not everyone experienced this change as an advance; for women and for slaves there was no direct benefit, and free Blacks actually lost rights they held under republicanism. Thus it is necessary to be quite careful in using terms like "democracy," "majority rule," or "individual rights." Most contemporary commentators may have agreed with Alexis de Tocqueville that such exclusions could take place without disqualifying America as a democracy, but others, like Frederick Douglass, were not convinced and in the cause of democratizing America urged the full rights of citizenship for women and Afro-Americans. As it went, the active citizenry was limited generally to men who were free, white, and twenty-one and could meet residency requirements and pay a poll tax. Considering those who were left out, this was a highly select group; but comparing only the position of white men in the United States and Europe, the selection was very broad, indeed, and the use of the term "democracy" should fall within that context.

The growth of political democracy was integrally related to the evolution of American capitalism. The transfer of the franchise from the householder to the individual citizen happened as part of the disintegration of the household as the basic unit of production. As the marketplace penetrated into the producer's household, freely competing entrepreneurs increasingly employed freely competing wage earners. Individualism burgeoned with expansion on the land, as well as in the cities; the migration of population westward accompanied by the demand for agricultural goods discouraged communal control over the economic practices of the small commercial growers of the trans-Appalachian region, and they, too, sought new political forms that suited their style of competitive individualism better than the old republican commonwealth.[37] The political arena became a marketplace of individual, unattached voters.

The United States was able to move toward mass political democracy before any other nation in the world because of the prior success of republicanism in eliminating monarchy and aristocracy, the traditional enemies of democracy. But republicanism, in turn, became an obstacle to democratic development, and American society in the early nineteenth century rejected the republican social order of deferential ranks; such a system was out of place in an environment that fostered equal access of all men to the political process. Consequently political leaders who urged electors to vote for their social betters went out of style; instead, leaders took to drinking hard cider, arranged to be born in log cabins, and acquired epithets like Old Kinderhook that showed they were just folks. Since economic success and social preeminence no longer led automatically to public service or conferred political power, candidates of whatever station in life had to compete with one another in selling their wares in the voters' marketplace. Men like Abraham Lincoln devoted a lifetime to perfecting the personal skills and party apparatus required for this process.[38]

The on-going problem faced by the democratic career politician was to reconcile equal access to political participation with social and economic inequality. The dynamics of the expanding capitalist economy generated the pressures for political democracy, but also generated new inequalities. Those citizens who wound up with smaller shares of wealth and power sounded the alarm that once again the Tree of Liberty was in danger, and urban artisans rallied to its defense. Some of their lines in Lynn collapsed rather quickly: for example, the community ignored the call for a town meeting to thwart the "gross impositions" of the bosses, and a slate of workingmen's candidates for town office in 1836 also went nowhere. But journeymen got at least some oratorical assistance in their struggle from regular party politicians, especially the Democrats. Journeymen voted for the candidates of all parties, but after Martin Van Buren captured a majority of Lynn's votes in 1836, Democrats usually won state and national elections, at least as long as they talked Equal Rights to journeymen voters. In 1848, the Democrats abandoned Equal Rights, and the journeymen abandoned the Democrats for the Free Soil party, which won in a three-sided contest.[39]

The man who epitomized the Democrats' links to Lynn labor in these years was George Hood. Hood was the young man who borrowed $1000 worth of shoes from Micajah Pratt and Nathan Breed in

1829 and went to St. Louis to seek his fortune. Success enabled him to return home and invest in Lynn real estate, a Boston leather supply firm, and the Lynn Five Cents Savings Bank, capstone of his financial accomplishments. Being a bustling small businessman did not prevent him from becoming a popular figure among the journeymen. He joined the Society of Journeymen Cordwainers, attended meetings of the group, and was the only prominent local politician to get favorable mention in the *Awl*.[40] He peddled the notions of Equal Rights, traded in the coin of bullionism, and sold the slogan that the laborer was worthy of his hire. In a time of status anxiety, such flattery was a commodity in great demand.

Hood's supply of this commodity was sufficient to put himself at the head of the movement to resist the incorporation of Lynn as a city in the late 1840s and then to become the city's first mayor. The pressure for incorporation arose from businessmen in the central manufacturing district near the main railroad station, while opposition coalesced around shoemakers and fishermen in outlying districts. The opposition chose a committee of five mechanics to draft a bill of "Reasons and Facts" against the charter of incorporation; among its twenty-two indictments was the complaint that wealthy businessmen were out to tax the whole community in order "to maintain and improve their numerous streets, their high school, their city hall, their police court, their night watch, their 'strong and efficient' police, their Mayor and City Marshal." This train of abuses would lead in only one direction—to the destruction of Equal Rights. Small taxpayers and the poor were urged to oppose the charter: "Because this City scheme was got up by a few individuals that have more money than they have actual use for, and it is believed they are desirous to expend their surplus means for preferment, office, honor, power, and to create inequality, caste, and an aristocracy of Mayors and Aldermen, nabobs and *nobles*."[41]

The Tree of Liberty trembled in the winds of change. Resistance to tyranny appeared to be shaken when the voters of Lynn narrowly approved the charter in the spring of 1850, after three previous rejections. But those who had gathered to defend their liberties regrouped around George Hood, a person who could be trusted to prevent the would-be nobility from growing fat and sleek off the public treasury.[42]

Turning defeat into victory, they elected Hood mayor. The people hoisted a commoner onto the nabob's throne.

The effect of Hood's election was to give his supporters the illusion of power without its substance. Elevating their man to the highest position of honor in the community provided powerful emotional satisfactions, and for some of the supporters there was the material benefit of patronage, to boot. But these satisfactions enticed them into a frame of government they had once conceived as a structure of oppression, and the structure did not change with their entrance or the elevation of one politician to sit at the top. Popular participation was not popular control, and the guardians of the Equal Rights tradition were absorbed into a structure which was designed by businessmen and which precluded certain forms of action. No politician urged taxation of the profits made by the stockholders of the Lynn Mechanics Bank; no successful politician proclaimed that the laborer is entitled to the *full* fruit of his toil. Journeymen were ready to listen to such ideas, but they were not forthcoming. Instead, journeymen heeded the message of politicians who told them that the election of antiaristocratic officials would suffice to cut the ties between private investors and public privilege. Thus the artisan participation in the democratic process channeled the radical impulse in the Equal Rights tradition away from a critique of the political system as a whole.

The economic experience of the journeymen in the central shop era engendered the awareness of an inescapable conflict of interest between labor and capital. Despite the attempts of business spokesmen to kill this idea, it would not die. But such is only the stuff of which an awareness of class conflict is made; it is *not* the full awareness of parallel conflicts in politics, society, culture, and economy. The development of such a belief was checked by the political experience of laboring people in the context of capitalist democracy. The ballot box was the coffin of class consciousness.

The political experience of Lynn artisans pruned the Tree of Liberty. Whereas the first American Revolution remained fresh in their minds, they did not see the need for another. As the primal event in the history of the Tree of Liberty, the Revolution was an inspiration to nineteenth-century radicals. Abolitionists invoked its equalizing spirit. Feminists rewrote the Declaration of Independence so it read "all men and women are created equal." Likewise, the artisans of Lynn called for a spirit of '76 to infuse the labor movement. The second issue of the *Awl* reprinted the entire Declaration of Independence; some journeymen compared their bosses to King George, and one proposed that workingmen assemble on Lynn Common on the Fourth of July to erect a monument to their forebears who marched to repulse the British at Concord in 1775.[43] The artisans remembered a Revolution in which the struggle for national independence was accompanied by a struggle for equality, a recollection that differed markedly from the businessman's memory of the victory of the rights of property. But if interpretations varied, both groups believed they had come out on the winning side. Unlike the Parisian sans-culottes or the English Jacobins, American artisans could identify with the State that emerged from the period of eighteenth-century revolution.[44] And every time a politician who posed as a friend of the workingman was elected to local, state, or national office that belief was confirmed. Tradition was recreated in experience, and so artisans had reason to believe that the structure of authority, if not particular officials and policies, rested on popular sovereignty (again, "popular" must be taken in the context of white men).

In contrast, English artisans saw something sinister in the whole structure of British government. Parliament appeared to be walled in behind the legal barricades of property tests for voting and officeholding, and the government was willing to use violence to preserve these walls, as it had proved by shooting 400 (killing 11) of the 80,000 peaceful demonstrators at St. Peter's Fields near Manchester in 1819. Partly as a result of the "Peterloo Massacre," English artisans defined reform as a change in the basic structure of political power. The political program of the English workers rested on the People's Charter, which called for a six-part reform that would bring universal manhood suffrage, voting by ballot, with each vote of equal weight, and the election of annual Parliaments whose members did not have to meet a property test and who would be paid a salary. After the collapse of the attempt to form a national union of all trade associations in the mid-1830s, the next two decades were consumed with agitation for the Charter, a movement with clear revolutionary potential.[45]

But where was the Charter of American artisans? Most of it was already written into the Federal Constitution, Article I, Sections 1, 2, 4, and 6, which together provided for a House of Representatives whose paid members were not subject to explicit property tests, and who met in annual sessions to represent the interests of equal numbers of constituents (though not equal numbers of *voters,* since qualifications varied from state to state, nor equal numbers of persons, since "Indians not taxed" were excluded and slaves fell under the three-fifths clause). The only remaining plank in the People's Charter—that calling for universal manhood suffrage—was enacted on a state-by-state basis into the laws of most northern and western states. And where was America's Peterloo Massacre? It did not yet exist. The massacres of American workers were still in a future industrial society which would generate more desperate forms of discontent among its workers and repress them violently out of a more intense need for regimentation on the part of its employers. The generation of American working people that confronted the first stages of industrial capitalism looked back upon their political heritage and remembered not exclusion but inclusion, not violence but peaceful change, and concluded that they could change the laws if only they would do so. In their eyes, the government was but the executive committee of the people.

3

FACTORIES

For two centuries after the initial white settlement of New England, profit hungry investors and frustrated fortune hunters encountered powerful restraints on economic development. They were impeded by Puritan strictures against profiteering, by mercantilist regulations of the economy, and by environmental backwardness. But they persevered, and by the second quarter of the nineteenth century their boundless ambition for gain had achieved significant breakthroughs in extending the principles and practices of marketplace directly into the sphere of production.

Leading the way were shoes and textiles, which stood first and second in the industrial statistics of New England from the first statistical surveys in the 1830s through the Civil War. Together these industries carved great basins of industrialization out of the hilly, rock-ribbed countryside that straddled the Merrimack and Connecticut River valleys and ran inland from the shores of Rhode Island and eastern Massachusetts. Lynn lay in one of these basins stretching from Boston to the White Mountains and including the major manufacturing cities of Lowell, Lawrence, Haverhill, Salem, Manchester, and Newburyport, plus several other smaller cities in Massachusetts, New Hampshire, and Maine. Furthermore, dozens of additional villages in the country imitated the enterprise of the more renowned urban centers, and in some of these hamlets outworkers for the shoe industry labored in the shadow of a local textile mill. Everywhere central shops, factories, and warehouses were shouldering their way in among the artisan shops, hay barns, livery stables, and grist mills that represented the vanishing era of economic restraint.

Lynn manufacturers joined the headlong rush toward unimpeded economic development. Between 1830 and 1836 they increased production by two-thirds, making this a time of "feverish excitement" when the character of the town changed "more rapidly and more essentially than at any previous period in her history." The number of streets and buildings nearly doubled in these years, and the physical strain on the community was compounded by social dislocation. The only thing that held back the rapacity of the entrepreneurs was the fearsome grip of panic, which took hold in 1837 and stopped them in their tracks. For the next seven years, they chafed at the restraints of the prolonged depression in the industry and organized through the Whig party to improve their prospects by increasing the tariff on imported shoes. But foreign competition was no longer a major factor in the industry, and when the domestic market finally responded to the proddings of the manufacturers in the mid-1840s, those who had survived congratulated themselves on being sounder and stronger than their fallen competitors and rushed ahead with renewed vigor. Another period of feverish expansion ensued between 1845 and 1850; boosted by the rapidly lengthening railroad network, shoe production came close to doubling. (See Appendix A.) Freed from the restraints of the past, the marketplace did not produce Adam Smith's version of stable, self-regulating progress, but manic cycles of expansion and contraction.[1]

The main resource for expansion was labor. Increased output in the prefactory era was directly proportional to an increase in the number of shoemakers, and employers calculated profits in these terms: so many hands, so many dollars. During business upturns, they hired hand over fist; for every three employees of a Lynn firm in 1845, there were five in 1850. (See Appendix A.) Like the declining dominions of the Old South which were sending slave laborers to the more profitable cotton lands of the West, rural New England yielded up its laborers to employers who mined the area as if it were filled with gold. Making the transfer from farming to shoemaking was not difficult for the rural inhabitants, who had worked with their hands from childhood. What teenage girl did not know how to stitch and sew? What man who mended harnesses and repaired saddles could not learn the gentle craft of shoemaking, especially now that cutting was done by specialists? So for a quarter of a century the land readily gave up its people.

But no resource, however abundant, is inexhaustible. Employers quickly depleted the areas close to the cities, and they had to range ever further afield. Driven by gold fever, shoe manufacturers ventured into northern New Hampshire and Vermont, while textile employers prospected as far away as upstate New York and Canada in search of young female operatives. Competition among the employers was compounded by the migration of labor out of the region; enough Massachusetts natives moved to New York to make the number living there in 1850 almost equal to the total number of people employed by the entire Massachusetts boot and shoe industry.[2] The shoe industry felt these pressures in the form of a diminishing marginal product in the branch where competition for labor was most keen—binding. In the 1830s each binder stitched an average of 934 pairs a year, but by 1850 the number had fallen below 700. The rates of output appear in Table 1.[3]

TABLE 1. Average Annual Output (in Pairs of Shoes) of Men and Women Employed by Lynn Firms, 1831–1860.

Category	1831	1832	1837	1845	1850	1855	1860
Women	941	842	1018	754	689	714	1438
Men	986	1024	980	894	1154	1031	958

Source: 1831: C. F. Lummus, *The Lynn Directory and Town Register . . .* (Lynn, 1832), p. 14; *1832:* McLane, "Documents Relative to the Manufactures in the United States," pp. 224–237; *1837:* John W. Barber, *Historical Collections* (Worcester, Mass., 1841), p. 197; *1845:* Palfrey, *Statistics,* pp. 8–38; *1850:* Shattuck, *Report,* p. 508; *1855:* DeWitt, *Information,* pp. 634–643; *1860:* author's calculations from Lynn census manuscripts.

Note: The figures were obtained by dividing total output by total employment in each category.

Because textile recruiters sent most of the ready women without children to the factories, the boot and shoe firms had difficulty finding full-time binders and, instead, had to rely on new recruits who bound shoes intermittently between their other chores at home. "Women's nimble fingers," wrote one observer, "were found inadequate to the demand."[4]

The geographical outreach of the outwork system heightened the manufacturers' dilemma by making production most sluggish at the frontiers of expansion. Transportation of raw materials to the fringes of the system 150 miles from Lynn consumed two or three weeks, and the return trip doubled the time lost in transit. When this delay was added to the easy going work pace logged by farmer shoemakers, the result was a waiting time that ranged as high as six to nine months before a pair of shoes was finished.[5] The further the system expanded without changing its technological base the more difficulty it encountered reaching its objectives. As the distance and time between the various steps in the manufacturing process increased and as it became harder to get binding done quickly, the method of sending work out of town, originally designed as a means of raising peak seasonal output, was beginning to have just the opposite result. The gold rush was coming to a close.

Deus ex machina

The manufacturers' problem was resolved by a deus ex machina in the form of a sewing machine. Minor modifications of the original invention enabled an operator to bind the uppers in a fraction of the time it took by hand. Therefore the manufacturer no longer had to expand the geographical frontiers of his labor force and instead could cut back the total number of female employees and hire a greater proportion from among residents of Lynn. The importance of the machine was emphasized by a newspaper closely identified with the manufacturers: "The introduction of sewing machines for stitching and binding of shoes was the result of an absolute necessity."[6]

Since the uppers were made of cloth or light leather, the same machine could be used for binding uppers and mending a dress. Initially, the cost of the machines restricted their use to people with substantial savings, but their price steadily declined from the $75 to 100 range of the early 1850s to a level around $20 in the early 1860s, before Civil War inflation drove the price up again. Newspaper ads were frequently addressed to "the lady operator and the shoe manufacturer" and strained to make the point that they were for family use, as well as for manufacturing. The ads were effective, and soon "almost every house" in Lynn sported a sewing machine;

the number of sewing machines per capita was more than the number of hogs had ever been in preindustrial Lynn.[7]

However, the trend in manufacturing was unmistakably away from the household and toward the factory. The first machines were tried out and proved in the shops of three of the larger manufacturers in 1852. Because they employed two to three times as many people as the average firm, these manufacturers were more deeply entangled in the contradictions of the outwork system than the smaller employers and were especially eager for a way out. Their initiative spread, and by 1855 most of the leading manufacturers had begun to use sewing machines. Sometimes smaller contractors set up independent stitching shops, but usually the manufacturers outfitted rooms of their own. From this point on through 1880 the trend in female employment was downward, even as total output rose; between 1850 and 1860 the number of women employed declined 40 percent, while their output doubled. Both speed and quality were enhanced by bringing operators and machines together under one roof, so that only one-fifth of the women employed in 1875 were left working at home.[8]

From the outset, the stitching shops looked strikingly like factories. The gathering of as many as three or four dozen women in one room and the clatter of their machines were such a contrast to the picture of a woman quietly at work in her own kitchen that everyone agreed a fundamental change had taken place.

The invention of the sewing machine opened a new frontier, which "soon transformed the old fashioned 'shoe-binders' into a new and more expansive class of 'machine girls' whose capacity for labor was only limited by the capabilities of the machines over which they presided. Iron and steel came to the aid of wearied fingers and weakened eyes. This was the beginning of a new era, which is destined to produce results big with lasting benefit to our flourishing city."[9]

Glowing enthusiasm for the factory system appeared in an 1860 federal census report on the boot and shoe industry. Describing the sewing machine as a "crowning invention," the article said that along with a sole-cutting machine it was bringing about "a silent revolution" in manufacturing. The report sensed the shoe industry was "assuming the characteristics of a factory system, being conducted in large establishments of several stories, each floor devoted to a separate part of the work, with the aid of steam-power, and all the labor-saving contrivances known to the trade. It is safe to predict that this change will go on until the little 'workshop' of the shoemaker, with its 'bench' and 'kit', shall become a thing of the past, as the 'handcard' and the great and little 'spinning wheel' have disappeared from other branches of the clothing manufacture."[10] This report jumped the gun by a few years, but because the major forms of factory organization were fully represented in machine stitching, and because the model of textile industry was so compelling, it is not surprising that the report assumed the inevitability of a full-scale factory system.

The Great Strike

The manufacturers' enthusiasm for machines and factories did not spread to the shoemakers. Binders and journeymen looked back over a quarter century of social dislocation, and now in the 1850s they feared that once again the manufacturers were up to no good. The first sewing machines introduced into the city "aroused the ire" of the binders, who saw them as another incursion on their household independence. A delegation of binders tried to block the spread of the new devices by visiting a central shop where one had been installed and requesting the operator to cease her work on the grounds that the machine "would ultimately be the ruin of the poor workingwomen."[11] These early machines, which cost a third to a half of a binder's annual income, were clearly implements designed to benefit only capitalists; both the binders who went into the stitching shops and the shrinking group of those who worked at home continued to regard the new methods of production with extreme distrust. Each binder knew that the labor the new devices saved could well be her own, and what good, she wondered, could possibly come of something that eliminated hundreds of jobs each season.

The binders' ire was mollified for a time by the declining price of the sewing machine (making it more accessible for family use) and by the persistence of high levels of employment in the shoe industry. But when the Panic of 1857 brought the shoe business to a standstill, and workers all over the city were given the sack, the twin pressures of depression and displacement converged on shoemaker families to force discontent to the surface again, as in the 1830s and 1840s. The tensions between shoemakers and their bosses were apparent at two mass meetings held on the edge of winter in the depression's first year. As journeymen shoemakers and other laboring men of the community filed into Lynn's rustic Lyceum Hall, the chill November air reminded them of the blankets, overcoats, cordwood, and provisions they would need in the coming months, and of the long winter layover looming ahead when they would have little or no income. They listened with growing indignation while businessmen and politicians proposed emergency public relief, as if the honest workingmen of Lynn were nothing but paupers. Were they not able-bodied men willing to work?

At a second community meeting the following week, these sentiments buried the proposals for public relief. "Would it not be better," asked one opponent of charity, "for the shoe manufacturers to give full price—to say to the workman we will give you a little something to do until business is better?" And he added, "Let the rich come forward and say we will give you ten per cent of the profits we have made." The idea was radical enough to prompt a quick rejoinder from a shoe manufacturer and leather dealer named John B. Alley that the purpose of the meeting was not to degrade business for the benefit of labor. Alley was an up-and-coming politician on his way to the House of Representatives polishing the techniques of rhetorical compromise; he endorsed the work ethic but argued present circumstances made public relief a practical necessity.[12]

Despite Alley's compromise, this debate set a tone of hostility for encounters between shoemakers and shoe manufacturers during the next three years. Eight months later several hundred journeymen sweltered through a July meeting in the Lyceum to consider a strike to raise wages. No action was taken immediately, but economic distress kept up a steady pressure, and by the spring of 1859 journeymen had established the Lynn Mechanics Association and had begun publishing the *New England Mechanic*.[13] The Association and the *Mechanic* continued operation for the remainder of the year, becoming a solid core of organizational strength among the journeymen. Finally, in the winter of 1860 all the years of anxiety over the effects

of machine stitching combined with the years of depression to produce a mounting frustration that burst forth in the Great Shoemakers
Strike.

The biggest strike the United States had ever experienced hit the
whole upper New England basin like a driving "Nor'easter." The
shoe centers along the North Shore bore the full brunt of the storm,
where a clear majority of shoemakers joined the strike, and it also
swept inland to secondary towns and outwork villages. All in all,
probably a minimum of 20,000 people quit work, somewhat more
than half the employees living in this region and a third of the 60,000
employees of all Massachusetts firms. The progress of the strike was
given large play in most of the region's major newspapers, and
national journals sent illustrators and reporters to the scene. The
experience left an indelible mark on folk memory, and for a generation it was recalled with the frequency and vividness people usually
reserved for earthquakes or hurricanes. Given the scope of the strike,
it is astonishing that it should have been totally ignored in the works
of John Commons and several of his followers. This gap was filled
by Philip Foner, who wrote an excellent overview of the strike, and
later by George R. Taylor, who recognized the event as "the greatest
strike in American history before the Civil War."[14]

Lynn was at the center of the storm. The strike began on Washington's Birthday, a date the journeymen picked to demonstrate they
were acting in the best traditions of the Republic. They believed the
producers were the bone and sinew of society, and in a community
of interdependent households the producers should be able to unite
and carry everyone along with them. The dimensions of their success
were revealed in the scope and style of demonstrations and parades
held in support of the strike. In six weeks, five processions passed
through the streets of Lynn, each with 1000 or more people in the
line of march, plus hundreds of sympathizers in the sidelines. The
largest demonstration occurred on March 16; besides strikers from
Lynn marching in ward units, the 6000 people who crowded into the
procession included companies of militia and firemen, brass bands,
and several out-of-town strike delegations. The order of march that
day was:

Lynn City Guards, Lynn Cornet Band; Lady stitchers, in wards; delegations of women from Swampscott and elsewhere; Fountain Engine Co. #3, Lynn; Co. #4 of Marblehead; Tiger Engine #4 of Lynn; Atlantic #1, Swampscott; Engine #5 and Chelsea Brass Band; strikers from Swampscott; Eagle #5, S. Danvers; Niagara #9, Lynn; delegations from South Danvers, Danversport, East Danvers with banners; strikers of wards 4, 5, 6 of Lynn; strikers of Saugus and South Reading; Volunteer Fire #8, Lynn; Worth #2 Stoneham with strikers from Stoneham and East Woburn; ward 7 strikers of Lynn; strikers from Beverly and Beverly Cornet band; Salem strikers; Marblehead strikers, escorted by Lafayette Guards, Glover Light Guards, Marblehead Band, Engine Cos. #1, #2; Washington Hook and Ladder #1, Gerry Co.[15]

The strikers immersed themselves in the pageantry of waving banners and brightly festooned uniforms to show that their strike had the support and expressed the will of the general community. The presence of the militia companies and firemen—themselves mostly laboring men in special uniforms—emphasized the interdependence among the householders of an artisan community. The organization of the strikers into ward units bespoke the ties of neighborhood fraternity and sorority. The joint participation of men and women expressed the solidarity of all who labored in the craft. The strike processions, therefore, emerged from the customs and traditions of preindustrial society. They were festivals of the old artisan way of life presented in the context of the new system of industrial capitalism. Influences from the past and forces leading to the future simultaneously fashioned the present event.

The presence of women was a noteworthy feature of the processions. Without the action of women, it is questionable whether the strike would have occurred at all, and certainly without them it would have been far less massive in its impact. Women's grievances helped cause it; their demands shaped its objectives; their support ratified it as a community undertaking. Whether they worked at home or in the manufacturers' shops, all women employees earned piece wages, and both home and shop workers focused their demands on an increase in wages. They held their own strike meetings, did their own canvassing in Lynn and nearby towns to win support, and turned out in strength for the big street demonstrations. The laborer, they contended, was worthy of her hire.

The demonstration on March 7 was held in their honor. Escorted by a detachment of musket-bearing militia, 800 women strikers started at Lynn Common and marched in the falling snow for several hours past the central shops on Lynn's major thoroughfares. Their action was a bold violation of the cultural code that stipulated women should not venture beyond kitchen hearth and church pew. The keepers of this code of True Womanhood were middle-class families in retreat from the disorder of urban life into their parlors, sewing circles, and church clubs. But workingwomen were bound to no such cult of domesticity. For several generations their labor had mingled with that of other producers, just as their protests had blended with the journeymen, and they were not about to renounce their own heritage of Equal Rights.[16]

At the head of their procession they carried a banner with an inscription taken from the Equal Rights philosophy: "AMERICAN LADIES WILL NOT BE SLAVES: GIVE US A FAIR COMPENSATION AND WE LABOUR CHEERFULLY." Slavery had long been the measure of the ultimate degradation of labor, the point to which the shoe bosses seemed to be driving their employees. With the execution of John Brown only three months before the strike, artisans felt the immediacy of the conflict between slavery and Free Soil, and analogies linking manufacturers to slavemasters flowed freely. One speaker at a mass meeting declared it was not necessary to go to "bleeding Kansas" to find oppressors of labor; there were plenty who had been "drawing the chains of slavery, and riveting them closer and closer around the limbs of free laboring men at home."[17] A similar note was struck by the first stanza of the "Cordwainers' Song," written during the strike by Alonzo Lewis.

> Shoemakers of Lynn, be brave!
>   Renew your resolves again;
> Sink not to the state of slave,
>   But stand for your rights like men!
>
> Resolve by your native soil,
>   Resolve by your fathers' graves,

You will live by your honest toil,
   But never consent to be slaves!

The workman is worthy his hire,
   No tyrant shall hold us in thrall;
They may order their soldiers to fire,
   But we'll stick to the hammer and awl.

Better days will restore us our rights,
   The future shall shine o'er the past;
We shall triumph by justice and right,
   For like men we'll hold onto the last!

The peaceable people of Lynn
   Need no rifles to keep them at peace;
By the right of our cause we shall win;
   But no rum, and no outside police.[18]

For all its resounding resolves, the song was clearly not in tune with full sexual equality. The Equal Rights tradition contenanced a limited version of feminism: women who worked should be accorded a place of honor among the ranks of toilers, should be paid a fair and equal compensation, and should take an active role in defending the rights of labor. But this was the extent of labor feminism; when it came to critical strike strategy, to political affairs, and to final arbitration in domestic matters, men ought to be in charge. Thus the cultural environment of the strike was filled with symbols of manhood which could hardly appeal to women strikers. The call to "stand for your rights like men!" must have left women seated in their chairs.

The "Cordwainers' Song" rallied shoemakers to the defense of the Tree of Liberty. Striking a classic Jeffersonian pose, the brave shoemakers prepared to shed their blood, should tyrants order their soldiers to fire. The tyrants of the song were the big shoe bosses of Lynn, especially those who practiced "dishonest competition" and affected an air of superiority in their dealings with the masses. But some of the manufacturers held the trust of the shoemakers, and four bosses received "Hurrahs!" when the Washington's Birthday marchers passed their central shops. One of the four reciprocated the holiday spirit by decorating his building with flags and bunting for the occasion. This was the kind of harmony between labor and capital many strike leaders hoped for. The week before Washington's Birthday, officers in the Mechanics Association had carried a bill of wages around to the manufacturers asking for voluntary agreement to pay the advanced rates. The committee even solicited contributions from the bosses to the strike fund! Shoemakers were not surprised when several manufacturers actually subscribed to pay; leading the list was a boss who "agreed to be taxed $300." Believing they represented the general will of their community, shoemakers found nothing strange in their plan to "tax" their neighbors.[19]

Shoemakers prepared for the strike as members of the "producing classes." As producers they felt they were entitled to a fair reward for their toil, which they defined as an exchange of the goods they made for an equivalent value of food, clothing, shelter, and enjoyments. Anything less was cheating. Thus "monopolists" and "grinders" who cut their prices or cheapened their wares to increase their sales practiced "dishonest competition." In their train followed a host of unfortunate laborers forced to toil for a pittance on cheap goods until their existence approached the pauper labor of Europe. The dire result was the degradation of the earnings and reputations of "honest labor." When artisans divided their employers into "good bosses" and "bad bosses," they were not indulging in meaningless moralizing; they expressed a view of reality that conformed to the heritage of a community of householders.

Yet reality itself went well beyond this view. The central shop was no simple producer's household. The marketplace compelled manufacturers to adhere to the laws of competition, opposing the interest of those who bought labor to the interest of those who sold it. Moreover, shoemakers did not control the instruments of public authority. In the course of the strike, shoemakers were forced to face these disturbing facets of reality. The image of the artisan seemed to dissolve before their eyes, and in its place they saw an image of the industrial worker taking shape.

Shoemakers had to come to terms with the fact that manufacturers did not behave like fellow household producers. Only one came through on his pledge to the strike fund; the rest either reneged completely or paid only a trifling sum, such as a $20 contribution from the man who had agreed to be taxed $300. Worse than that, the manufacturers connived to break the back of the strike by hiring scab labor. They sent agents to ransack the surrounding states for workmen and hired "everything in the shape of a shoemaker." To the manufacturer, business was business, and the laws of the marketplace were more compelling than the will of the majority. With debts to pay, orders to fill, and customers to keep, manufacturers were not about to suspend the quest for profits just because the shoemakers desired it. But to the shoemakers, the manufacturers' effort to keep up production, after promising "to help us through, if we would strike and stick for a few weeks," was an outrageous betrayal. In a retrospective article fuming with indignation, two strike leaders snarled that the manufacturers, virtually without exception, tried to "defeat and disgrace us." One of the leaders told a group of binders in early April that the events of the past few weeks proved "the interest of capital is to get as much labor for as little money as possible."[20]

Shoemakers had interests and compulsions of their own. Money wages were the staff of life; no one could survive any longer on home-grown pork and greens. Because shoemakers were wholly dependent on their industrial income, the wages of industrial unemployment were debt and destitution. Going into debt during the winter layover was a normal experience for shoemakers, but every year since the Panic of 1857 getting out of debt in the spring had been unusually difficult. The manufacturers were "grinding us down so low that men with large families could not live within their own means."[21] Neither could young men with little experience (who were given low-paid tasks) nor women of any age and skill (whose wages were the lowest in the industry). Wage earners of all types concluded that the degradation of free labor was at hand.

In a mood of bitter determination shoemakers vowed that if the manufacturers would not willingly raise their wages, then they must be compelled to do so through a complete cessation of labor. This feeling motivated some strikers to use force to win their objectives, a marked contrast to the holiday atmosphere of the strike processions. On the morning of the day after Washington's Birthday a crowd of strikers gathered in front of the Central Square railroad depot. It was apparent that most manufacturers intended to maintain business as usual, because they continued to send cases of shoe stock to the depot for shipment to outworkers. A considerable portion of the crowd was in favor of preventing all such cases from leaving Lynn. Many who assembled that morning were piqued by a hoax played on them the previous afternoon, when they had carried what appeared to be a case of shoe stock back to its owner, only to discover it was filled with leather scraps and floor sweepings. This provocation was heightened by the local city marshal who addressed the crowd in insulting terms that "only served to increase irritation and excitement among the strikers who heard them."[22]

The marshal got another crack at the shoemakers the same afternoon. With a few deputies in tow he fell upon a handful of men who were dumping cases destined for scab outworkers off an express wagon. The marshal's force succeeded in replacing the cases on the wagon, but in the eyes of the strikers, the marshal was now firmly identified with the shoe bosses, and his office lost whatever majesty it might have had. Pursuing their own justice, the strikers attempted to cast down the cases once again, and when the marshal stood in their way, they pummeled him and his men with their fists. It was reported that one of the strikers drew a knife. Overpowered in this fracas, the marshal refrained from further adventures that afternoon, and several more cases were taken from the train depot and returned to the central shops. In addition, the pugnacious expressman who tried to defend his cargo was "badly hurt," and strikers roughed up at least one journeyman on his way home with fresh materials.[23]

In the eyes of the manufacturers the interference with the flow of trade and the attack on the city marshal constituted a vile threat to the social order bordering on insurrection. Through friends in city government, they prevailed upon the mayor to call out the militia. In his letter to the commander of the Lynn Light Infantry, Co. D, Eighth Regiment of the Massachusetts Volunteers, the mayor took note that "bodies of men have tumultuously assembled in [Lynn], and have offered violence to persons and property, and have, by force and violence resisted and broken the laws of the Commonwealth; and that military force is necessary to aid the civil authority in suppressing the same." The men were called to appear at their armory the next morning "armed, equipped with ammunition." Then while the mayor went off to counsel moderation before a mass meeting of shoemakers, other city officials got in touch with the state attorney general, the sheriff of Essex County, a major general in the state militia, and the city officials and police chiefs of Boston and South Danvers. The manufacturers were taking no chances with unruly employees.[24]

The next day, February 24, shoemakers arose with dawning amazement to find their community occupied by outside police and armed militia. In the morning a detachment of deputies from South Danvers stood guard at the train station to see that there was no more interference with the shipment of shoe materials, and at 1:00 o'clock a posse of twenty uniformed Boston policemen arrived at the depot. These professional law officers joined the militia at an inn named the Sagamore House, which had been converted into command head-quarters for the day. Decisions were in the hands of the attorney general, the major general, the city marshal, and several aldermen; conspicuously absent from the Sagamore were the mayor, who had fallen ill, and the city councilors. Apparently with the aim of arrest-ing those who were disorderly the day before, the Boston regulars were sent back into the streets. Led by the hated city marshal, they roved through town for two hours, stimulating near riots where ever they went. Hounded by hoots and hisses, pelted by stones and brick-bats, they ran the gauntlet of a hostile crowd, participated in a "gen-eral melee in which several of the crowd were knocked down," and finally ended their tumultuous trek through town at the railroad depot in Central Square where it had begun.[25]

Most residents of the community were outraged at this incursion on their right of self-government, and it was a man who lived by his wits, not his hands, that wrote:

> The peaceable people of Lynn
>   Need no rifles to keep them at peace;
> By the right of our cause we shall win;
>   But no rum and no outside police.

Widespread indignation apparently blocked the prosecution of the five men arrested that day. Though they were spirited away to Salem for safekeeping and arraigned and bound over to the grand jury in Lynn a few days later, there is no record that the grand jury was ever convened or that any of the men were ever convicted of riotous conduct. The five benefited from community opposition to the odious actions of manufacturers and public officials, even though only one of the men arrested was a long-standing, propertied resident of Lynn. The others were newcomers, immigrants living in poverty, including the Irishman reported to have pulled a knife.[26]

The turmoil of the first three days of the strike was the worst fury of the storm. On the evening of the third day the outside police and state officials left town, and the temporary soldiers dismantled their rifles and went home. That was the end of violence. But the passions stirred up in these days imparted a force and momentum to the strike that carried it through six weeks of mass organizing on a scale never before seen in American industry. While manufacturers hunted for scabs, teams of strike canvassers combed the neighborhoods of Lynn and visited a score of other shoe towns to mobilize support. Thousands of people were organized into strike processions, with thousands more watching. On the days of the processions, dozens of kitchens kept up a steady outpouring of food to provide refreshment to those who marched. In addition, there were rallies in Central Square, mass meetings in Lyceum Hall, and frequent meetings of the strike leadership in the Mechanics Association and the Ladies' Association of Binders and Stitchers.

Support of nonshoemakers was also mobilized. Besides other laboring men who marched in the fire and militia companies (with the conspicuous absence of the infamous Lynn Light Infantry), the city's retail businessmen were called upon to aid the strikers. Most grocers and provisions dealers were compelled to defer collection of shoemakers' bills, regardless of their opinion of the strike, but because of neighborhood ties and revulsion against the military invasion of their community, many retailers actively sympathized with the strikers. One lumber dealer, for example, gave shoemakers free access to a stand of trees he owned so they would not have to purchase cordwood. Several politicians also came forth, though their effort to curry favor with the voters led them into some strange political contortions. Congressman John B. Alley sent a donation of $100 to the strike fund, but after bending over backwards to be identified as a friend of labor he spun around and lectured the shoemakers on the foolishness and futility of their strike, intoning the perpetual murmur of the manufacturers, "the interests of the manufacturer and the journeymen are identical."[27]

The strike was carried through March on high spirits, but by the beginning of April it was fast losing momentum, and within another two weeks it had subsided. Though a substantial number of manufacturers were paying higher wages by the end of the strike, the shoemakers were completely frustrated in their other goal of getting their employers to sign the bill of wages and thereby accede to the principle that shoemakers collectively had a voice in determining their wages. In this regard, the strikers were defeated partly by the decentralized character of bottoming (enabling manufacturers to get shoes bottomed by outworkers with less organization and militancy than Lynn artisans) and partly by the very economic factors that had caused the strike in the first place. To someone with no means of support except his labor, even low wages are better than no wages. Finally, the manufacturers' ability to lay their hands on the instruments of institutionalized violence (even though the effectiveness of the local police force on their behalf was nullified by the shoemakers) put the coercive power of the state on their side and tipped the balance of power their way. Coming after several decades of social dislocation caused by the growth of industrial capitalism, the Great Strike exposed the class fears and hatreds generated by the rising order. In the expanding marketplace, the manufacturer was both the hunter and the hunted, predator and prey. He sharpened his weapons, knowing that creditors and competitors did the same. Thus when a committee of his employees politely asked that he disarm, he politely refused, and when disorderly bands of employees broke his weapons in the street, he gave them a taste of martial law. For their part, the workers knew that the weapons of competition, though they be aimed at business competitors, struck them first. When it came to businessmen buying cheap and selling dear, employees' livelihoods could only suffer. And unless they could act collectively and effectively in their own cause, each would stand alone, the hunted and the prey.

The System of the Factory

Enclosed in a wooden box like a miniature casket, the vital processes of the factory time clock went on unseen behind the stark white mask and black Roman numerals of the clock face. As the hands on the front face edged toward 7:00 A.M., the hidden workings were convulsed with a spontaneous whirring of wheels and a lifting of levers that tripped the hammer that struck the bell that signaled the start of the day's work. Outside behind the factory a man pushed against an iron rod that threw a level to engage a wheel that caught the motion generated by a steam engine. Inside the factory on the first floor, gears transmitted energy upward to the ceiling where other gears and shafts and wheels and belts began to spin and whirr until all was ready for the machines and operatives below to begin the day's production. If the clock was an emblem of the mechanical inventiveness of an earlier age, surely the factory was the crowning symbol of the mechanical arts of the nineteenth century. The factory itself was a kind of supermachine—a gross, cacophonous exaggeration of the elegant principles of the clock.

The outer shell of the shoe factory was sometimes fashioned of wood in the traditional style of the central shops and sometimes of stone, but most often it followed the functional, almost military, style of classic factory architecture—several stories of densely regimented red brick, which surfaced iron support beams that carried the weight of the structure and permitted rows of large windows to parade along the walls in brigade formation. Behind the flat, rectilinear facade lay the inner workings of the factory, a jumble of discordant sounds and motions which appeared to the self-important factory owner as a marvel of technological efficiency. In his eyes everything appeared as part of a larger system; every gear and lever, every machine and work table, every foreman and operative hastened the swift, smooth flow of production.

On the first floor the leather was cut and sorted into drawers according to size; the drawers were loaded together and set on a small cart which was wheeled on rails to an elevator and hoisted to the top floor. The uppers were taken from the drawers and prepared by the stitchers, assisted by an assortment of pasters, liners, and buttonhole sewers. Then the completed uppers were replaced in their appropriate drawer on the appropriate car and lowered to the second floor, where other operatives matched them with the appropriate soles. Back in the drawers again, the elevator rose to the third floor where, in a series of short, quick motions, each shoe was passed along a row of workmen to be lasted, bottomed, heeled, finished, and packed. This process could infatuate those who watched it: "The arrangements of this buliding are perfect in their way. It is a complete beehive of industry; everthing is systemized, everything economized, and each part made to act in concert with every other part. There is no clashing or jaring, and the harmony that prevails speaks volumes for the master mind that planned and controls its operations."[28]

The masterminds who established the factory system had long been preoccupied with the technological and managerial problems associated with prefactory production. Simple hand-tool technology imposed labor intensive conditions on the shoe industry, and expansion in this context created an increasingly inefficient flow of materials from the central shops out and back, and out and back again. Equally significant, the manufacturers could not control the process of production at its most crucial point—in the artisan household—and this hurt their ability to compete in the marketplace. First, it hampered efforts to standardize their wares, something entrepreneurs had been trying to do since the eighteenth century. Manufacturers yearned to tell their retail customers that every shoe they sold had the same shape and overall quality, but because individual artisans had different styles of work and disparate levels of competence, their work lacked uniformity and sometimes showed poor workmanship. Second, manufacturers were stymied by the artisan control over the rhythm of production. Among outworkers, in particular, irregular work schedules meant that sometimes several months went by before finished shoes came back to Lynn. Conditions were somewhat more efficient among the resident journeymen of Lynn, but even here the manufacturers were frustrated by the absence of direct supervision over production. Journeymen sometimes neglected work they had promised to do, occasionally failed to keep the shoes clean, and were also at liberty to break off work when they felt like it. Manufacturers concluded that the "employer's interests were allowed to suffer for some momentary enjoyment which was not always conducive to health or good morals."[29]

The factory system resolved the contradictions and conflicts of the household era in favor of the manufacturers. It gave them the means to make the employees act in the employers' interests. Under the new industrial discipline, workers pursued their own momentary enjoyments at the risk of a head-on collision with the boss or his foreman and the loss of a job. Order, therefore, rested on the power of the manufacturers, and harmony in the beehives of industry was founded on economic compulsion, rather than on some instinctive dronish desire on the part of wage earners to cooperate among themselves for the owners' benefit. The manufacturers were eager to take charge of the new industrial army, and, like other men on horseback, they were confident of their right to command and convinced they were astride the forces of progress: "The problem as to how best to bring in and concentrate the vast army of men and women employed in the shoe manufacture of Lynn is one that has attracted the attention of many thinking minds among our business men, but it has never been satisfactorily solved until now."[30]

The catalyst for conversion to the factory system was the adaptation of the sewing machine. Since shoe uppers were made of light leather or cloth, the original invention was quickly altered to suit the task of binding, but since sole leather was harder to sew and bottoming was a more complicated process, it took another decade for a clever inventor to figure out how to apply the sewing machine to that branch of the trade. Finally, Lyman R. Blake of South Abington, Massachusetts, hit on the right combination of moving metal parts to take the needle and thread out of the hands of journeymen cordwainers. Like many another industrious inventor, Blake was pushed aside by a hustling businessman who attached his own name to the machine and sold the first "McKay stitcher" in Lynn in 1862.[31]

The productivity of the McKay operator was far greater than the hand bottomer. The machine allowed an operator to stitch *eighty pairs* in the same time a journeyman could sew the seams on only *one*.[32] However, this ratio of eighty to one was not the final measure of the overall gain in productivity, because the McKay stitcher actually did only part of the journeyman's job. The machine did not last the uppers, position the sole, or shape the leather; for each of these steps, additional hands were necessary, so the journeyman's job was parceled out to a series of workers stationed along the factory production line. At least three other workers were required to put the uppers and bottoms in position to be sewn, and two more had to finish the bottoming process after the shoe came off the machine. Without these other workers, the machines would have been useless, no matter how fast their needles pumped up and down.

The system of the factory was built on the twin foundations of mechanization and the division of labor. The McKay stitcher divided bottoming into half-a-dozen separate steps, and, overall, mechanization broke down the process of shoemaking into thirty-five or forty discrete operations. Prior to the introduction of mechanical labor-saving devices, certain efficiencies had been realized by the specialization of hand laborers into separate branches of the trade. Besides the basic division of labor between binders and bottomers, there were cutters, finishers, and packers working in the central shops.

On the eve of conversion to the factory system, heelers appeared in the trade, and their branch carried specialization further than it had ever been. David Johnson, who was born in 1829 when plenty of men still could make a whole shoe from start to finish, described the various steps in heeling in a passage that echoes Adam Smith's famous account of pin manufacturing: "A man working exclusively at this branch of the craft soon became an expert, even though he knew nothing else of the art of shoemaking. The 'heeling' was afterward subdivided into 'nailing,' 'shaving,' 'blacking,' and 'polishing;' and from this gradually came that minute division which is now the marked feature in this business, distinguishing the new order of things from the old."[33] Of course, this minute division of labor was itself a cause of mechanization, since the simplification of a task only invited the development of a machine to perform it.

The ever finer divisions and the new high-speed machines imparted a revolutionary dynamic to the industry. As speed and efficiency increased in one branch of production, other branches strained to catch up, and to restore equilibrium it was necessary for the whole industry to move at a much faster pace. In this fashion the introduction of the first sewing machines for binding created an imbalance in the rhythm of production. Once, it had been necessary to hire more binders than bottomers to keep the latter supplied with materials. Now the reverse was true; while binding was done at great speed with fewer and fewer binders, bottoming lagged behind. Balance was restored by the McKay stitcher, which vastly increased the velocity of bottoming, but this change, in turn, created new imbalances vis-à-vis cutting, lasting, shaping, trimming, nailing, and buffing. By 1880 every operation except cutting uppers and lasting had been brought up to the faster pace by the invention of new machines. In this period of rapid technological advance, one increase in productivity beckoned forth another . . . innovation sparked further innovation . . . change begat change.

The factory system cracked the whip on production. With technological advance as the pivot, the production line swung around at an ever faster clip, so that out at the tip of the line, productivity streaked ahead at breakneck speed. Each year the average factory worker processed nearly three times as many shoes as a prefactory counterpart. On a daily basis, the increase was about the same. Comparing the statistics from 1875 and 1855, the factory system enabled approximately 2,000 fewer workers to produce 7,000,000 more shoes! There is little wonder that the manufacturers were so effusive in their praise for a system that yielded such wondrous results.[34]

Conversion to the factory system was virtually complete by 1870. Such an enormous changeover in such a short time required larger sums of capital than had ever before been necessary in the shoe industry. In one inner city ward there were half-a-dozen firms valued at $100,000 or more in 1870, whereas no firm in the entire city was worth even half that much before the factories.[35] For a short time this capital expansion could be financed on loans from the local Mechanics Bank (rechristened the First National City Bank in 1864) or from investors in other cities, but sooner or later the bill had to be paid with profits from the shoe industry itself. The manufacturers counted on two factors to provide sufficient profits: mounting productivity and soaring inflation. In terms of productivity, the factory system financed itself by reducing the unit cost of labor and generating the enormous increase in output. Concerning inflation, the manufacturers benefited from a Civil War bonus in the form of large increases in the price of shoes. Although no government contracts were let in Lynn, the inflationary effects of the Union's fiscal expenditures and greenback monetary policy drove up prices on manufactured goods at the precise moment that manufacturers needed extra funds. The average price of a pair of Lynn-made shoes zoomed up from under $1 in 1860 to $1.65 in 1865 and remained at this level through 1870. The rising price made the risk of investing large sums in buildings and machinery seem to disappear. Hoping to get in on the bonus, dozens of small entrepreneurs rushed into the shoe business during the mid-sixties, and were rushed out again just as quickly, but larger manufacturers held on more firmly and carried the conversion through successfully.[36]

The fighting itself caused a temporary loss of the vital southern market, but it was not long before the difficulties of the rebellion began to look like blessings. New orders from everywhere except the deep South arrived in Lynn with cash generated by federal financial policy, a most welcome substitute for the six to eight months credit manufacturers were accustomed to give.[37] This solidified the resources of well-established firms and boosted their capacity to build. Thus with bottlenecks in the rhythm of production breaking up, with unit labor costs dropping, and with ample cash on hand, the manufacturers had a heyday of investment. Stashing away their profits in bricks and iron, gears and machines, they embarked on a period of rapid capital accumulation, and brought Industrial Revolution to the ancient and honorable metropolis of the gentle craft of leather.

By substituting machines for simple hand tools and by eliminating the time lost in transporting the goods to and from the workers, the factory generated an intense concentration of human energy on the productive process. The factory worker did not take an afternoon off because he had a headache or wanted to go fishing; he did not postpone the completion of a case of shoes because he needed to begin the spring plowing. He worked steadily at a pace set by the external forces of the production line and enforced by the line foreman. If he slackened his pace, he threatened his own standard of living, either by risking firing or by cutting down his piece-wage for the day. Since he had no other source of livelihood, it is no wonder that a visitor to one of the factories noticed "the men and boys are working as if for life and scarcely stop to bestow a look upon the visiting party."[38] Such were the requirements of "system" in the factories.

The conversion to factory production appeared as nothing short of revolutionary. David Johnson named the period from 1855 to 1865 "The Great Revolution." It was commonly felt that the changes of those years were not confined to the shoe industry but had effects that pervaded the entire society. The sense of revolutionary change is fully conveyed in the following comment on the factory system which appeared in a local paper of 1863: "Of course, the system is yet in its infancy—the business is yet in a transition state; but the wheels of revolution are moving rapidly, and they never turn backward. Operatives are pouring in as fast as room can be made for them, buildings for "shoe factories" are going up in every direction, the hum of machinery is heard on every hand, old things are passing away, and all things are becoming new."[39]

4

THE CITY

The system of the factory was a model of smooth-working efficiency compared to the life of the city outside its walls. Through the tangled web of ill-planned streets, past a careless jumble of architectural styles, the city's inhabitants went their own separate ways to private destinations giving the helter-skelter appearance of molecules in random motion. They collided in the home, the neighborhood, and the workplace to form unstable aggregations of families, neighbors, and coworkers that were themselves separate, discordant elements in the social system: the dangerous classes, the higher sort, the middling interest, the churchwomen, the men's drinking clubs, Papists, Baptists, Irishmen, Yankees.

The social system of the industrial city was a study in contradiction: the regimentation of factory discipline against the chaos of the streets; the rational calculations of individual businesses against the irrational character of the whole; the functional architecture of the factories against the ostentatious opulence of the owners' homes; bureaucratic forms of social control against the voluntary association of individuals. All of these opposing features of urban life arose out of the contradictions within industrial capitalism, and it is worthwhile to view the nineteenth-century city in that context.

The Politics of Capital

This chapter examines four aspects of urbanization where the rise of industrial capitalism compelled Lynn to modernize in accordance with the new economic and social realities: (1) the emergence of the Republican party; (2) the creation of a professional police force; (3) the attempts of reformers to reach the new working class; (4) the spread of new styles of architecture. These aspects were selected because they provided ample and revealing information on the links between industrialization and urbanization; under other circumstances in other cities the links could be explored through other aspects, such as city finances, taxation, schooling, fire fighting, water supply, sewage removal, and poor relief.

The history of local government paralleled the development of the shoe industry. As long as the industry was conducted by household artisans and shopkeepers, the ancestral town meeting sufficed to manage local affairs. However, the central shop induced changes in the community—chiefly, a rising population of increasingly anonymous voters and a new group of improvement-minded manufacturers —that could not be contained within the traditional frame of government, with the result that the town meeting was cast away in 1850 and replaced by a mayor-council system based on ward representation. However, voters often elected traditionalist candidates to fill the new offices, and no other changes were made in the basic structure of local government, until the 1860s, when the coming of the factory system generated new pressures, and the Civil War gave factory owners the opportunity to push through the changes they wanted. In a short span of intense activity, the city acquired professional police and fire departments, its first water supply system designed for industrial use and fire protection, a stingy program of poor relief, a new system of bureaucratic administration, and a grotesque new City Hall as a monument to the wealth and achievement of the shoe industry. Since these changes occurred during the Civil War and its immediate aftermath, the struggle against slavery, the coming of the factories, and the transformation of city government merged together in the minds of the city's residents to form an image of revolution, a feeling that "old things are passing away and all things are becoming new." Breathing hardest down the neck of change were representatives of industrial capital, and their surge to power marks the period of the Civil War as a revolutionary advance of the bourgeoisie; indeed, it was, as Barrington Moore reminds us, "the last capitalist revolution."[1]

The precondition for power in a democratic system is control of a political party. After the Mexican War, the party system disintegrated; the Democrats divided into factions along sectional lines, the Whigs crumbled into oblivion, while the Free Soilers and Know-Nothings could not muster sufficient resources and appeal to become major parties. The cause of the disorganization of the old party system was the conflict between slavery and industrial capitalism, and this ultimately caused the reorganization of the party system along new lines. The Republican party emerged from the disarray as the only organization appealing to industrial interests with a coherent economic program and energetic leadership. At the same time, the Republican position was broad enough to appeal to other businessmen, farmers, artisans, and industrial workers, which was the crux of its success at the polls.

Workingmen in Lynn regarded the Republican party with mixed emotions. They warmly endorsed Republican opposition to the expansion of slavery, just as they had supported the Free Soil party in its struggle against slavery's monopolization of the land in the western territories, but they coldly rejected the Republican party's close identification with the interests of capital. In practice, they split their tickets, giving stunning majorities to Republican candidates in state and national contests, but withholding their votes from Republicans in local elections.

The Republicans tried to elect a mayor in Lynn three times before the Civil War, and each time they failed because of labor's opposition. In their first outing, they put up George W. Mudge, one of their foremost local organizers and a merchant whose blaring boosterism of the shoe and leather industry was matched only by his unrestrained enthusiasm for the principles of the Republican party. Although not a manufacturer, he was allied in business to the heads of leading shoe firms and was a spokesman for them in local newspapers and national trade journals. In politics Mudge pleaded the cause of these same interests, urging the "conservative portion of the community" to abandon the secrecy of Know-Nothingism, forsake the antagonisms of previous political campaigns, and form a northern party: "Let it be truly and firmly so, not only on the question of slavery, but in every respect, and the result would be highly beneficial to our industrial, mercantile, and commercial interests, many of which have been blighted and stunted by the baneful influence of slavery." Mudge's dream of a "northern party" became a reality by the fall of 1855, but his hopes of leading it to victory were dashed when he failed to win election the following year.[2]

The most prominent Republican in the city, indeed, the most prominent native son Lynn ever produced, was John B. Alley. Alley's career was the stuff of which myths were made. With common origins as a shoemaker's apprentice, Alley drove himself through successive careers as a Yankee trader in the Ohio Valley, a shoe manufacturer in Lynn, the head of a wholesale shoe and leather house in Boston, a banker, and finally a director of the Union Pacific railway. Alley was already a perfect representative of the self-made man when he launched a new career in politics with the Free Soil party, and from that time on he banked heavily on the slavery issue to reward him with political office. In 1858 his investments paid off with a seat in the House of Representatives from the Essex district. As a businessman directly connected to the new industrial wealth, as an uncompromising foe of slavery expansion, and as an ardent war Republican, Alley came from the same mold as Henry Wilson, a Massachusetts shoe manufacturer who became a Republican senator and vice-president of the United States, and Thaddeus Stevens, a Pennsylvania ironmaster who led the radical Republicans in the House.[3]

Like these other archrepresentatives of industrial capitalism, Alley's mastery of the new forces of production propelled him into a position of political leadership. There was no coincidence in the fact that Lynn's most prominent politician was also first in wealth and standing in the community. Worth a quarter of a million dollars, Alley was the richest man in town in 1860, and with diversified investments in manufacturing, wholesale trade, and banking he was supremely qualified to become president of the Lynn Board of Trade. The main function of the Board was to allocate prestige among the city's businessmen based on rank in the organization. In addition, the Board was the Republican party caucus in local business circles: when the Republican party was just getting under way in the middle 1850s, *all* of the officers of the Board who can be identified politically were Republicans.[4]

Secure in the esteem of his peers and in the stability of his personal fortune, Alley boldly proclaimed the demands of his class for greater influence in the affairs of the nation and for the weakening of his great and perpetual adversary, the Slave Power. In a pamphlet prepared for the Presidential campaign of 1860 on the "Principles and Purposes of the Republican Party," Alley admonished the Slave Power to beware the wrath of northern citizens: "When they consider that their commercial, their manufacturing, and all their political interests are neglected and sacrificed, and everything made subservient to the interests of slavery . . . they will rise in their might and demand their rights under the constitution and laws." Alley had no doubt about the ultimate victor in the contest between slavery and capitalism, nor was he uncertain about the cause of victory: the business of the North would prevail because the laws of economics compelled the South to purchase northern manufactured goods like shoes, even if fire-eating politicians didn't like it. Speaking with the fearless arrogance of a man whose class had risen to dominance in one sphere and looked forward to further conquests elsewhere, Alley proclaimed that the talk of a southern boycott of northern industry was simply ridiculous: "trade will seek the best markets in spite of popular clamor."[5]

Alley's contention that economics was the foundation of political power had a distinguished intellectual pedigree going back to the first generation of American revolutionaries who sought to embody the concept in their foreign treaties, their acts of nonintercourse and embargo, and their Union under the Constitution. Recognizing the economic significance of the southern market, Alley vowed never to permit the Slave Power to break up the Union or overthrow the Constitution. Far from being an abolitionist (his pamphlet promised protection for slavery where it currently existed), Alley stood squarely with the man his pamphlet was designed to elect as president and would have agreed that the permanent objective of the North during the Civil War was "to save the Union . . . and not either to save or to destroy slavery."[6] Like Lincoln, Alley did not seek war with the South, but neither did he shrink from that possibility by withdrawing his claims against slavery interests for federal policies on the tariff, transportation, and finance that favored manufacturing.

If the only Republicans in Lynn had been wealthy industrialists like Alley, the party would never have gotten more than a few dozen votes. To develop a mass voting base, the party tapped middle-class voters by espousing the marketplace values which most small businessmen and professionals shared with the industrialists. At a time when the typical unit of industrial capital was a local firm headed by a single individual who competed in the market with other firms similarly situated, the economy still provided all businessmen with like experiences, whether they were manufacturers, merchants, or shopkeepers. Thus the traditional values of industry, frugality, and temperance struck resonant cords at all levels of business activity before the Civil War, as did the newer values of individual freedom and mobility. Using the common cultural denominators of middle-class experience, the Republican party hitched the wagons of small farmers, independent artisans, and shopkeepers to the rising star of industrial capitalism.[7]

Republicans also made headway among workingmen by appealing to their antislavery sentiments and flattering them as being the bone and sinew of society, as its producing classes. But when the Republicans turned their attention to the newer industrial workers, their perceptions filled with blind spots. During the shoemaker strike of 1860, when workers were growing bitter and venomous over their condition, a Republican editor cast his glance upon labor in the shoe industry and could see only a happy and contented group of people:

> We do not believe that the laboring class of Lynn, or of any other city of Massachusetts, is "ground down in the dust" and "oppressed" by a "cruel and heartless class of capitalists." That is all moonshine and flummery, and is abundantly refuted by the fact that the laboring class in our community is, in the main, a free, happy and independent class; that from it come a majority of our wealthiest and most respectable citizens; that in our free states property is constantly changing hands, and the poor mechanic of to-day becomes the wealthy capitalist of to-morrow.[8]

With Republican spokesmen spouting such palpable absurdities, it is hardly surprising that the party was not popular with labor in Lynn.

In fact, the local election of 1860 pitted the Republican party against a Workingmen's party hastily organized in the aftermath of the strike to wreak vengeance on the politicians who had connived with officials of the state militia and the Boston police to defeat the workers. The decision to call out the troops was an overreaction of panicky officials who confused the level of violence, which was slight, with the scale of the strike, which was huge. Since the Democratic mayor became ill when the police were summoned and since Lynn was infested with outside authorities, the regular chain of command in city government broke down, with the result that much of the responsibility for the course of action fell on the aldermen, who, in turn, looked to Roland G. Usher for leadership.[9]

Usher was a retail merchant and the son-in-law of a shoe manufacturer when he was first elected to the Board of Aldermen in 1859. He had been a Know-Nothing and was a Republican by the time of the strike. Usher's special passion was military affairs. As a member of the state legislature in 1856 his only committee assignment dealt with the state militia. His biographer says, "He was always a great enthusiast over everything connected with military life," and at the time of the strike was a lieutenant colonel in a local militia company. Usher was a unique combination of business motivation, political influence, and military authority, which is probably why he was entrusted to coordinate police and militia actions when the mayor collapsed under the strain.[10]

The anger generated against manufacturers and city officials like Usher provided the energy for the successful Workingmen's campaign against the Republicans in the city election held a few months after the strike. In the words of a Democratic editorial, the time had come for workingmen to declare that they were "competent to carry on the city government, to administer its affairs, and to preserve peace and good order, without calling to their aid the Boston Police to overawe and control the people." The new mayor, Hiram N. Breed, was an old cordwainer who received the news of his election while working on the bench. Shortly after taking office, Breed replaced the old city marshal with a man who had been one of the top leaders of the strike. With that matter taken care of, the Workingmen had fulfilled their mission and enacted nothing else by way of a labor program for the remainder of their term of office.[11]

The Workingmen's movement became a political casualty of the Civil War. The party entered the race for mayor again in 1861, but this time the Republicans were running the country in a patriotic war against secession and that made all the difference. Opposition to the Republicans collapsed as citizens came to the defense of the Union, the war, and President Lincoln. The Workingmen vanished; abolitionists who had long refused to vote now rallied to the cause; so did peace-minded Quakers who packed away their pacifism for the duration. Welcoming hosts of old enemies to the fold, a Republican paper proclaimed, "There is no difference between us now." During the war opposition to the Republicans withered away to nothing. Literally *nothing*. In 1863 not a single vote was cast against the incumbent Republican mayor, prompting a newspaper to remark, "Almost everybody seemed to have forgotten that it was election day."[12]

The stunning impact of Civil War lifted the Republican party from a minority organization to the dominant force in city politics; it won every local election during the war and held the upper hand for the next thirteen years after it was over. In the course of this political reorganization, opposition to the business interests behind the Republican party was critically weakened. During the Republican tenure in City Hall, shoe manufacturers were more fully represented in local government than ever before, and their goals were translated directly into policies.[13] They wanted and received better police and fire protection for their property, a bureaucratic system of city administration, a tight-fisted welfare policy, and a costly new building to house the new city government. The Republican party was the manufacturers' instrument of urban reorganization; the Civil War was their opportunity.

Urban Reform

In the form of society founded on industrial capitalism, people encountered one another in the bits and pieces of their lives. The great cleft between home and work divided people from themselves and their families. The ever finer division of labor cut apart broad occupational groupings into ever more specialized segments. The new patterns of geographical and social mobility made people perpetual strangers to their surroundings. Every person played a multitude of separate roles but rarely combined them into a well-rounded synthesis of occupational, family, and community identities. In this setting the older forms of social control which relied on personal, face-to-face contact within the household and the community became obsolete, while, at the same time, the massing together of large numbers of dispossessed and unattached individuals heightened the tensions that generated the need for control in the first place.

Though the problem of social control is an issue inherent in any society, the period of conversion to the factory system was a time of especially anxious searching for new methods to keep the ranks of society marching in place. This search was graphically described by a Lynn resident in a superlative metaphor of nineteenth-century industrial imagination: "Steam was a tremendous force and under the restraint of an iron boiler and a heavy piston it worked well. Man must be surrounded with like restraint to keep him where he ought to be."[14] With the explosions of the Civil War echoing in their ears, with the Industrial Revolution moving ahead at breakneck speed, many residents saw iron restraints as the only protection against chaos, called for stricter discipline in the administration of the city, and demanded the creation of a professional police force to keep order in the streets. Although many further developments in the bureaucratization of business, government, and labor and many further steps toward the militarization of society awaited the twentieth century, the journey along these paths was well under way in the 1860s.[15]

In Lynn the strongest pressure for "iron" reforms came from shoe manufacturers, who pressed their demands through the Republican party. When the Republicans took over in 1862, the police force was a loosely organized collection of part-time officers unable to cope with disorder in a strike or to control criminal behavior in the rapidly growing population. The question of strengthening the police force had been posed before, but until the Republicans took over, strengthening simply meant increasing the number of constables. The Republicans strengthened the police by *reducing* the number and turning them into a professional corps of full-time, gun-toting, uniformed officers ready to move quickly to any trouble spot in the city.

The Republicans raised the police issue at their first opportunity. The new mayor in 1862—a well-to-do Quaker businessman who abandoned the pacifism of his church during the war on the grounds that "there are evils worse than war"—called for a smaller force of full-time, professional policemen, and his call was answered by a city council appropriation of $5000, three times greater than any appropriation in the past and ample enough to support four full-time officers instead of one. The creation of professional force had begun. The mayor justified the expense in social and economic terms:

It was deemed advisable, last year, to make a larger appropriation than usual for police, as many young persons, without families or friends here were thronging our city from neighboring places, in search of work, some staying but a short time, and then leaving to try their fortunes elsewhere. It is always harder to govern this class of persons than those who remain in a place long enough to make it a home. All are strangers to them, and they seem to think that a certain amount of bravado is necessary to let their consequence be known.[16]

Complaints about intemperate and rowdy behavior had been common in the past, but this was the first time the problem of policing the city was described as an offshoot of labor migration.

The new attitude reflected the emergence of the factory population. For the first time, large numbers of people congregated together on city streets each day as they went to and from work. Unlike the household shoemakers, the factory workers were not subject to the personal authority of the householder; unlike other congregations of people in church or public meetings, the behavior of factory workers was not overseen by any of the traditional institutional guardians of morality. Businessmen complained that unwatched workers were the recruiting ground for "gangs of rowdies" who trailed respectable citizens, particularly females, through the streets in the evening, making loud and indecent remarks. The businessmen warned the temporary residents not to mistake a "mild government for a powerless one."[17]

The reorganization was brought to fruition by the next Republican mayor, Roland G. Usher, the military-minded alderman who had coordinated police action during the strike of 1860. In his first inaugural in January 1866, Usher spoke of the need for professionalism and recommended reducing the number of police, substituting a "permanent force" for the remaining part-time officers, and putting all the regular policemen on a salaried basis. He believed that only this would give the men on the force the inducement "to perfect themselves for this duty," and he contended that a small, well-trained, tightly-disciplined organization would be far better able to "preserve the peace, quell insubordination, and ferret out criminals than a large number deficient in such discipline."[18]

Although Usher did not make an explicit comparison between the kind of police force he envisioned and the organization of the Union army, it seems likely that he was using the military as a model for his reorganization plans. He had entered the army at the first call in April of 1861 and served until the end of the war as a paymaster of his old militia company, the Eighth Massachusetts Regiment. Usher's biographer said the army experiences had a deep effect on him: "This was his period of mental development and discipline. . . . the army was his college, and from it he graduated *cum laude*."[19]

The man in charge of the police department during the pivotal months in 1865 and 1866 was Daniel N. Barrett, son of a well-to-do Congregational minister, and a Republican party organizer. His fervid passion for organizational discipline more than met the high standard set by Roland Usher and caused him to be thoroughly disgusted with the lax and irregular procedures he found when he took office. Because he could see no reason why "the rules of business should not be as rigorously applied to police matters as to other affairs," he recommended that the city council: (1) require the department to keep full and complete records; (2) make permanent appointments instead of annual political handouts; and (3) adopt a written code of rules and regulations.[20]

Concerning the relations of police and the community, Barrett insisted on the need for a professional image:

In police matters, as in military affairs, uniformity of discipline, practice and dress is considered an indispensable condition of efficiency, and wherever a city is patrolled by a well organized police force, the same importance is attached to the proper uniforming of such officers as to their discipline and good behavior. To those unwilling to conform to the requirements of the laws, police officers are constant reminders of the necessity of good behavior, and a uni-

form being emblematic of power, and strongly suggestive of authority, he who wears it is enabled to exert a great influence over such
persons, and brave the violence of the brutal with increased confidence; and I believe that an order requiring every member of the
department to appear in uniform would contribute as signally to the
effectiveness of the force as to its neatness and appearance.

Like his boss, Barrett used the military as his model and felt martial
authority was necessary to overawe the "floating population" of
temporary residents who came to Lynn from all parts of New England
and Canada and who did not have "the slightest interest in sustaining
the good name of our municipality."[21]
    Barrett and Usher got most of the things they wanted, including
another large increase in expenditure, and by the end of the decade
the cost of policing the city rose to nearly $18,000, more than ten
times the cost at the beginning of the decade. The size of the force
multiplied even more rapidly from one full-time man in 1860 to an
1870 contingent of nineteen salaried, uniformed, full-time policemen,
supplemented by three part-time officers, plus a reserve force of
twenty special police who were on call for emergencies and were
paid by the hour.[22]
    The main duties of the police consisted of preventing disorderly
behavior and protecting the business property of the city. The largest
number of police were on night duty patrolling the streets on the
lookout for burglaries and fires (though even this did not satisfy
some of the wealthier businessmen who hired specially deputized
police as night watchmen in their shops and factories). Judging by
the number of arrests, the police saw action most often in the running
battle against disorder. The highest number of arrests was for drunkenness, followed by assault and battery, with larceny usually in third
place. Police reports also listed the number of "disturbances sup-
pressed" without an arrest involved, and this total was usually somewhere between the arrests for drunkenness and assault.[23]
    Barrett's overweening zeal got him into trouble with the city
council's committee on police affairs and with some local residents.
The controversy began with a hassle over the administration of certain details of police work, such as who would determine the hours
of the night watchmen. It expanded into a full-scale debate between

Barrett and people hostile to a new system. Barrett felt that "success in police matters depends largely upon secrecy," and he posted signs in the City Hall offices of the police closing the area to anyone not there on police business. This action offended some of the older citizens who liked to hang around the police station. Barrett referred to their visiting as "the prying curiosity of newsmongers." When the committee ordered Barrett to remove his "Police Only" signs, he resigned in May 1866.[24]

Opposition to the new regime of police administration surfaced in the fall elections of 1866 alongside other sources of opposition to Usher on the grounds that he spent too much money and favored business interests over the needs of "soldiers, sailors, and laborers." Opposition organizers included the city marshal in the Workingmen's administration of 1861 and a few other strike leaders from 1860, but their campaign was hastily assembled only a few days before the election, and when their candidate for mayor did not accept their nomination, they were unable to find a replacement.[25]

The next year, however, the forces of opposition did much better. They won a few seats on the city council and polled 1300 votes to Usher's 1500. Usher had the backing of the Republican organization, and, according to stalwart George W. Mudge, of "the active, enterprising businessmen of the city," while his opponents included a newly revived Democratic organization and a small group who called themselves Workingmen. However, the opposition was unable to overcome the Republican momentum of Civil War popularity, and so the reorganization of the police proceeded uninterrupted.[26]

The change in the police force occurred as part of the whole reorganization of Lynn's social structure; the rise of the industrial worker and the rise of the professional policeman went hand in hand. First, the appearance of a floating population clearly established the need for professionalism in the eyes of the city's businessmen. Second, the new factory worker could no longer be both shoemaker and policeman. The artisan who controlled the day-to-day conditions of his own labor could stop his work at any time to serve a warrant or arrest a drunk, but the factory worker could not.

Within this general context, the specific cause of the reorganization and its character and timing arose both from the narrow economic need of shoe manufacturers for better protection of their property and from their broader need to protect the social order in which private property was a fundamental institution. Shaken by disorder in the strike of 1860, manufacturers lost faith in the traditional methods of policing the community inherited from the preindustrial era when class antagonisms had scarcely existed and laboring men often had the same attachment to private property as businessmen. But in 1860, after a half century of industrial erosion of the old society, a police force drawn directly from the ranks of laboring men could only have represented the increasing hostility of that class to the prerogatives of capital and its increasing rejection of the manufacturers' personal authority and standards of behavior. The corresponding anxiety among manufacturers about social disorder and the lack of means to control it only intensified as they pressed forward in setting up a factory system and watched their streets become filled with factory workers. Who among these strangers to the city were thieves or disorderly persons? Which ones lacked respect for private property? Unable to tell, the manufacturers set up a professional police force, an efficient, highly visible body of men responsible not to the community as a whole but to the Republicans in public office and to the manufacturers in the private offices of the city's leading business establishments.

The idea of a professional police force was not invented in Lynn, and the change was not associated only with the factory system. Boston, for example, established the police on a professional footing after a series of mob disorders in the 1830s stemming directly from the tensions of urbanization and only indirectly from the migrations and occupational changes induced by the Industrial Revolution.[27] Also, a Republican administration was not a necessary precondition for the reorganization; even a Democratic administration in Lynn that was more sympathetic to the concerns of workingmen would eventually have been forced to take the same steps. Nevertheless, the simultaneous occurrence of Republican political ascendancy and the rise of a factory system pushed the change so far so fast in Lynn and made the police an instrument used by one class in the community to discipline another during the critical years of industrial conversion.

The manufacturers did not stop at remaking the police force; they went on to reorganize the entire network of city services. They professionalized the fire department, installed a new water system, improved waste removal, overhauled the system of poor relief, and topped off their achievements by building a new city hall.

The reorganization of the fire department duplicated the process in the police department. At the beginning of the 1860s the fire companies were still volunteer organizations only loosely tied to the administrative apparatus of the city. Like the prefactory police force, they grew directly out of the community life of the artisan. "Our fire companies are composed almost entirely of mechanics—men who labor hard for a living; and they join the department, not for the pay they receive, certainly, for that would not renumerate them for their labor at one such fire as we had a week or two since. They love the excitement attendant upon their duties at fires, and at friendly trials of skill."[28]

The manufacturers felt the volunteer system lacked the discipline and efficiency necessary to protect their burgeoning investments and also felt the existing hand pumpers were inadequate compared to the more powerful steam engines. In the 1860s, gradually the city replaced hand engines with steam engines, and, since the steamers required fewer men to operate them, the volunteer companies were disbanded. In their place the city hired a corps of permanent, full-time firemen who stayed on alert in the fire stations instead of waiting in their homes and shops like the artisans to be summoned by the fire-bell. The new system was administered by a Board of Engineers responsible to the city council, and, as in the case of the police, professionalization and bureaucratic administration of the fire department withdrew direct control over the service from the hands of the community at large.[29]

The problem of fire protection continued to bother the manufacturers until the city improved its water system. The need was recognized as early as 1860, but the cost of doing something about it deferred action until the end of the decade when a series of spectacular fires in the winter of 1868–69 heightened the pressure for taking action. In the largest blaze, $300,000 went up in smoke, most of it from shoe factories. The following summer the city voted on a referendum to increase the water supply, but to the dismay of the manufacturers, the proposal was overwhelmingly defeated 1,396– 326. The manufacturers immediately shifted their attention to the city council, and by scaling down their demands they won approval for a system of pipes capped by a series of fire hydrants bringing the "fire-quenching fluid" to the factories.[30]

By 1873 the city had spent $800,000 for the new system, but the depression of that year wiped out the business enthusiasm that was the foundation of such generous spending. The smaller taxpayer who had originally defeated the proposal for a water system reappeared in the 1873 election and urged a complete cessation of spending. By the next election, everyone was talking retrenchment, and the new mayor in 1875 noted that business stagnation required the city to "live within its income." The city incurred no more big debts through the rest of the decade.[31]

In respect to poor relief, a spirit of retrenchment had set in several years earlier, and it was not intended to benefit the poor. Rather, the new emphasis of the relief agency by 1870 was to avoid giving aid to the "undeserving." This contrasted with the predominant attitude of city officials in the 1850s, who defined charity as a natural public duty and who were not stingy, even in periods of business stagnation. As one said, "The greater our benevolence, the greater will be our own happiness." During the Civil War the city was heavily involved in providing aid to families of servicemen, and, even though the regular expenditures for poor relief increased to unprecedented sums, city officials expressed virtually no concern over the rise in cost.[32]

After the war, however, a new feeling crept in. In a long city council debate over relief expenditures, several councilmen argued that the old system of administering relief upon request might be appropriate in a small town but was far too lenient in a city the size of Lynn. Given the large number of requests received by the Overseers of the Poor, it was impossible for these men, who were paid only a nominal salary and who had businesses of their own, "to give each case of application for public aid proper attention and close investigation." Thus, according to one councilman, "there were many instances of unworthy subjects receiving aid"—chiefly workers who "lived high" for ten months during the work season and then expected the city to take care of them at slack times. After the debate the council voted to reorganize the Board of Overseers of the Poor, and later hired a Republican shoe manufacturer as a permanent case investigator to scrutinize each and every request for aid. The city's mayor for 1870, another Republican shoe manufacturer, credited the new tight-fisted system with saving the city several thousand dollars in relief expenditures.[33]

Moral Police

To the factory owners the internal system of the factory was an allegory of harmony, an agency of progress, and a microcosm of the well-ordered society. Since they saw the system through the self-interested eyes of its beneficiaries, it is hardly surprising that they had a rose-colored view or that they sought to reform urban life in keeping with the factory principles of efficiency and discipline. Their introduction of bureaucratic management into city administration and professionalism into the police department represented the blood-and-iron side of urban reform, the military force of arms linked to the boiler, cylinder, and piston of social restraint.

Other segments of the community, however, were not so sanguine about the social consequences of the system nor so ready to remold the city in its image. To the guardians of public morality—church women, clergymen, educators, and men of letters—the factories were moral battlegrounds where the forces of good and evil waged terrible struggles for the hearts and souls of those that labored within. It seemed to them that the land of the Puritans had been taken over by dark Satanic mills. Since they viewed the factories as outsiders, and since they had vocational inclinations toward the milk of human kindness rather than blood and iron, they sought to reform urban life in keeping with their principles of Christian charity and individual self-discipline. Whereas the manufacturers were hard, objective, and authoritarian, they were soft, subjective, and manipulative. Despite their differences in style, the two groups never quarreled over the fundamentals of private property or the moral right to private profits; such a debate was beyond the pale of even those "soft" reformers whose views shaded over into Labor Reform. (See Chapter 8.) By defining the worst evil of the factory system as the creation of a laboring population of shiftless, underpaid hirelings, the moral reformers led an effort that was less an attack on the rights of property and the factory system than a calisthenic exercise in middle-class morale-building and a condemnation of the character of the new working class. They were the moral police for middle-class virtues.

They saw the factory system as a threat to the social order because it crushed the household system of production and took the laboring class away from the old restraints of home life. The most threatening segment of the working class was the floating population, people who only resided in the community for a few months at a time. The fact that they moved so often and formed so few significant connections in the community made them seem as alien as the original settlement of Irish immigrants in the late 1840s, even though they were commonly seen as Yankees. One minister identified them as a wholly separate community—"floating Lynn" was his phrase.[34]

The reformers regarded the boardinghouses that sprang up to give the floaters temporary lodging as the night-time counterparts of the large, impersonal factories, and just as dangerous in terms of moral impact. They longed for a restoration of the authority of the household and hoped in vain that "men of property would combine to build some healthily constructed and well-planned boarding houses, and place them under the management of some sensible, competent, motherly woman." Reformers were especially sensitive to the plight of young, single women workers: "Far from friends, they lack sympathy, crowded in boarding houses they are deprived of the comforts and restraints of home, confined all day at a fatiguing and dull round of labor they need healthful and innocent recreation."[35]

The reformers' sympathy for unattached factory workers was balanced by their hostility to those workers who were attached to the Knights of St. Crispin. The greatest flurry of reform activity occurred between 1868 and 1872, the very years of rising Crispin militancy. (See Chapter 7.) A few months after the first Crispin strike, a major general in the moral police force, Reverend Joseph Cook, made an inspection tour of several local factories and publicized his findings in a series of lectures from January to May 1871. Cook's critical views stimulated a flow of letters and editorial com-

ment in the newspapers, brought out hundreds of people to more
than a dozen mass meetings, provoked a public defense from the
manufacturers, and in general "aroused our community as no other
occurrence has for a long time." Cook's lectures, as well as other
documents from the controversy, were published in 1871 under the
title *Outlines of Music Hall Lectures on Factory Reform*.[36]

In Cook's eyes, the factory was a veritable den of iniquity. Wholly
ignoring the issues of wages and power, Cook concentrated on two
social aspects of the factory—the rootless condition of its transient
population, and the mixing of men and women in the workrooms—
both of which introduced "startling moral perils" into the community.
In regard to the floating population, he argued that mechanization
reduced the level of skill and increased the rate of output, with the
result that production was compressed into seasonal cycles which
drew thousands of low-skilled workers to Lynn each year who maintained no permanent homes there. Cook felt that the rootless condition of the floating population contributed to an unhealthy moral
environment in the workrooms, and he contrasted the floaters with
those who had strong family ties in the community: "He who comes
home at night to a circle that know him well and watch his daily
course has a kind of daily appearance to make before a moral tribunal." He found no such tribunal in the life of the floater.[37]

Cook felt that the floating population was the wave of the future.
He argued that the requirements of factory production created a
class of wealthy capitalists who owned the factories and a class of
impoverished workers who operated them. The irrepressible tendency
was for the capitalists to become increasingly superior and the workers increasingly inferior in terms of moral, intellectual, and economic
development. Eventually, he predicted, America would resemble
Europe and become divided into two classes, "the unemployed rich
and the unemployed poor, the former a handful and the latter a
host!"[38]

In regard to the mixing of the sexes, Cook reported gross violations
of the Victorian sexual code. He cited the common occurrence of
men and women working at close quarters where the foul talk and
careless behavior of a few disreputable employees could easily corrupt the virtue of others. Because the manufacturers would hire any-

body, the workroom door was not a "moral sifting machine." As another preacher cut from the same cloth as Cook put it, "The overcrowding and herding of people together would sometimes make devils out of saints."[39]

Cook then delved more deeply into the exact meaning of corruption by reporting a conversation with a local physician: "Take a room twenty-five or thirty by fifteen or twenty feet in size; put a dozen men and a dozen women, and boys and girls into it; and let tobacco smoke, and profanity, and foul talk take their course." The result of this polluted atmosphere, from Cook's point of view, was that many young girls grew coarse in appearance, lost the "natural freshness of complexion," and no longer showed a "lustreful flash of the eye." Not only did the "machine girl" contradict the minister's idea of womanhood, but Cook uncovered another aspect of the factory system that shocked his sexual code even more deeply. He said local physicians told him of an alarming increase in the incidence of the "infamous diseases" among the floating population. "I was moved as if smitten by an electric bolt."[40]

Cook's prurient interest in promiscuity and venereal disease was not at all well received by the women he was evaluating. A few female employees felt singled out by his remarks and printed a notice in the newspaper denouncing his views as "unjust and unchristian." The women were backed up by their employer, Samuel M. Bubier, who uttered some uncharitable words about Cook's character, for which he made a public apology. The reputation of the women was also defended by the local Catholic priest, who evoked pathos-filled pictures of the poor young girls walking to work on cold winter mornings trying to earn an honest livelihood for their families.[41]

The priest's entry into the controversy pointed to any underlying nativist theme in Cook's message. Cook championed the belief in the superiority of white, Anglo-Saxon Protestants over inferior stock like the Irish Catholics. Anticipating the racial arguments in the twentieth-century debate over the new immigration, he traced the progress of the race from the forests of Germany through the Magna Carta and ended his remarks with the proud observation that the Anglo-Saxon "rules the world today."[42]

For all his willingness to argue with the factory owners, Cook believed in the same bourgeois values that they did. Although he temporarily accepted the idea of collective bargaining in 1870, it was because the manufacturers were also willing to put up with it, and because it diminished the fearsome prospect of class conflict. Although he favored higher wages, he was opposed to strikes in order to get them. He viewed the working class as increasingly vulgar, coarse, and inferior to the men of property. He was both ethnically and sexually prejudiced. In his construction of the world, Irish were not the equal of Anglo-Saxons, and women were no more independent than children. Thus it is little wonder his ideas for "factory reform" were more criticisms of the working class than an attack on the factory owners. In his eyes, factory reform did not mean challenging the power of factory owners so much as it meant a combination of uplift and discipline for factory workers.

The same mixture of uplift and discipline characterized the work of Lynn's City Missionary. The idea for a mission to the poor originted among half-a-dozen local churchmen, including Joseph Cook, along with a few of the city's businessmen. This group began to enlist support for the project in the spring of 1871, and by September of 1872 they had engaged a missionary by the name of W. F. Mitchell whose job was to give both economic assistance and spiritual encouragement to the poor and especially to the floating population. The missionary dutifully enclosed a religious message in each dollar or second-hand coat he gave out. The following excerpt from Mitchell's diary showed how he combined relief with religion, benevolence with a lesson in social discipline.

Then a lady calls and desires the Mission to become security to a grocer for a workingman, for provisions to the amount of five dollars; which request, as the lady is known, I comply with, especially as the party aided is becoming interested in religious things. . . . Then an unhappy deserted wife, aided and cheered. Then another workingman to be tided over. He is trying to be a Christian, tempted and tried every day. He is helped. The young man who comes after him has been aided, but will not be this time, as he is not exerting himself to get employment.

Mitchell's manipulation of misfortune is what the supporters of the mission described as "showing our Christianity."[43]

For five years Mitchell administered to the unchurched workers of the city, but the amount of money he dispensed was trifling. His annual cash payments were less than his own salary of $2000, yet he claimed to serve the needs of 400 poor families in Lynn. In order to receive the pitttance he gave to each applicant, it helped for the recipient to demonstrate resignation to poverty and humility in the face of desperation. Mitchell said he was quickest to come to the aid of well-behaved workmen who showed a "crushing of pride" as a result of unfortunate circumstances. He criticized the tramps who took free lodgings from the city without looking for work as a "very dangerous element in the society." His diary showed an increase in cheeriness and satisfaction almost in direct proportion to the misery of his subjects. He confided that he had a special "feeling for lame boys." Unable to do anything for one sick old man, he did not criticize his own ineffectiveness but instead congratulated himself on showing such magnanimous Christian sympathy for the unfortunate. With the onset of the depression in 1873 the benevolence of the businessmen began to decline in direct proportion to the increase in requests for aid. For the next two years the mission stayed alive only through emergency appeals for funds, and finally, after taking one cut in his own salary, Mitchell decided to resign in 1877.[44]

Although no one was hired to replace him, a measure of his work was carried on by the Young Men's Christian Association. Interest in the Y dated back to the early 1860s, but a permanent branch was not established until the coming of the factories focused attention on the floating population. In 1868 businessmen and churchmen set up a Y office to assist young men "who have no homes here other than their boarding houses." Growing slowly but steadily, the original reading room expanded to a full building in 1880. Although it was not a relief organization, the Y did take over some of Mitchell's missionary work among the poor, holding temperance and prayer meetings, and finding jobs and lodgings for newcomers.[45]

A sister organization called the Women's Union for Christian Work was set up in 1869 by women representing the "wealth and benevolence of the city," with the object of providing innocent recreation in the form of a reading room and a few classes in drawing and sewing to floating women workers. The Union also directed newcomers to job openings and rooms for rent and attempted to be what the factory was not—a moral sifting machine—by sizing up the character of the applicants before making a referral. One woman who was asked to leave the Union's office because it was "no place for vagrants" made a public protest over her rude reception. The Union replied that the woman in question looked extremely dirty and ragged, seemed drunk, and replied sharply to a question asked in the office. The Union advised it had nothing to offer such "disorderly" persons. The sentiments of the City Missionary, exactly.[46]

The directors of the Women's Union assumed some of the duties of the mission when that folded. They also tried to coordinate all the benevolent activities in the city to improve the process of weeding out the "shiftless" applicants for aid. They set up a charity clearinghouse in 1879 where all applicants could be sent to receive aid and where records would be kept on each person, to avoid giving assistance to the same person twice. The clearinghouse also coordinated home visiting to make sure there was "genuine destitution" behind the application. The directors of the Women's Union urged all relief agencies not to give out one cent before investigating, "as the use of it will generally be doubtful," and they stressed that employment was preferable to cash donations.[47] Again, the disciplinary function of private charity went hand in hand with benevolence.

How effective were the new missionary-relief organizations? The City Mission was clearly a failure. The paltry offerings of the Missionary and the time consumed in each home visit prevented the daily work of the mission from touching more than a very small part of the lives of a very small part of the poor people of the city. The YMCA and the Women's Union for Christian Work reached a larger number. Each day an average of three women visited the Union inquiring about a job, and the total number of daily visitors of all sorts to the Y reached 160 at the end of the 1870s. Yet most of the energy of these associations was not consumed in making contacts with the poor but in organizing the middle class to do good! According to the records of the Women's Union for Christian Work, fully five-sixths of the visitors to the offices of that organization were not workingwomen but people representing the "wealth and benevolence" of the city. Nor did the organizations even claim to have great success in uplifting large numbers of the poor. Instead they singled out individual cases where one person started going to church regularly, or another became a temperance advocate. Thus these attempts to build bridges between the property and the poverty of Lynn achieved weak and insecure results.[48]

The results of reform in other fields were even less significant than in charitable work. Reformers generated numerous proposals for putting working-class housing under more rigorous moral supervision, but in practice their ideas boiled down to a short-lived Boarding House Association which drew up a blacklist of "irresponsible parties" whose immorality consisted of skipping town without paying rent.[49] Reformers were also alarmed about juvenile crime and pleaded in vain for the creation of a juvenile reformatory to prevent it. They focused attention on the boys who were disorderly in school or who were habitually truant, and they warned that these boys "will furnish recruits to the army known to the police of every city by the cant terms of 'tramps,' 'beats,' etc., for only slang language can accurately describe them." The reformers identified the boys with the floating population, and many were, no doubt, among the 400–500 children under fourteen at work in the local factories in the 1870s. In place of the workroom and the street, the reformers proposed to substitute the reformatory, where "the youthful devotees of vice and crime may be trained in habits of virtue and industry, and be taught the nature and need of law, the wisdom and benevolence of penalties." Despite their plea, the reformatory was not built.[50] An idea for evening schools to teach basic subjects to adult workers got further than the idea for the reformatory when an evening program was launched in 1869 amid predictions of great benefits for the poor and the uneducated. But the program had a disappointing attendance record, and the schools just barely limped along until 1874, when they were shut down for good.[51]

A more durable change occurred within the existing schools when a strict system of grade levels was introduced. In the prefactory school, grading lines were loosely arranged with students of widely different ages present in the same classroom, but by the early 1870s the lines were tightened into an orderly progression of grade ranking. The School Committee compared the new classification system to the

dinarily complex sentence
a factory production line:

eel in a Waltham factory,
y cunning machines and the
it of men and women, each
grand result, issue at length
am watch, so from the little
r Primary, to the youth with
teacher has a limited sphere,
:ure a more perfect execution

very limited because most of
inessmen, believed the existing
rm. They saw the school as an
owntrodden and relied on it to
ass child.

iprocal position of governor and
governed. He learn... that the guidance and self-control of the
individual are, after all, the great sources of happiness and prosperity
of the commonwealth at large. . . . He is an addition to that moral
police which, in every enlightened and virtuous community, watches
over the virtue and happiness of the humblest as well as the greatest
individuals. Such are not the men who fill our jails, nor are they
likely to become the demoralizers of their country.[53]

The speaker of this nugget identified himself as a member of the
"middle class" and said his "class" was "a medium of communication
between the upper and lower." Quite so: middle-class educators attempted to teach the lower class to respect the governing position of
their betters.

The reformers looked to religion for similar results. Joseph Cook
declared that the chasm between capital and labor could only be
bridged by "the Bible laid on the buttresses of the Sundays and the
Common Schools." He hoped the church could mediate in social
strife and occupy the same position in respect to the "different classes
in society at large as the Industrial Board of Arbitration . . . has in
particular cases of conflict." He had faith that wealthy church mem-

bers could be motivated to do good works for the poor and that workers would cease to feel hostile toward their bosses once they could be persuaded to put on clean clothes and go to church.[54]

Yet Cook's view of the church as a bridge only betrayed his anxiety about the existence of the chasm. The other prime movers behind the City Mission, the Women's Union, and the YMCA shared his doubts that the existing church structure could do the job. In the early 1870s they asked themselves, "How Shall the Church Reach the Masses?" and they were uncertain about the answer. Despite the existence of an assortment of temperance groups, and despite a small-scale revival in 1877, it was clear that the churches and the crusades for moral reform that had been so important in prefactory Lynn were not attracting large numbers of workers.[55] The new patterns of migration discouraged regular church involvement, and the notorious indifference of nineteenth-century workers to religious issues hampered the efforts of middle-class reformers to propagate their beliefs in harmony, obedience, and self-discipline outside their own social stratum. The moral police were most effective in enforcing their beliefs among the already converted. Charity began, and ended, at home.

The Mark of Business Rule

Architecture is a splendid field for the study of human relations. The buildings erected by a civilization over years of development are the sediment deposited by the moving streams of social and economic events. Secrets of social organization are molded into cornerstones and crevices, textures and geometry, the arrangements of wood, stone, and glass, and the secrets are revealed to the eyes of imaginative observers who can see the social existence of people in the physical appearance of the things they make. To see in this fashion it is necessary to look at a society's architecture as it actually was, and not as the most privileged members in the society would have us see it. The magnificent temples of dead rulers that arose all over the ancient world leave one wondering—if so much labor and so many resources were expended in providing housing for the dead, what was left over for the living? Following this angle of vision, a study of nineteenth-century urban architecture would be obviously incomplete if it only described gilded mansions and ignored the tenements, and, further-more, a study of mansions alone would be incomplete if it treated them only as expressions of upper-class taste and not as the results of the gap in income between rich and poor that made their construction possible. Fruitful study might begin with the questions of Bertolt Brecht:

> Who built the seven towers of Thebes?
> The books are filled with names of kings.
> Was it kings who hauled the craggy blocks of stone?[56]

Neither kings nor craggy blocks of stone could be found in pre-industrial Lynn. At the time George Washington visited the village on his postelection tour of New England, the closest thing in American experience to a royal visitation, the townscape presented him with a view of republican architectural simplicity. The rustic, clapboard-and-shutters style that appeared in most of the private homes reap-peared in the retail stores and artisan shops that were interspersed among the dwellings. The uniform scale of construction and homoge-neous appearance befitted a social order that rested squarely on ethnic homogeneity and economic equality among heads of house-holds. None of the farmer shoemakers, master artisans, and shop-keepers who presided within the household rose to any great height above his fellow citizens. The loftiest building in town was the church, though it certainly did not dominate the townscape and did not reflect the presence of a wealthy religious establishment.[57]

Over the next half century the town grew considerably, but its basic style remained the same. Homes and shops increased in number and grew somewhat larger, churches multiplied and their spires reached higher into the sky, but none of these changes altered the traditional format. When a Town Hall was constructed, it followed the old specifications and fit in so comfortably beside the plain wood shops that a shingle might have been hung oustide announcing the town was now open for business and inviting the public inside to examine the assortment of official wares—selectmen, assessors, fence viewers, and hogreeves. Contemporary drawings and paintings of the town revealed the open, uncluttered feel, the textures of earth and wood, the green and brown colors of vegetation everywhere. In a similar vein a group of mechanics circulated a broadside in 1850 opposing the move to acquire a city charter; their first reason for opposing incorporation as a city was architectural: "Because the Town of Lynn is not compact and piled up in high blocks of buildings."[58]

But the position of the old structures was being gradually undermined by the forces of industrial capitalism after 1815, and by the middle of the nineteenth century the townscape included a few craggy blocks of stone hauled in by laborers and stonemasons and hoisted into place in two or three of the new central shops that belonged to the town's rising shoe manufacturers. In addition, the church spires no longer stood alone above the roofs and treetops; a pair of brick smokestacks carrying the smoke from two steam engines also stood out against the sky. And in the 1850s, the city (the mechanics had lost their battle) acquired a few four- and five-story warehouses and stitching shops whose rectangular flat-roofed appearance revealed the unmistakable mark of the factory system. By 1860 the church spires were still the most prominent feature as one looked out over the city, but their position was clearly threatened by the economic tremors shaking the ground below.

Those tremors gathered the force of an earthquake in the 1860s. In the central business section old buildings collapsed in a heap of rubble, and in their place new structures squatted across old foundations and empty lots, filling the area with the chunky geometry of the factories. Some were of wood, but the largest were red brick bullies whose imposing magnitude transformed Lynn into a compact city piled up in high blocks of buildings. A series of pictures taken at High Rock in 1879 and pieced together in a sweeping cityscape captured the features of a nineteenth-century industrial city: an outer residential band converged on the inner heartland where church spires were outnumbered by smokestacks, boardinghouses were squeezed in between stores and factories, and the functional purity of the single factory was lost amidst the disorganized jumble of the whole scene.[59]

Striking contrasts in residential housing appeared by that time, reflecting the increasing gap between the city's rich and poor populations. (See Chapter 6.) Evidence of newly acquired wealth stands out in large, three-story homes that occur at several points and in the two or three ornate, mansard-roofed homes with carriage houses that prominent businessmen built to establish their membership in the ranks of mansion dwellers. Where poorer tenants occupied buildings of a size equal to the mansions, several families, or as many as forty boarders, lived under the same roof; otherwise, the double houses or single-family bungalows in the residential band housed the laboring population. The physical appearance of the city in the factory era mirrored the increasing gaps in economy and society. The old uniformity in the styles of residential, commercial, and industrial buildings was as far gone as the homogenous order of household producers.

Nothing epitomized the transformation better than the contrast between the old Town Hall, a study in classical New England simplicity destroyed by fire in 1864, and the dazzling, new, gay-plumed phoenix that rose from the ashes. Whereas the old was a Doric composition of pure geometry, all rectangles and triangles, its painted white surfaces free of ornament, the new was a Corinthian composition in brick and stone of swoops and swirls, cornices and columns. When an engraving of the old Town Hall was included in the *History of Lynn,* the author apologized for its homely appearance and admitted it was "not presented for its architectural elegance." Other observers were even more offended by its common look; a committee of the city council set up to consider erecting a new hall branded the existing building "almost a disgrace."[60]

In the late 1850s, the city council decided to submit the question of getting rid of the Town Hall to a popular vote. Apparently, the only other issue besides the "disgraceful" appearance of the building was the need for a better city jail, which at the time was simply a room in the same building. However, the popular feeling against the old building was not strong enough, and the proposition was defeated by a three-to-two vote.[61] That did not stop the patrons of civic improvement, who prevailed on the city council to purchase a piece of real estate without holding another referendum, and, at the same time, the Republican mayor who had initiated police reorganization urged the city to go ahead and construct a new building, despite the heavy financial burden resting on the city from expenses connected with the Civil War.[62]

The new City Hall was ready for use in 1867. It was designed as a monument to the business interests of the city, a point emphasized in several of the speeches at the dedication ceremonies. One orator was quite explicit about the symbolic connection between the City Hall and the other architectural innovation in Lynn—the shoe factory. He boasted of "the long stride from the unpretentious shoemakers' shops, the 'ten-footers' of 1827, to those magnificent shoe factories of the later day—from the old Town House on the common, with its bare beams and scraggy walls, to that great model of architectural beauty and grandeur, the new City Hall of Lynn"[63] This imitation Italian Renaissance model of "beauty and grandeur" represented the wealth and confidence produced by the factories, but it was far too pretentious to resemble the factories themselves. Instead, it looked like an exaggeration, almost a caricature, of the new Victorian houses in which some of the factory owners lived, and where, in their private retreats from the intense pressures of the marketplace, they felt free to express their tastes for luxury and ostentatious display.

Some of the speakers at the dedication ceremonies felt uncomfortable in the presence of such extravagance. They tried to play down the break with the past and appealed to working people in the audience to think of the City Hall as their monument, too. One wealthy manufacturer flattered the shoemakers by saying, "The old lapstone of our shoemakers is the real corner or foundation stone."[64] But none of the speakers mentioned the new factory population or the floaters; apparently these people were not yet regarded as part of the community. Moreover, many hardhanded toilers were not very pleased with the new City Hall or what it represented. They disliked the building's ostentation, looking upon it as an "elephant." The sentiment of distrust and resentment was described in the "Poem of the Day:"

> Some come admiring; some with reverence;
> Some sneering, crying, "What extravagance!"
> Good judges, not a few, have thought it queer
> That there's no public hall hid somewhere here.
> In all this mass of brick and stone and lime;
> Where any man might come at any time,
> For any purpose and in any way,

Through any period keeping up his stay,
A place for liberty's peculiar use.[65]

The poet expressed a feeling that had been roused a year earlier when
City Marshal Barrett posted his "Police Only" signs around his
offices. It also had arisen many years before, when the town meeting
was abandoned in favor of a system of ward representation under a
city charter. Now in the new City Hall, common people were again
excluded, and they resented the absence of a room belonging to the
people, seeing only a maze of chambers belonging to government
officials.

Speaking at the dedication, Mayor Usher addressed himself to this
feeling of resentment. The mayor acknowledged the city government
possessed "less of the democratic form" than the old town meeting,
but he asserted it was free from "the evils incident to such gather-
ings." Under the new government, there was more talent, responsibility, and "system." Usher hoped the City Hall, as a monument to
the new order, would inspire devotion to it. He described the building as "a living voice, ever speaking of good order in society, protection to the weak and security to the strong." Challenging the
people who scoffed at it, Usher retorted, "If it shall strengthen the
bonds that bind a single one more closely to Lynn, as his or her
home, it will not have been reared in vain." To the poet, the building
symbolized the separation of the city government from the average
citizen, but to the mayor, it was just the opposite: "It is a monument
of the thoughts and purposes and feelings of this people."[66]

To be more precise than the mayor, it was a monument to the
ascendancy of Republicans and shoe manufacturers. As one of the
dedication speakers observed, "appearances, though sometimes deceitful, quite as often possess a ruling power," and with the construction
of the new City Hall, it was clear to the community who ruled. The
manufacturers were acutely conscious of their dominant position in
the city. As they marshaled the forces of change in the city's economic
and political structure, they spoke in eager and determined tones of
their historic mission. Describing the demise of the "old Lynn" and
the rise of the "new," a newspaper closely identified with the manufacturers summoned them to their task: "Let us throw off the supine-

ness which has rested upon us and awake, fully determined to be equal to the occasion."[67]

They were more than equal, and by the opening of the 1870s, they had achieved practically all they had hoped for. They had revolutionized the production of shoes. They had defeated slavery and subdued the South. They had set up an efficient fire department supplied with water piped through the business district to protect their factories from fire. They had created a professional police force to protect them from theft and social disorder. And they placed their splendid City Hall upon the community as the crowning glory of their achievements.

5

WORKERS

Driven by hidden movements, moving at an invisible pace, the hands on the face of the factory clock marked the early morning hours before the start of another workday as the sun, hidden behind the horizon, began to seep through the walls of nighttime darkness. While the gears and spheres of machine and nature wheeled and turned toward day, several thousand factory workers of Lynn rolled over for the last time and got out of their beds. Standing in the still damp and darkened bedchambers, they fumbled for their clothes, bent over a wash basin to splash themselves with water, and then, after a short breakfast, left home in the still tentative light of morning to reach the factory gate just before the hands on the clock touched 7:00.

Family Portrait

Among the multitude of men and women whose morning ritual hinged on the clock, and for whom the rising of the sun was somehow an aftereffect of mechanical time, was one man who will forever be known to history by the lone initial of his last name "S." He was number XLIII in a series of capsule biographies of laboring people compiled by the Massachusetts Bureau of Labor Statistics in 1871.[1] "S." had been a shoemaker for forty of his fifty years, and for half-a-dozen years prior to the publication of his biography he had worked in a shoe factory. Recently, he was accompanied to the mill each morning by his three older children; their combined earnings, plus the piece-wages his wife earned sewing baseballs together in the home, enabled the family to rent a seven-room house about fifteen minutes walk from the factory.

After work hours "S." devoted much of his time to the union in his trade, the Knights of St. Crispin (KOSC). One or two nights a week from 7:30 to 10:00 he passed his time in the company of other shoeworkers at the Crispin lodge room. He valued the fellowship of the lodge and also recognized the importance of the union's resistance to the arbitrary rule of the manufacturers. "But for the Crispin order," he affirmed, "shoemakers would to-day have been virutally beggars." After work hours he might roll ten-pins or play baseball, and on Saturday nights he could accompany fellow shoemakers to the weekly dances. He was also an avid reader, keeping himself abreast of current events through a daily newspaper subscription, plus readings in two weekly and two monthly journals. When it came to religion, however, his interest waned; though he mentioned that shoemakers in Lynn generally honored the Sabbath, he failed to say whether they ever kept it holy by going to church or whether they simply took advantage of a day of rest.

His cultural activities helped overcome the boredom he felt on the job; like virtually all who perform semiskilled machine labor, he complained his job did "not exercise the mind at all." Another measure of his alienation was his wish that his children not follow him in the trade. But the family needed income, so what else was there to do? Since he had job contacts in the mill, his children became factory workers like himself because "necessity compels it." No doubt, his sons also found fraternity in the lodge room and pleasure in learning the mysteries of the Crispin ritual, and perhaps they took delight in the ceremonies of brotherhood and the singing of the Crispin "Closing Ode," to the tune of "Rock of Ages":

> Brothers, now, before we part,
> Pledge anew each other's heart;
> Then, as brothers stronger be,
> Working out our destiny.[2]

With strong roots in the community and a certain degree of economic security, the "S." family represented the stable core of laboring people around whom the new factory population of the city coalesced. It was the sort of family that neighbors relied on during periods of duress, like the Great Strike of 1860, when the family used its $75 in cash savings and provisions to sustain themselves and, in addition, to help "others that were needy." The family's inner history spanned the revolutionary years in the shoe industry and bridged the world of the artisan and the world of the factory worker; one member had spent most of his years as a household journeyman, while others had experienced little else besides the factory. With intimate links to the past and strong ties to the present community, families like this brought strength and cohesion to the new working-class residents of Lynn.

The "S." family was not a "household" in the traditional sense of the term. Even though census takers, statisticians, and writers continued to use that term to help organize their own thoughts, the unit they described no longer engaged in social production or functioned as a cooperative work team. The erosion of the household had begun with the rise of the central shop, when binders and journeymen came to be hired as separate individuals, and now the factories shut down the ten-footers, put an end to the sharing of kit among the shop's crew, and split experienced workers off from young helpers. (One redeeming feature of this extreme economic individualism was that family members in the shoe industry were not driven to exploit one another, as in the sweated industries where parents sometimes responded to starvation wage rates by compelling their children to work beyond endurance.) The disintegration of the old work team also isolated boarders from the families with which they lived, since boarders now obeyed the summons of the factory clock and the rules of the production line rather than the authority of the head of a family or the owner of the house they lived in. Since the units in which people lived were no longer the units in which they worked, the traditional household, once the major link between economy and society, ceased to exist.

Instead, laboring people lived in a new social and economic matrix which placed few institutional buffers between themselves and the larger aggregations of class, sex, and ethnicity. People increasingly lived in neighborhoods segregated along class or ethnic lines—or sometimes both, as in the poverty-stricken Irish sections of Lynn and other American cities and the Yankee neighborhoods which contained only wealthy business and professional people. Cutting through every neighborhood, the ancient sexual division of labor in the household was replaced by a cultural division between men's sphere (outside the home) and women's sphere (inside the home). Even in families where both sexes were occupied outside the home, domestic chores were normally assigned exclusively to women.

Although the creed of individualism beclouded the perception of great social divisions, the amassing of Americans into broad groupings based on class, sex, and ethnic identification was plainly evident in the voluntary associations they formed. Separate churches, fraternal orders, and charitable societies demonstrated the importance of ethnic divisions among such groups as African-Americans, Irish-Americans, and Yankees. The existence of a women's movement and its assertion of the collective interests and rights of all women emphasized the growing impact and visibility of the cultural division between the sexes. And the rise of mutual benefit societies, trade unions, and strikes emphasized the emerging solidarities among laboring people and their collective opposition to their employers, who organized, for their part, into boards of trade and exclusive businessmen's clubs.

Just as contemporary paintings and photographs of exterior factory architecture revealed much about the system of industrial organization, so pictures of people at work inside gave revealing hints about the class experience of factory workers. Photographs showed women stitchers frozen to their posts behind whirling sewing machines, wearing plain white cotton shirtwaists with collars buttoned tight around the throat and shirtcuffs rolled back to avoid catching a sleeve in the works. With their hair drawn up and knotted atop the head, they sat with heads bowed over their work as if in prayer, a silent congregation surrounded by the cacophony of moving machinery. In the next room men in floppy coveralls inclined to their machines, and on the floor above cutters standing under tall windows plied their craft, dressed in vests and shirtsleeves with starched white collars and sometimes wearing ties.[3]

Unlike the close conviviality of the ten-footer, the factory workrooms heard little conversation and saw little human movement. In confining men and women to the isolation of their solitary work stations the factory duplicated the Common School practice of seating young children behind rows of desks and compelling silence unless spoken to, a practice which provided a basic course in industrial discipline for future factory recruits. Paradoxically, the one thing all workers had in common was this experience of confinement and subordination. Each one knew that her isolation was like that of the others, that her boredom and weariness were akin to the feelings of those on either side, that her resentment of the foreman peering over her shoulder was a shared passion of mixed fear and contempt for the man whose ability to move about the factory and speak at will set him off from the common worker. A special contempt was reserved for the type of foreman who flaunted his relative freedom, who swaggered from room to room acting as if he were first in command, and who did not acknowledge that he, too, was just an underling and had to answer to the owner like everybody else.

From the lowest ranking unskilled subordinate to the foreman, the basic production worker carried out orders from above issued by the one man who answered to no superior. Though the owner rarely put in an appearance in the workrooms, he was omnipresent. His authority was engrained in the wooden planks of the floor, cemented into the stubbled brick and mortar walls, cast into the iron implements of

Shoe Factory Cutting Room, circa 1910. *Courtesy of the Lynn Historical Society*

the trade. There was no mistaking the inequalities of power and status in the factory. The very enormity of the building in comparison to the tiny ten-footer and the great surge of productive capacity that jolted through its beams when the machinery was started up seemed to demonstrate that the person who owned this fortress of technology was a giant in comparison to the dwarfs who toiled within.

Of course, the factory apparatus itself was not what subordinated worker to boss. After all, the worker on the shop floor knew how to handle the machinery better than the men who minded the office. Rather, the worker's subordination was a consequence of his exclusion from ownership, since property ownership in a marketplace economy conferred control over the means of production. This disparity between giving orders and taking them set up powerful antagonisms and engendered a deep anger—sometimes muffled and turned inward in self-hate, sometimes turned outward in defiance— among people who believed all men should be equal. The spicy taste of anger was on the lips of "S." when he told the Bureau of Labor Statistics, "The employer knows just how much it costs to keep the breath of life in his employees, and if he finds they are getting ahead, he cuts wages down just low enough to prevent it."[4] Such passions formed the enduring basis of class conflict long after the low wages and bare-knuckled social relations of the nineteenth century gave way to higher wages, softer personnel policies, and washroom welfare programs in the twentieth century.

Social Origins

To establish the social origins of the factory work force and to answer questions about the impact of the factories on artisans living in the city, it was necessary to conduct a lengthy, detailed process of research in local census manuscripts. (See Appendix B for a complete description of research methods and Appendix C for a discussion of the correction of a statistical error in the census data.) Some of the results appear in Table 2. All male shoeworkers in the census of 1870 were divided into three occupational subcategories used by census enumerators and then divided again into two groups of "stable" and "mobile" workers.

The table represents the basic statistical framework for analyzing

TABLE 2. Composition of the Labor Force in 1870.

Category	Stable	Mobile	Total
All shoeworkers	1152	2585	3737
Factory	504	1931	2435
Cutters	145	159	304
Nonfactory	503	495	998

Source: U.S., Eighth and Ninth Census manuscripts for Lynn.

the composition of the industrial work force. It indicates that "stable" workers like the "S." family were less important numerically than culturally. The stable workers—members of shoemaker families who resided in Lynn for at least a decade—were clearly a minority of the total work force and an even smaller proportion of factory workers (504 of 2435 or 21 percent).

The stable workers were more significant as recruits for the cutter aristocracy and as hand workers carrying on in the small central shops and the few remaining ten-footers. Considering wages and prestige, a man did well to become a cutter. The other hand workers, however, looked toward a bleak future. They continued for a time to meet the demand for fine grade, hand-sewn products, but fierce price competition was forcing their employers into more efficient factory methods, and their days were numbered. David Johnson spoke of their ten-footers as relics of the past that "remind us of a former age," and by the end of the 1870s the hand workers had taken their place alongside the master mechanics in the artisan graveyard with the factory as their mausoleum.[5]

Most factory workers were new to the city, or new to the trade, or both. Men who fit one of these descriptions are combined in Table 2 to form the category of mobile workers, who constitute 79 percent (1931 of 2435) of the factory work force. They were a heterogeneous group with social backgrounds ranging from Irish Catholic peasant immigrants to Yankee Protestant urban artisans. Whatever their origins, virtually none of them had ever set foot in a factory, and, therefore, the dislocation of their migration was compounded by the disruption of becoming a factory hand.

In both numerical and cultural terms, the most significant segment of mobile recruits were the former outworkers of the New England shoe industry. As the central shops evolved into factories, causing the collapse of the outwork system, people whose well-being once depended on what the freighter brought each month were sent reeling about in search of work. Large numbers found their way to Lynn, a fact reflected in the statistics on shoeworker nativity. Census manuscript data on factory workers in 1870 indicated an unusually high proportion from the outwork states of New Hampshire and Maine. As reported in Table 3, 23 percent of this group were New England-

TABLE 3. Nativity of Shoemakers: Factory, Nonfactory, and Cutters, 1870 (Percent).

Category	Mass.	New England	Other U.S.	Foreign
All shoeworkers	60	20	1	19
Factory	56	23	2	19
Cutters	81	12	2	5
Nonfactory	61	16	1	22

Source: U.S., Ninth Census manuscripts for Lynn.

ers born outside Massachusetts, and, according to tabulations not shown in the table, practically all of these were from New Hampshire and Maine.[6] In addition, almost half of the group born in Massachusetts were not Lynn natives but migrated to the city; some of these were also former outworkers.[7]

The outwork system was a giant watershed for labor migration which would look exactly like a river network if it were mapped out. The outer tributaries of the network originated in the rural hamlets to the north and east of Lynn. Before the factories, the flow of labor from these communities was only a trickle, but afterwards it became a substantial stream. In one of the hamlets, Northwood, New Hampshire, the number of shoemakers steadily expanded from 1840 to 1860, but in the next decade the number declined dramatically. Not all of the local shoemakers who left the trade also left Northwood, and not all of those who left Northwood went to Lynn, but the prior existence of outwork made it more likely that a refugee shoemaker would seek work in Lynn, where he already had job contacts, than in some other industrial or commercial city where he might have no contacts whatsoever. Knowing a boss in Lynn made a move there more a hopeful matter of opportunity and less a hazardous matter of sheer chance. As a result, the pattern of Northwood was repeated again and again as outworkers from dozens of such hamlets joined one another in ever larger streams of migration flowing into the channel that led to Lynn.[8]

Just before reaching Lynn, the stream from upper New England joined the stream of people born in Massachusetts outside the city limits of Lynn. From Marblehead came young women, not as forlorn as the Hannah of Lucy Larcom's bathetic poem, but every bit as dependent on income from shoe binding, and from Danvers and Peabody came outworkers running for cover like their New Hampshire counterparts. Completing the roster of native-born migrants, men with no previous connection to the trade came to Lynn, having heard how quickly one could learn the basics of factory work. At the point where all these streams united to pour their contributions into Lynn, the flow of people amounted to several hundred each year.[9]

At times, the older residents of Lynn felt innundated by all these newcomers. "Operatives are pouring in as fast as room can be made for them," a newspaper editor said. A minister watched the arrival of young people "fresh from a New Hampshire farm never having seen a factory" and coined the phrase "New Lynn" to describe this growing segment of factory recruits. The city's public health officer made this report: "During the last two or three years, in consequence of an important change in the method of manufacturing shoes, large numbers of young persons of both sexes have removed from the country towns in the vicinity to the city where they are collected together in large bodies during the day, and suffer the inconveniences and discomforts of crowded boarding houses after the labor of the day is over."[10]

These Yankees rubbed elbows at the boardinghouse table and in the factory with Irish workers, who constituted the strongest current in the stream of foreign immigration. Driven from their cottages in rural Ireland by the spector of starvation, hounded by terror across the seas and sailing with death aboard ship, the Irish experience of

social apocalypse made the uprooting of the Yankee farmer shoemakers, an experience harsh enough in its own frame of reference,
something rather mild in comparison.[11] Most of the Irishmen who
moved into Lynn settled in the central manufacturing district and
worked as laborers, morocco dressers and finishers, and shoemakers.
Reflecting their position in the occupational structure at large, Irishmen in the shoe industry tended to be concentrated at unskilled and
semiskilled levels, so that virtually none of the Irish became shoemaker aristocrats (Table 3). Although a sprinkling of Irish names
began to appear among the ranks of the city's grocers, morocco manufacturers, and other small businessmen, the overwhelming number
of Irish were poor working people, and if some found fraternity in
neighborhood "drinking clubs" (while others joined the local chapter
of the Father Matthew Temperance Society), the most active segment
found solace for their condition in trade unionism. Irishmen were
more prominent in the Knights of St. Crispin than their numbers in
the shoe work force would warrant, and the same held true during the
reign of the Knights of Labor, as well.[12]

Still, despite the visibility of the Irish in the first two decades of
the factory system, and despite the growing number of French and
British Canadians, who became the largest immigrant stream after
1880, the work force was largely native born. In fact, Lynn had a
larger proportion of native-born workers than nearly every other
major manufacturing center in the state, a consequence of the development of large-scale shoe manufacturing before the existence of a
factory system.[13]

All the above information applies to men, but one-third of the
work force in the factory era were women. (See Appendix A, Table
8.) Much of Lynn's labor history was made by women, who had been
binding shoes in Lynn almost as long as men had been bottoming
them. The full-time commitment of women to the trade in the last
two decades of the eighteenth century made possible the conversion
to large-scale manufacturing, and by 1850 more Yankee women
made shoes than men. Women were the first to encounter the factory
system through the stitching shops of the 1850s and were the first
to feel the corrosive effect of the factory on the household. Women
came to the factories from the same places as men, and in about the

same proportions. Slightly more than half (52 percent) of the female shoeworkers in 1885 were natives of Massachusetts, another quarter (23 percent) were from elsewhere in New England, 22 percent were immigrants, and a small fraction (3 percent) were from elsewhere in the United States.[14]

The Floating Population

One of the major social consequences of the factory system was the creation of a floating population composed of people who moved about from city to city like vagabond peddlers of labor. The floaters were without property, personal connections, or essential skills. Other workers may have moved to improve their situation in life; the floaters moved to eat. The term itself was of prefactory origin, sometimes invoked when a large number of strangers appeared, like Irish day laborers roving through eastern Massachusetts in search of work, but it gained currency and was applied to shoemakers only with the coming of the factories.

The cause of floating migration in the shoe industry was the seasonal production cycle. A local newspaper affirmed that "Lynn must, from the nature of its business, contain a large transient population." Including both men and women, the transients remained in the city "only during the busy season."[15] The Massachusetts Bureau of the Statistics of Labor in 1871 and 1873 attested to the existence of two well-defined production seasons, one running from January to June, and a second beginning in August and extending to the end of October. The bureau's observations were confirmed by the monthly curve of shoe output, reports of which began to appear in the newspapers in the late 1860s. Invariably the statistics showed a peak in early spring and then another peak at a lower level later on in the year, usually in September.[16] The consequence of this cycle was a regular cutback in the number of employees during the slack periods. The 1880 census commented on this situation: "It is a well known fact, especially in midsummer and mid-winter, when demand is small, or between the changes from the heavy goods of one season to the light goods of another, that the force of employees at many establishments is greatly reduced, frequently from a third to a half."[17] (Light goods were for spring and summer wear and were made during the first season; heavy goods were the thick-soled shoes made for fall and winter wear during the second.)

The demand for additional labor at certain seasons had been the critical factor in creating an extensive outwork system in the three decades before the factories. Now, as the factories became the manufacturers' solution to the problems and limitations inherent in outwork, the floating worker took over the function of added seasonal help formerly held by the outworker. Under the new system, the seasonal high tide in the demand for labor could only be satisfied by bringing extra workers into the city. Then when production slackened and layoffs began, the floating workers were carried out again in the ebb tide of unemployment. The floaters were at the mercy of the tides in production because they had neither property nor skills to anchor them to the community, a fact which turned the manufacturers' needs directly into misfortune.

Because of their unsettled life style, statistical evidence on the floaters is very hard to get, but there is some quantitative information hidden in the records of free lodgings, which the city customarily provided in the lock-up for people who had nowhere else to sleep. Some of those who took advantage of this arrangement were only passing through, but others used the lock-up for a night or two until they could find employment and other lodgings in Lynn. For many years before the factories, particularly in the cold months, an occasional workman who could not afford a bed at the Lynn Hotel found a place to rest in the jail. In 1860 the city marshal said the lodgers were "mostly travellers in search of employment, without means of support, and without friends to assist them in their search for business." Up through the 1860s the city cheerily bestowed a place to sleep and a small ration of food upon them, but in the early 1870s the attitude of city officials changed to wariness and then hostility as the depression turned the jail into a boardinghouse for as many as twenty men. In 1874 the marshal referred to the lodgers for the first time as "tramps," and in the next few years the reports grew more alarmed, depicting unemployed workers as "professional tramps with no particular destination, and no object in view." The marshals identified the tramps as a criminal element—in the words of one official report: "an unclean, indolent, shiftless class of people." Since the lodgers were still workers on the tramp, the change in the attitude of city officials provides a glimpse of the deepening social gulf between the city's middle-class and working-class residents.[18]

The statistics on free lodgings also provide some information on the genesis of the floating population. The figures depicted in Graph 1 show a dramatic rise in the number of lodgings after 1866, reaching a peak in the depression year of 1874.[19] The timing of the rise seems clearly to be associated with the impact of the factories and reflects the fact that large numbers of single, unattached workers were being drawn to the city as factory jobs opened up.

In addition to this long-range trend, monthly figures also show a relationship between tramping and employment in the shoe industry. Until the depression set in late in 1873, the statistics on shoe pro-

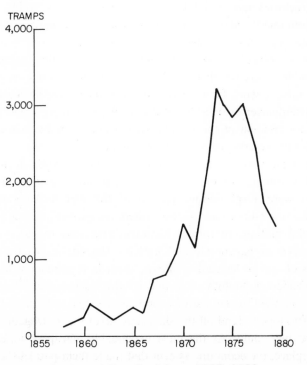

Number of Free Lodgings, 1857–1880

duction and the number of lodgings rose and fell at roughly the same time during the year. Workers without means of support were attracted to Lynn as shoe production got under way in the spring, when the number of lodgings usually rose; then as production declined in June and July, fewer people arrived and the jail became less crowded. (Beginning in October 1873 and running for the next several years, the long-range condition of industrial depression tended to blur the seasonal pattern of tramping that had developed beforehand.) [20]

The very movement of the migrant workers makes it difficult to estimate their numbers. Seasonal fluctuations in output were large enough to cause the discharge of one-third to one-half of all employees, though it is impossible to verify whether all these discharged workers actually left town. [21] Even if company payroll records were available, they would not provide an answer to this question. As for city directories, they maintained a bias against the less stable residents of a community, and the census manuscripts, appearing at ten-year intervals, were about as helpful as a dime-store microscope in magnifying a molecule. Given the limitations of statistical sources, it is impossible to say whether the floaters made up as much as one-third of the factory work force. It is enough to recognize that even if they were one-quarter or one-fifth of the whole, they represented a significant new creation of the factory system and an important contribution to "the reserve army of surplus labor."

The floaters were an extreme case of labor migration in the Industrial Revolution. [22] Like a movie film being shown at triple speed, the floaters were a speeded-up version of the typical American; they existed at the end of the spectrum where occasional migration became perpetual motion. In former historical eras they would have been stigmatized as vagabonds and perhaps singled out to become the objects of special legislation affixing them in a permanent place, like the Elizabethan Statute of Artificers. But such mercantilist notions were outmoded in the age of economic freedom, and so the floaters were left alone to fend off the slings and arrows of outrageous fortune as best they could. As the most expendable, cheapest wares in the marketplace, the economic system that made them part of the regular circulation of commodities dumped them like surplus cloth goods at the first sign of slack in demand.

Who Were the Knights of St. Crispin?

The organization of labor to resist the depredations of organized capital was the historical imperative of the industrial working class. Everywhere that the Industrial Revolution brought new sectors of the working class into being, the imperative was expressed in forms ranging from spontaneous turnouts to nationwide trade unions, from shop talk that bad-mouthed the boss to platforms that defined an injury to one as the concern of all. Often the attempt at organization failed or succeeded in ways that divided the class into suspicious and hostile segments along lines of occupation, ethnicity, sex, and geography, yet the pressure to unite in opposition to the common enemy was unrelenting and in certain historical circumstances resulted in the formation of classwide institutions.

With the aim of organizing all who labored in the trade, industrial workers in Lynn's shoe industry established a local of the Knights of St. Crispin in 1868 and a local of the Daughters of St. Crispin shortly thereafter. They enrolled a representative cross section of the new factory work force and sustained the organizations against the disintegrating effects of seasonal unemployment, high rates of labor migration, diverse social backgrounds, occupational jealousies, and sexual divisions for all but two of the next ten years.

This picture of the Crispins as modern industrial workers conflicts sharply with the bulk of historical scholarship, which paints Crispins as oldtime artisans outside the new working class. The fountainhead of misinterpretation is none other than the founder of American labor history, John Commons. Commons attempted to relate successive types of labor organization to a sequence of stages in the development of the shoe industry in America. His method was to begin with labor documents—the constitution of a journeyman's society, the transcript of a trade union conspiracy trial—and read back from there the nature of industrial organization at the time. His scheme of stages in economic history was derived directly from Carl Bücher's *Industrial Evolution,* his documentary method replicated the work of George Unwin's *Industrial Organization in the 16th and 17th Centuries,* and his approach was conceived as an alternative to Marxian analysis.[23]

He redefined the conflict between labor and capital as a conflict between labor and the market. From the seventeenth century onward, the ever-widening market reduced prices, brought increasing numbers of people into production, and depressed their wages. Thus he argued the basic fight of the nineteenth-century shoeworker was with the forces of the market, not with his boss. In his view, the Knights of St. Crispin were less concerned with waging a struggle against the bosses than with preventing green hands from taking their jobs. Under the terms of this green hands theory, the more experienced shoe-makers felt their jobs threatened by new machinery and new workers, and they organized the Knights of St. Crispin to protect themselves against both.[24]

The early followers of Commons merely elaborated his theory in greater detail. The year after Commons' original article appeared in 1909, Don Lescohier published a study based on the same Crispin convention proceedings and constitutions that Commons had used. Not surprisingly, he reached similar conclusions about the importance of the green hands issue. John B. Andrews followed the same inter-pretation in the multivolume, *History of Labour in the United States,* a milestone in its comprehensive treatment of American labor move-ments, prepared under Commons' editorship. Following this, Blanche Hazard wrote the standard study of shoemaking, *The Organization of the Boot and Shoe Industry in Massachusetts Before 1875,* which reiterated the Commons theme, as did A. E. Galster's monograph on *The Labor Movement in the Shoe Industry.* Norman Ware picked it up in his study of *The Labor Movement in the United States 1860–1895,* concluding that the Crispins were old fashioned "co-operators," an anachronism in an era of trade unions and machine production. In sum, every major work that dealt with the Knights of St. Crispin accepted the basic tenets of the green hands theory.[25]

The theory is wrong on two counts. First, it mistakenly construes the question of hiring new hands as a central issue; in fact, it was only a peripheral matter. Not a single strike was undertaken in Lynn over the issue of green hands. Wage disputes were always of primary concern locally, and more recent scholarship has demonstrated that the same was true in other towns where Crispins were active.[26] The second fault of the theory is that it incorrectly locates the sources of Crispin strength among workers who were either outside the factories or else did not yet accept the permanence of factory organization. The Commons' view of the Crispins as "lifetime" shoemakers battling the inrush of "newcomers" is no longer tenable.

Who were the Crispins? To answer the question, the names of union members were compared with names of shoemakers from the local census tracts of 1860 and 1870. The members were listed in a dues book containing just under 2000 names of dues-payers who joined Unity Lodge (one of two local lodges) from 1868 to 1872. It was possible to find 995 of these names in the 1870 census. (The remaining 1000 who were not found included men who joined in 1868 or 1869 and left town before the 1870 census, men who moved to town and joined after the census, and men who were not recorded in the Lynn census. The last group is made up of men who worked in Lynn, and joined the Lynn local, but lived elsewhere, plus residents who were simply overlooked by the census enumerators.) Since the other major shoe centers organized by the Knights of St. Crispin went through the same industrial transformation as Lynn, and since Lynn was the largest and perhaps the most active local branch, the city was an unusually important crossroads of experience of New England shoemakers as a whole. The conclusions from the study thus reach beyond the boundaries of the city itself.

The most telling result of the study is that *the bulk of the Crispins were factory workers*. Three-fourths of the members were so listed in the 1870 census.[27] Factory workers joined the union at a higher rate than nonfactory workers; the latter made up one-third of the labor force, but only one-fourth of the union membership. Perhaps one-half the 1870 factory work force signed up and payed their dues, and, in addition, hundreds more participated in Crispin mass meetings and strike actions.[28] The major dichotomy in the work force was not between lifetime shoemakers and green hands but between factory and nonfactory workers. Indeed, most of the lifetime shoemakers who resided in Lynn did not even become Crispins; only 22 percent of the residents who remained in the trade from 1860 to 1870 joined the union (248 of 1152).[29] The previous conception of Crispins as stable craftsmen trying to protect their skilled position against the competition of unskilled machine workmen breaks apart on these facts alone. The decision whether or not to join the union was made by and large along lines of industrial cleavage opposite to those suggested by the green hands theory.

But perhaps the Crispin factory workers were different from other factory workers. Perhaps they were a more highly skilled group, an elite.

No. The true elite corps among the shoemakers did not join the Crispins at all. There were but three cutters among the nearly 1000 members in the study, and there was no mention of joint action of cutters and Crispins in any of the Lynn strikes. In fact, when the cutters organized, they imitated the manufacturers. During the strike of 1870, instead of supporting the Crispins, they formed their own exclusive organization called the Lynn Cutters' Board of Trade, emulating the manufacturers' organization of the same title. Not until the cutters had had over a decade of experience with the factories were they ready to join the labor movement. Even into the twentieth century, however, they still considered themselves a cut above the ordinary worker.[30]

Perhaps, then, the Crispins were better off than the average factory worker. Perhaps they had higher incomes and owned more property.

No, again. In terms of property ownership, three-quarters reported they owned nothing of value. This was slightly better than the factory workers as a whole, who showed 81 percent without property, but if the test is raised to people with property worth $500 or less, the gap between Crispins and all factory workers falls to only 2 percent.[31] No measurement of income has comparable accuracy, but the absence of labor aristocrats, the prominence of lasters (underpaid skilled workers),[32] and the presence of many semiskilled operatives make it likely that income statistics, were they available, would reinforce the bond between the Crispin and the average factory worker.

Still, it might be possible that the Crispins were more stable members of the community threatened by outsiders.

Not so. In fact, Crispins experienced more uprooting than even the factory workers as a whole. Exactly one-half of the Crispins were born outside Massachusetts, compared with 44 percent of the factory workers. Nearly one-quarter originated in New Hampshire and Maine, and the remaining 25 percent were foreign born, mostly Irish. The green hands theory has no place for such a large group of newcomers, especially the Irish immigrants. To take a second measure of stability, only 25 percent of the Crispins had been members of shoemaker families in Lynn in 1860, whereas these ex-artisans made up 30 percent of the entire shoemaker population in 1870. Thus the Crispins had a smaller portion of long-time local residents than the shoemaker population at large. Furthermore, the Crispins probably had their share of floaters, too; among the names in the Crispin dues book which could not be matched to names in the census were men who stayed in Lynn for only one or two seasons or perhaps commuted to the city during the peak months of production.[33]

In every measurable category, the Crispins contained a cross-section of the factory work force. They did not represent the highly paid, highly skilled labor aristocracy. They did not represent old-time, stable members of the community. Thus, in order to understand who the Crispins did represent, it is first necessary to recognize that they were factory workers. To the extent that the factory work force was recruited among "lifetime" shoemakers, these old-timers would in turn be present in the union. It is not so much that the green hands theory is wrong in describing the Crispins as lifetime shoemakers, but that the whole division of shoemakers into newcomers and lifetime workers is confusing and misses the point. Ex-artisans, both rural shoemakers and urban mechanics, undoubtedly made up the bulk of the Crispin membership, but that is because they first made up the bulk of the factory work force.

Knowing who joined the union makes it possible to understand why they joined. Writers in the Commons' tradition answered this second question through a process of circular reasoning. They made assumptions about the membership of the KOSC on the basis of Crispin speeches and by-laws. Then they turned around and interpreted the speeches and by-laws in terms of their assumptions about membership. Take the study by Lescohier. He assumed from the green hands theory that the Crispins were skilled artisans losing their jobs to machines and factory workers. Then he argued that the old artisans joined the union to protest against the competition for jobs and the resulting economic hardship.[34] To be sure, Crispins hated competition and suffered hardship, but they identified the manufacturers as the prime cause of their troubles and organized to fight them, not green hands.

In sum, the Knights of St. Crispin emerged from the encounter between prefactory artisans and the factory system. Accustomed to making their own day-by-day decisions about production, the old artisans were subjected to a new order wholly under the control of the manufacturer. Used to setting their own work pace, they were subjected to a rhythm dictated by machinery. Expecting to work close to their homes and families, they were thrust together with dozens of strangers among whom they were strangers themselves. Self-reliant and proud, they found themselves treated as objects. And even though their standard of living did not decline much, if at all, they felt, in a word, proletarianized.

When they sought means of dealing with their new situation, they found their own heritage rich in the experience of collective action among workingpeople. They were familiar with the forms of voluntary association and jealous of their right to join whatever group they wished. Many of them had direct and intimate experience of prefactory combinations among workers to raise wages, and many had been involved in the strike of 1860. Thus they possessed the tools of historical experience with which to build an organized expression of their anger. The Knights of St. Crispin, therefore, represented both the experience of being a factory worker, and the reassertion of an alternative, less regimented way of life.

6

THE POOR AND THE
LESS POOR

Gilded Age industrialists stood atop a growing mountain of wealth built upon investments in mines, mills, and railways. They accumulated capital in the means of production and acquired prestige through conspicuous consumption without pausing to calculate the cost of their acquisitiveness in burgeoning slag heaps, swelling river effluents, and smoke-choked skies that begrimed their environment. Further down the slope of the mountain, small shopkeepers, petty traders and working professionals staked their claims to lesser portions of the new wealth, living in fear that every disturbance in the economy would trigger an avalanche that would cast them still further down the mountainside. Thus they twisted and turned from awestruck imitation of those above them to resentful condemnation, from procapitalism to antimonopoly. Below them in the foothills and plains at the base of the mountain lived industrial workers, whose wealth was measured negatively by the goods they needed but did not have, and who were always the first to pay the costs—ecological, economic, psychological—of the Industrial Revolution.

Wealth and Poverty

Although the topography of wealth had always been uneven, the new order of factory capitalism exerted a massive impact on the system of production and distribution, causing the earth to buckle and heave, thrusting the hilltops sharply upward to become mountain peaks, and depressing the level of the plains below. Never before in Lynn had the wealth of the wealthy and the poverty of the poor been so far apart. Residents measured the change by contrasting the richest businessmen of the factory era with their less wealthy prefactory counterparts and by counting the rising number of propertyless workers.[1] The conclusion was inescapable: wealth and poverty were increasing apace. An ardent defender of the factory system analyzed the recent upheavals:

Machinery creates wealth; and a large part of the increase naturally falls into the hands of capital that employs the machinery. Colossal fortunes are piled up in a few years, apparently making wider the gap between rich and poor.

A critic of the factory system called attention to the same gap:

Those who look beneath the surface of things, with unprejudiced eyes, are painfully conscious that wealth, though year by year still on the increase, goes now into fewer hands; that the results of industry are very unequally divided; that the advantages which machinery and division of labor bring, have been altogether in favor of capital and against labor, and that these evils are dangerously increasing from year to year.[2]

The overall impact of the factory system on the civilizations of Europe and the United States had long been a matter for debate between those who acclaimed the new wealth and those who bewailed the new poverty. Did the system raise or depress the living standards of the mass of the population? Did it lighten the burden of toil or increase it? Did it elevate or corrupt popular morals? Did it narrow or widen the gap between social classes? And ultimately the question was asked, did the factory system mark the decline and fall of western civilization or its ascendancy? The two sides of this debate were crystallized in the words of two American intellectuals with wide experience of the conditions of industrial society. Speaking *for* the factory system was Carroll Wright, bureaucrat and statistician, who sanctified the new system as a "most potent element in promoting civilization" and a force which "outstrips the pulpit in the actual work of the gospel, that is, in the work of humanity." Speaking *against* was Wendell Phillips, abolitionist and labor reformer, who declaimed, "I am ashamed of the civilization which makes 5,000 needy men dependent on one."[3]

The same debate was conducted in Lynn, with pessimists like the Reverend Mr. Cook depicting the factory as a den of iniquity, and optimistic factory owners depicting it as a benevolent school of industrial discipline. Images of lewd workers in need of moral uplift battled images of loyal operatives who responded well to discipline.[4] Such contentions between divergent flights of bourgeois fantasy offered real-life workers nothing to choose from, so workers kept their dignity and stayed away from this theater of debate. Of more direct interest to the working population was the question of the material impact of the factory system: Did workers live better than before? Usually this boiled down to a dispute over property ownership. Debaters argued whether or not industrial workers measured up to a social ideal of small artisan and agricultural producers who worked their own capital, or, in the language of the day, the argument turned on whether or not workers could acquire a "competence."

Competence meant the ability to get along well in economic terms —to possess real estate or savings sufficient to house a family, or tide it over during hard times, or support husband and wife in old age. As a bare minimum, a competence would provide a base for stable membership in a community, reduce the terrors of falling into debt, and keep a family from the throes of dependency and destitution. For working-class families, it was a ticket out of poverty to the regions of minimal security. For middle-class families, the competence was a more liberal endowment of property or savings that generated income through rent or interest to sustain the family through adversity at its accustomed level of prosperity. In his celebrated essay on "Wealth," Andrew Carnegie defined competence in middle-class terms as "moderate sums saved by many years of effort, the returns from which are required for the comfortable maintenance and education of families."[5] In these terms, a competence would have required investments of several thousand dollars, something completely out of reach of virtually all industrial workers, who would not have been wage-earning employees in the first place had they been able to live off rent or interest. In working-class terms, a competence could be secured for much less; a worker's annual income was only a few hundred dollars, and the small wooden cottage he could afford to purchase cost one or two annual incomes. Thus the family worth $500 or more was in possession of at least a minimal competence.[6]

With the competence as the main focus of attention, one round in the on-going factory controversy occurred in successive issues of a local newspaper whose editor took the optimistic position in reply to the pessimism of an adversary who signed his letters to the editor "Scrib." Scrib's opening volley was a broadside against the wealthy classes of "idle loafers" like Gould and Vanderbilt who basked in the luxury of Newport and Saratoga and accumulated enormous sums of wealth, while the worker who rose early each morning to toil all day long found it hard to gain even a small competence. In a follow-up letter Scrib outlined the conflict between the capitalist and the worker: "The interest of the laboring man is to receive for his labor a fair and equitable reward. The interest of capital is to divert every dollar that he can from the channel above indicated into his own pocket or bank account. How *can* the two interests be identical?" The editor shot back with the contention that workers acquired a competence more easily now than in the past, and he added a series of rapid-fire denials of the existence of class antagonism. Capital, he insisted, could not be hostile to labor because capitalists were generally hard-working individuals: "We are all working men. The drones in American society are few." By the same token, labor should not be hostile to capital because laborers with savings were capitalists: "The capital of the country is not made up of the wealth of a few Jay Goulds. Every man who has a hundred dollars to invest is a capitalist, and the same law, whether written or unwritten, that protects the wealthiest in their possessions protects him."[7]

What was absent from both sides in the debate was factual information on the extent of property ownership. Was it, in fact, easier for a factory worker to gain a competence than it was for an artisan? The answer is no. On the contrary, factory workers had a harder time gaining the prize than their prefactory counterparts. Comparing all male shoemakers in 1870 with the respective group for 1860, the proportion of workers with a competence dropped from 25 percent in 1860 to 21 percent in 1870. To sharpen the comparison by measuring ordinary shoemakers of 1860 (excluding cutters) against factory workers of 1870 (again excluding cutters), the drop-off became steeper as percentages fell from 24 percent with a competence in 1860 to only 15 percent in 1870, as Table 4 shows.[8]

TABLE 4. Property Ownership of Male Shoemakers, 1860 and 1870.

Year	Percent without a competence[a]			Percent with a competence[b]			Total percent[c]	Total number
	I ($0-100)	II ($200-400)	I + II ($0-400)	III ($500-1900)	IV ($2000 and over)	III + IV ($500 and over)	II + I + III + IV	ber of shoe-makers
1860								
Shoemaker	59	16	75	16	9	25	100	2569
(Cutters excluded)	61	15	76	16	8	24	100	2306
1870								
Shoemakers	72	7	79	9	12	21	100	3737
(Factory only)	81	4	85	7	8	15	100	2435

Source: U.S., Eighth and Ninth Census manuscripts for Lynn.

[a] The subdivision of people without a competence into two columns is designed to compare the size of the subgroup that had little or no property (col. I, $0–100) with the subgroup that had some small holdings (col. II, $200–400).

[b] The subdivision of people with a competence into two columns is designed to compare the size of the subgroup that had medium holdings (col. III, $500–1900) with the subgroup that had large holdings (col. IV, $2000 and over).

[c] The total percent is the sum of those with a competence plus those without a competence. The sum, of course, is equal to the combined percentages of the four subgroups.

These are conservative figures. They measure the gap between factory and prefactory workers at its narrowest point because they contrast understatements of the higher percentages in 1860 with overstatements of the lower percentages in 1870. That is because the 1860 figures had been depleted by three years of hard times and six weeks of strike; because outworkers (who made up half the roster of 1860 employees and were more likely to own property than shoemakers residing in Lynn) were not taken into account; and because the 1870 figures had been swelled by several years of prosperity and by inflation. All in all, the figures are an irreducible measure of the minimum decline in property holdings among male shoemakers. Underestimating the true decline in this fashion may have its advantages; nothing establishes a fact more firmly than conservative understatement.

The decline in the percentage of property owners was accompanied by a rise in the actual number of employees. Like two waves colliding in the sea to produce a swell larger than either of them, these two numerical movements combined to produce a vast increase in the number of men *without* property: the net increase across the decade of conversion was 1162 men. Owing to the sheer increase in the number of employees, the number of men *with* a competence also increased, though the net gain was a meager 139 individuals. Further elaboration of this point emerges when net gain in overall employment is contrasted with the net gain in employees with a competence. In these terms, one man acquired a competence in every twelve additional employees.[9] The conclusion was clear that factory capitalism blocked opportunities for gaining a competence and that poverty among wage earners was increasing faster than security, at least as measured by property holdings. In regard to the debate over the opportunity for factory workers to acquire wealth, the net results of this information prove the *Transcript* wrong and "Scrib" correct.

At this point our intrepid newspaper editor would have to recalculate his position. A smart man would know that net changes do not register all the movement taking place. They are but the visible manifestation of a lot more movement taking place behind the scenes, so to speak, just as the net change in the position of the hands moving around the dial of a clock is the end result of an intricate interplay of many different movements—clockwise and counterclockwise, fast and slow—taking place within the mechanism. Concerning occupational and property groupings, net changes are the result of many more movements in and out of the group; if ten men cease to be shoemakers and eleven take up the trade, the net change is only one.

Thus the editor could rebuild his case on evidence from behind the scenes; in the face of facts demonstrating an overall decline, he could bring forth examples of *some* groups of shoemakers who improved their standing. The most dramatic improvement was registered by heads of households who owned absolutely nothing in 1860: ten years later one-third had acquired a competence. Another group of stable shoemakers who also showed some improvement were the men who became factory workers in 1870: the proportion of those with a competence rose from a little over one-fifth in 1860 to one-third a decade later. The key variable seems to be residential persistence, because shoemakers who remained in the city for a long stretch of time were likely to wind up better off, no matter whether they went into the shoe factories or some other line of work. Long-term residence in the same community was geared directly to the process of accumulating a competence month by month, year by year, through tiny accretions added to savings, building up a competence the way coral polyps build a reef.[10] At the same time, many of the accumulations were not newly established; some of the individuals who acquired a competence were merely taking over the possessions of the previous generation when the elders died off.

The optimists in the debate over property ownership would thus be reduced to the position that the factories did not foreclose all possibilities for acquiring a competence. This argument had the merit of being tenable in the face of generally contrary statistical evidence, but for the same reason it was hardly an enviable position. Every gain the optimists could point to was swamped by overwhelming losses; every time someone left the ranks of propertyless shoemakers, several additional men moved in to take his place. Observers who watched the number of propertied shoemakers grow at a snail's pace, while the number without property grew by leaps and bounds, might have gauged the declining position of shoemakers in the community by comparing shoemakers with their bosses: the actual net gain in propertied shoemakers from 1860 to 1870 was about equal to the net gain in propertied manufacturers, despite the fact that the former outnumbered the latter ten to one! A friend of labor drew the following conclusion in 1873:

Within five years real estate has enormously increased in value, and it is largely held by a few rich men. No longer is there opportunity for an operative in a shoe shop to save his earnings, and finally purchase a home. Very few indeed of the working people of Lynn have been able to save anything or even to keep out of debt, the last two or three years; and it is only too evident that the cause now at work in Lynn may render it rich and prosperous as a city, but with a population of overworked, underpaid hirelings, hopelessly dependent upon employers who act upon the good old rule, the simple plan

—that they may take who have the power, and they may keep who can.[11]

Income

Feeling the burden of evidence weighing against him, our indefatigable editor might have reassessed his position again and shifted the discussion away from the distribution of wealth to the distribution of income. At first brush, this would seem to be a wise move on his part, since the personal income of the average shoemaker almost certainly increased, but, as we shall see, other factors tended to minimize the contribution of higher personal income to family finances. Family living standards are determined by several converging influences; besides the obvious factors of wages and prices, standards are set by the kind of material goods and services available at a particular level of technology, by the general quality of the environment, and by the structure of the family.

Starting with the question of hourly or daily wages, much of the available information is virtually useless, since it is impressionistic and fragmentary. Company payrolls no longer exist, and in the absence of payrolls or comparable sources to tell exactly how many workers earned $2 a day, how many $1.50, and so on, numerical wage rates do not mean much by themselves. Information on *annual income,* however, does exist and is more valid as an approach to understanding living conditions. The state Bureau of the Statistics of Labor frequently looked into the question, and after several years of testing it produced an extensive and apparently reliable report in 1876 measuring incomes of wage earners for the previous year. Given the fact that the bureau was moving into a relatively uncharted area, the fact that it compiled a survey of 71,000 individuals is quite impressive. Among that total were 1,653 male shoemakers in Essex County, and they will form the basis for the following income analysis. (Since Lynn shoemakers comprised a large segment of those surveyed in the county, it will be assumed that the Lynn rates were at the same level as the countywide figures.)[12]

The average annual income of these shoemakers was $440.[13] This figure should actually be taken down a peg to give a better picture of the income of the majority. Although the published survey data does not permit an exact tally of the median, it does show that the largest group of shoemakers (classified "undesignated" in the report) earned an average of $420 a year. Bottomers, by contrast, earned $500, and cutters took in $521. The undesignated shoemakers were a clear majority (921 of 1653), and their income will be used as the point of comparison with the prefactory period.

Since the bureau's survey was a pioneering effort, there is no information that is exactly comparable for the earlier period. However, estimates of income can be extracted from the federal census manuscripts on the statistics of industry. In 1860 each manufacturer listed the average number of his employees alongside his total monthly wage bill. Men and women were figured separtely. Calculations from these returns for 132 Lynn manufacturers show an average annual income of about $260 for all male shoemakers.[14] Here again, the median is no doubt slightly lower, though the nature of the data does not permit a calculation. But if the median is estimated at $250, and if this is compared with the $420 reported for 1875, the result is an increase of 68 percent over the fifteen years.

The amount of money a person actually had to live on was the product of the intersection of nominal income and prices. Because prices rose during the years of conversion, the growth in real income was not as great as the face value of the preceding figures. In 1875 the bureau responded to criticism that it had overlooked the question of prices in previous studies and set out to compare cost of living with income. The study, though very limited, depicted a general pattern of rising prices eating up wage gains. The bureau was moved to recommend a "minimum-wage plan," under which employers would voluntarily tie their wages to a cost-of-living index.[15]

The recommendation vanished into thin air, but the problem remained. To get an idea of its dimensions, there are several national price indexes running from 1850 to 1880, and although they do not all coincide on precise levels, they parallel each other on general trends. They show a slight increase from 1850 to 1860 followed by a sharp rise after 1862 that brings the post-Civil War level to roughly 70 percent above that of 1860. Then there is a gradual sloping downward, so that by 1875 the level is one-quarter to one-third above 1860. Thus between 1860 and 1875, a rise in prices of one-third would have reduced the 68 percent rise in *nominal* income to an actual increase in *real* income of one-third.[16]

Before the income picture is complete, women's earnings and family pooling of incomes must be considered. Women sold their labor for about two-thirds the going rate for men. The Bureau of Labor report on 1875 disclosed that the majority of women were working as stitchers and earning an average of $270 a year, compared to $420 for the majority of men. It is not possible to use the 1860 census information to get an average wage for women to compare with the factory wage, since the reports in the industrial statistics for 1860 include a large segment of part-time workers. To get information on full-time Lynn binders, it is necessary to go back to local reports for 1850, when the annual average was put at $168. That figure increased slightly over the next ten years to the point where women in 1860 probably made about two-thirds of the $260 that males took in. Thus the factory left women's relative position unchanged.[17]

However, the factories shifted the burden of industrial employment from working wives to young, single women. The state census of 1875 counted only 600 married women among the total of 3167 female employees.[18] Reflecting this trend, the term for a woman shoemaker changed from "lady shoebinder" to "machine girl," or just plain "girl." Many of these young women were floating workers with no permanent home in Lynn, and some had been outworkers who left home to become self-supporting rather than staying behind to become a burden on the family when outwork ceased.

Sons living in their parents' households were also becoming less significant in the economic life of the family. In 1850 sons at home constituted one-third of the total number of local male shoemakers; in 1870 sons at home made up one-quarter. This is not to say that the age structure of shoemaking was moving to older levels nor that married men were taking over all the work. *Single* men made up 43 percent of the work force in 1850, and the proportion was just about the same in 1870. Combining this steady percentage with the decline in the proportion of dependent sons, the conclusion is that young men who would have been working in the ten-footers next to their fathers in 1850 were working on their own away from home in 1870.[19]

Thus the trend of rising individual income was at least partially offset by the contrary trend of a decline in the sources of support for the family as a unit. In the prefactory era, husbands, wives, and children all tended to stay within the nuclear unit and contribute whatever income they earned directly to the family kitty. But as jobs were taken out of the household, the number of wives working to contribute was reduced, and both male and female dependents were forced to withdraw from the family circle. The result was a loss of some of the advantages of cooperative living of the sort implied in the old adage that two can live as cheaply as one. If the two live separately, they must each bear the costs of maintaining a household, such as separate sets of furnishings and utensils, with a resulting erosion in the level of living of both.

Taking all the factors together, they yielded some improvement in income but not enough to make the elusive goal of the "living wage" a reality for most shoemakers, who continued to be haunted by the spectors of debt, disease, disability, and dependence. Poised between the realms of poverty and meager subsistence, most shoemakers never knew the flush feeling of prosperity. Applying this conclusion to the debate on the factories, the material on income is the first major body of evidence that does not support the pessimists, but then, it does not offer much support to the optimists, either.

Occupational Mobility

At this point in the debate, the optimists are still unable to validate the claim that the factory system elevated the general condition of labor in the shoe industry. They have been forced to the defensive positions that the opportunity to acquire a competence was not altogether foreclosed and that the real income of shoemaker households apparently was not depressed. For optimists, these are not very reassuring arguments, so we might expect a new thrust in the debate. If the general lot of the shoeworker was not improving, the obvious point to argue is that shoemakers had the opportunity to make something better of themselves by getting into some other line of work where property was more widespread, income was greater, and status was higher.

Pursuing this point, optimists never tired of citing examples of successful manufacturers or illustrious public figures who had "risen from the bench." Local businessmen like Protestant high-achiever Benjamin F. Newhall and frontier shoe dealer George Hood were paraded in the same ring as Roger Sherman, the ex-shoemaker who signed the Declaration of Independence, and Henry Wilson, the vice-president of the United States who was known as "the simple cobbler of Natick." The argument implies its own rebuttal: if shoemakers had to leave the trade to do well, then the material condition of the average shoemaker could not have been very favorable. But it also poses a direct question which needs to be investigated on its own terms: What chance did the ordinary shoemaker have for success?

To answer this question, it is necessary to count the wage earners who achieved fame and fortune and match the total against the less fortunate workingmen who still marched in the ranks of the poor and downtrodden. Using Lynn census manuscripts, supplemented by city directories, a survey of occupational mobility was taken. It spans two decades and includes some 3000 individuals. Starting in 1860 with all shoemakers and sons of shoemakers, 1657 men were found in the city's records in 1870, and 1061 were found in 1880. The occupational distributions recorded at the end of ten and twenty years are tallied in Table 5.[20]

The categories used in Table 5 reflect the census listings and at the same time combine occupations that shared common functions, job conditions, and types of training. There are three general categories: manual occupations, nonmanual occupations, and farmers. The farmers are set off because they combined aspects of both manual and nonmanual labor, and because cultivating the soil was associated with conditions not experienced in the urban occupations. The manual category is more or less self-explanatory, though in some cases where the job includes supervisory roles, such as master artisans, policemen, and foremen, the taxonomy is somewhat stretched. They were included because none of the jobs required formal education, none were carried on in business offices, and all required a considerable amount of physical labor. The nonmanual category includes the owners and managers of the local economy, plus other men, such as ministers and clerks, who worked with their wits instead of their hands. These occupations are grouped together, not only to set them

TABLE 5. Occupational Mobility of Stable Shoemakers and Sons, 1870–1880.

Category	1870		1880	
	Number	Percent	Number	Percent
All manual	1351	83	761	78[a]
Shoemaker	1152	71	569	58
Craftsman	99	6	72	7
Laborer	26	2	15	1
Other manual	74	4	105	11
All nonmanual	257	16	200	20
Manufacturer	96	6	51	5
Shopkeeper	78	5	68	7
Clerk	68	4	60	6
Professional	15	1	21	2
Farmer	18	1	17	1
Total occupations	1626	100	978	100
No occupation	31		83	

Source: U.S., Eighth and Ninth Census manuscripts; city directory for 1880.

[a] When broken down into subcategories of manual workers, the combined percentage does not equal 78 percent because of rounding.

Note: See Appendix B for a description of methods used in compiling the table.

off from the manual jobs but also because they shared a social and cultural milieu generated by the institutions of higher learning and the business environment (though they did not represent a *class* in the sense in which the term has been used throughout this work).

Shoemakers experienced widely different rates of mobility into different occupational categories. Taking the category described in Table 5 as "craftsman" (basically, the artisan trades such as carpentry, carriage making, and tanning), there were 99 ex-shoemakers among the total of about 1800 employed in this category, or only 5 percent of the total.[21] Ex-shoemakers also accounted for only 5 percent of the common laborers in Lynn (26 of 518). The pattern is readily apparent—stable artisans and their sons contributed only small shares to the manual work force outside shoemaking in 1870.

The contrast with nonmanual occupations was dramatic. Where a smaller percentage might be expected because of the relatively privileged status of these occupations, the percentage actually was 16 percent—three times greater.[22] The most striking case was the manufacturers; ninety-six ex-shoemakers accounted for almost one-quarter of all the manufacturers in Lynn in 1870! Taking the proportion for *shoe* manufacturers alone, the result was even higher; out of 310 in the city, 91 had been members of shoemaker families in Lynn in 1860. The proportions for other business occupations were not as impressive as this, but shoemakers were generally well represented; for example, seventy-eight ex-shoemakers comprised 13 percent of the total group of 600 shopkeepers in the city in 1870. Among clerical occupations, such as clerks, salesmen and bookkeepers, the ex-shoemakers also contributed 13 percent of the total, and among the doctors, lawyers, and public officials they were 8 percent. The dimension of the shoemaker contribution was highlighted by the fact that in absolute as well as relative terms, more shoemakers moved into business, professional, and clerical jobs than into other manual occupations—257 compared to 199. Extending the study to 1880 amplifies the proportion of shoemakers who moved into nonmanual jobs; it increased from 16 to 20 percent.[23]

At last, the optimists seemed to have something to cheer about. There were paths running from the plains up the mountainside, and the paths were well traveled. This had always been assumed in the days of the artisan, but now it appeared that the factories may have even widened the paths by creating new opportunities for ownership through industrial expansion. But before this round is given to the optimists, other matters must be explored. Did the shoemakers on the way up start their climb from the bottom? Did other well-traveled paths lead down the mountainside?

Concerning the first question, the place to begin is with an analysis of the characteristics of the group of 257 shoemakers who went into nonmanual occupations. It is not possible to get very extensive information about them, but a few items can be squeezed from the census material. For one thing, a high proportion of ex-cutters were in the group; of all shoemakers who became manufacturers, 44 percent (42 of 96) were from cutter families, though cutters made up only 10 percent of the pool of 1860 shoemakers. Another point is that the 257 who moved into nonmanual jobs had strong connections to occupations other than shoemaking. Information on the father's occupation of 99 men can be located, and although most of these (71) had shoemaker fathers, 16 percent (16) had fathers who were manufacturers or shopkeepers. Clearly some of the shoemakers who moved into nonmanual jobs were actually returning to the occupational level of their fathers. Many of these men were sons of shoe manufacturers who were being given a few years of manual experience in the shop to become familiar with the basic arts of the trade before assuming their prepared place in the business end of manufacturing. Their stint as wage earners was only temporary, and they could reasonably be excluded from the mobile group altogether. If these well-placed sons are combined with the descendants of the cutter aristocrats, and if all these exceptional shoemakers are taken out of the picture, the number of *ordinary* shoemakers who moved into occupations at the nonmanual level is cut down considerably. In this perspective, the mobility of the common shoemaker into positions of relative ease and comfort becomes less impressive than at first glance: *barely 10 percent made the jump.*[24]

At the same time, the fact remains that the line between manual and nonmanual occupations, and even the boundary between the realms of labor and capital, was by no means impossible to cross. This was particularly true for manufacturing, where men of property gave their sons training in manual labor, while manual laborers who held property set up small manufacturing enterprises. The cutters were in the best position to fall into this pattern: 24 percent of the 1860 cutters had become manufacturers in 1870. The cutters took advantage of an unprecedented gain in the number of positions open to prospective manufacturers. Between 1860 and 1870 the number came close to doubling, an increase that was considerably greater than the rate of expansion in the number of manual jobs in the industry. Because the cutters held substantially more property than the ordinary shoemakers in 1860, and because they were familiar with the organization of a central shop, they were in a favored position to seize the opportunity for going into business. Thus some became owners of small factories, perhaps still using hand methods and avoiding the costly machines, while others became contractors for the larger manufacturers, hiring a room and a handful of employees to do heeling, stitching, or special types of hand bottoming. Contracting was the most open field of opportunity; while the number of firms directly involved in putting shoes together increased only slightly, the number of small contract and accessory manufacturers increased fourfold.[25]

It would be desirable to get some measure of the changing occupational structure as a determinant of mobility.[26] One indication of the impact of structural changes appears between 1870 and 1880: the number of shopkeepers, clerical workers, and professionals expanded at a rate almost as high as in the previous decade, but the number of manufacturers actually declined, as is shown in Table 6.

TABLE 6. Males in Four Occupational Categories, 1850–1880.

Category	1850	1860	1870	1880
Manufacturers	138	213	395	307
Shopkeepers	345	359	600	782
Clerks	93	259	508	665
Professionals and officials	88	115	172	252

Source: 1850: Shattuck, *Report,* pp. 504–505; 1860: U.S., Seventh Census manuscripts; 1870: U.S., Eighth Census manuscripts; 1880: *U.S., Tenth Census,* I, 885.

From this observation it might be expected that the ex-shoemakers would experience less mobility into manufacturing than into the other three categories, and this is just what happened. The proportion of ex-shoemakers who were manufacturers in 1880 was smaller than the proportion who were shopkeepers or clerical workers, whereas in 1870 it had been greater (see Table 5). It is clear that the net contraction in the number of positions available in manufacturing tended to choke off this channel of shoemaker mobility. In more general terms, therefore, the overall changes in occupational structure had an important effect in determining the future job prospects of 1860 shoemakers.

To deal with the question of downward mobility, we have followed the careers of the men in nonmanual jobs in 1870. It is possible to locate 161 in 1880, and after setting aside 18 who listed no occupation, 41 percent of those remaining (59 of 143) had *returned to manual jobs*. Thus not many more than one-half of the shoemakers who became shoe manufacturers, grocers, clerks, and the like had long-range security in their new jobs.

With so much crossing back and forth, the pattern of mobility might be compared to a network of railroad tracks: only about one-half of the shoemakers who got on the track in 1860 and rode straight through to 1880 got off at the end as shoemakers. The remaining half had crossed over to other tracks along the way. Some made only one switch of occupation, but others crossed and recrossed occupational lines, leaving a trail that vanished too quickly to register on the decennial census. Even among the 482 shoemakers who appeared stable in the census were some who shifted to another occupation after the first census year and switched back before the next. Summarizing the data, it is clear that at least one-third of the original group of shoemakers and sons experienced some form of mobility between manual and nonmanual occupations.[27]

But *mobility* was not the same thing as *success*. Not only did 41 percent of the upwardly mobile return to a manual occupation, but this group had been recruited from the ranks of the more prosperous shoemakers in the first place. The occupational structure provided a good deal of movement, but rather than moving from rags to riches most of the shoemakers moved within a much narrower range of wealth, prestige, and power. When the common shoemaker found a better position, it was likely to be another manual job that paid slightly higher wages, a job behind a store counter selling clothes, or perhaps a venture in flush times in a little corner grocery store or petty contract manufacturing. Even the cutter who became a shoe manufacturer doing contract work for a larger owner did not really move a great distance and was in fact liable to return to his starting point with only a fleeting taste of success in the business world.

And what of the great debate? As men rose and fell through the occupational ranks, was the optimist correct in celebrating the factories as engines of opportunity because so many individuals "rose from the bench"? Or was the pessimist correct in putting down the factories because they confined the great majority of shoemakers who remained in the city to the lower rungs of the occupational hierarchy? In terms of statistical evidence both were correct. The fact that most shoemakers circulated at the level of manual, or lower level non-manual jobs is consistent with the fact that a few became successful in business or the professions. If the claims of both sides were correct, then each would have to modify its position to conform to the opposite truth. The pessimists would have to give up their oft-made assertion that the factories split society into two wholly isolated castes, while the optimists would have to stop pretending that the path to success was open to all who would travel it. After eliminating these exaggerated claims, the debate over occupational mobility ends in a stand-off.

At this point the debate over mobility resolves into something else. The argument over the rate of upward mobility becomes an argument over which end is up. Statistical problems become ethical problems. To describe the change from shoemaker to manufacturer as a move upward may very well describe an actual improvement in an individual's wealth and standing, and in this sense it may be an objective description, but it also joins itself to the values that supported the type of society in which such a move was, in fact, upward. In this sense the objectivity of the description is subverted. It becomes aligned with the process it seeks to describe because it restates those values. It becomes subjective.

Thus in the name of a fuller objectivity, it behooves social analysts to consider a wider range of values and terminology than those that happen to predominate at a given time. In the context of nineteenth-century Lynn, the dominant ethics of the capitalist marketplace which identified the man of property as the paragon of society were challenged by the ethics of Equal Rights which identified labor, manual and mental, as the cornerstone of civilization. In this latter view, movement from shoemaker to capitalist manufacturer was upward only because the world was turned upside down.

Cycles

To return to the metaphor introduced at the beginning of the chapter, the factory system widened the gap between the plains of poverty and the mountain peaks of wealth, but it did not block off the paths of mobility between different levels of living. Individuals moved through the various latitudes, some going up, others going down, in a constant scramble for position that was glorified by tough-minded Social Darwinists as the battle for survival, the race of life, or the survival of the fittest. But it need hardly be said that these crude rationalizations for inequality offered little to explain the actual ways in which people found their places in the uneven landscape. In reality, the competitive struggle for success was not a free-for-all in which the best man won, because individuals were not free to move across the landscape. Instead, their opportunities were constrained within cycles of experience which extended over only part of the ground.

The following discussion is offered as a guidebook to observers of mobility. It abstracts certain general categories of behavior from the countless multitude of individual place-changes in an effort to make individual experience intelligible as social experience. Surely the advantage of subduing chaos outweighs the obvious disadvantage that the general categories will not apply in each specific case. So, pursuing the advantage and shunning the disadvtange, we will look at the phenomenon of social mobility from the perspective of four broad categories: *poverty, subsistence, prosperity,* and *opulence.* *Poverty* was the condition of paupers entirely dependent on charity, the "dangerous classes" (so-called by the men of property and standing who felt that thieves, prostitutes, drunks, and disorderly street crowds were recruited among underemployed, unskilled urban workers), and the laboring poor (men and women who held more or less steady jobs, but whose wages were below subsistence). *Subsistence* was the condition of people who earned a living wage and who could, therefore, spend small portions of their income for the enjoyments of life and in flush times accumulate savings or petty property holdings. *Prosperity* was the condition of people whose incomes enabled them to make significant choices about what to purchase; they might afford either a larger home, or a new piano, or a new tailor-made wardrobe, though they could not afford all of these things at the same time. They also had an estate that was sufficient to bridge a calamity like the loss of one source of income without going into dire poverty. *Opulence* was the condition of those who could spend according to whim, and did.

Poverty was the involuntary servant of wealth. Like a combination cook, coachman, butler, and maid, poverty always saw to it that the master was comfortable and well fed. The master's well-being could only increase through an increase in the number of servants who attended him, and, by a perverse twist of circumstance, the number of servants also increased when the master's condition declined. This was because the surest cause of poverty was unemployment, and unemployment was sure to increase at every downturn in the business cycle or at seasonal gaps in production. But a nineteenth-century industrial worker did not have to lose her job to be poor; plenty of people with steady incomes still could not afford all the necessities of life because their wages were so low. Even a person who earned enough to support one or two dependents in good times would be overtaken by poverty if he happened to suffer some unexpected calamity like a major illness or disability, or if he had incurred the mixed blessing of a large family.

Most full-time women factory workers earned less than $300 a year, most men a little over $400. Since these income blankets barely covered a single person's basic needs for food, shelter, and clothing, most self-supporting factory workers lived at the knife edge of poverty in constant fear that an increase in their needs would make the blanket too small to cover essentials. A person who had others to support besides himself could never make the blanket stretch far enough to prevent the family from being out in the cold, and sometimes people literally slept outside in the cold because they were unable to afford lodgings. Otherwise, the poor rented a back room in a private home or found accommodations in a boardinghouse and went into debt or skipped town when they could not keep up with the rent. What they took from their housing was used up before it had gone far enough to buy an adequate diet; the only regular feature of their diet was its inadequacy. And since nearly all the money was used up to pay for food and shelter, little remained for clothing (much of which was acquired by picking up the castaway garments of the prosperous, and an occasional donation of a blanket and winter coat from the Women's Union for Christian Work), and less for recreation (which, nevertheless, sometimes came first).

With money going out of one hand faster than it came in the other, how could anything be stashed away in savings? How was it possible to practice the first commandment of the middle class to accumulate little by little until a home could be purchased? Those shoemakers who possessed a competence (one in five in 1870) had already left the cycle of poverty, and their home was the clearest emblem of their greater well-being.

The precondition for working-class accumulation was a stable inflow of decent wages, and, for the most part, the only workers who could count on this were skilled in some difficult operation that made them indispensable to their employers. Without essential skills, a person could expect neither decent income nor job security. Lacking these things, the laboring poor also lacked property and savings, and since they received only token assistance from the overseers of the poor, they had nothing to lose by leaving town to look for work elsewhere. If they ended another season of labor in the next town with nothing, their only recourse was to move again and become one of the floating population, whose perpetual motion revealed their helplessness before the vast economic forces of the marketplace.

Such was the experience of the marginal laborer in industrial society. He was caught up in an oppressive cycle of low skills, low wages, propertylessness, unemployment, and migration to another town to begin the cycle again. As some individuals escaped the cycle, others were ensnared to take their place. Given the unplanned, uneven character of factory capitalism, given the seasonal and long-range fluctuations in the business cycle, given the competitive pressures on wage rates, and given the manufacturer's right to hire and fire, the result was bound to be a rapid and ruthless turnover in the labor force. Whether one individual or another was reduced to marginal status may have been a matter of social discrimination, personal character, or sheer chance, but the existence of the group was no accident. However expendable they were as individuals, the laboring poor were essential as a group.

To move out of poverty, a person needed the right combination of pluck, luck, and social background. Someone whose Irish brogue did not trouble his employer and whose sex enabled him to qualify for the better jobs in the factory might have stopped by the hiring office on just the right day when the superintendent needed another edge-setter or channeler, and might have said "yes" with a clear voice and straight face when asked if he knew how to run a machine he had never operated before. Barring the failure of the firm or a general depression, the rest of the story would be a matter of knowing how to take orders and piling up experience to become one of the good steady workmen that manufacturers counted on as much as the marginal hands. Through such a process a man could move out of the cycle of poverty into the cycle of subsistence.

Subsistence was just that—no frills, no fat, no feeling of plush comfort—just getting by and nothing more. To exist at this level, a family had to have a steady source of top wages from a highly skilled worker, or else have more than one breadwinner. In either case, the income of $500 or $600 a year was enough for a single *man* to live on without fear of want (a *woman* wage earner almost never made this much) and for a family simply to make ends meet. The family could afford meat on Sunday and perhaps once during the week, as well, and could furnish the home with rugs, chests, bureaus, and rocking chairs, though not with sets of china and silver. A succession of prosperous years or the accession of adult wages from an older child would enable the family to rent an entire four-room house instead of a two-room apartment, or, in a smaller number of cases, to put enough aside to begin paying on a mortgage for their own home. Though the family might move out of town to satisfy some itch or discontent, it would move more for improvement than for survival. At the same time, the family's position was anything but secure. The children would eventually move away, and adversity was always close by, for no skilled worker was immune to the effects of business failure. Since there was considerable movement within the working class between the levels of poverty and subsistence, and since subsistence was still an existence based on scarcity, the boundary between the two levels cannot be located precisely. In the nineteenth-century industrial city there was no "poverty line." There were only the poor and the less poor.

Beyond the reach of all but a handful of wage earners, lay the alluring realm of *prosperity*. Unless a worker inherited an estate or married a paid-up mortgage, he had to travel an extremely difficult road to get there. Along the way he encountered a set of rules that read like a series of "Keep Out" signs: Don't Get a Disabling Injury; Don't Get a Serious Illness; Don't Get Too Old to Work; Don't Get Laid Off. Since a person had little individual control over these matters, obeying the rules was more a function of circumstances than of human will, but if the circumstances were favorable, a wage earner might arrive at prosperity. There he became a labor aristocrat who tucked a gold watch into his vest pocket and had more than one fine, tailor-made suit hanging in the closet of his ample, if not spacious or sumptuous, home.

Among the shoeworkers of Lynn in 1870, 11 percent of the cutters (33 of 304) reported holdings of $4,000 or more, and, of these, five individuals were very well-to-do indeed, with estates valued at more than $10,000. A smaller percentage (4 percent) but a larger number (126) of the ordinary shoeworkers in the city also owned $4,000 worth of property and were as well off as most of the city's teachers, doctors, grocers, dry goods dealers, and smaller manufacturers. They were better off than some white-collar employees who earned only subsistence salaries and who called their condition "genteel poverty." The notorious parsimony of the clerk and the abstemiousness of the schoolmistress were necessities made into virtues by people whose pride lay in the prestige of being close to the social elite, and whose manner and style imitated the more commanding presence and sumptuous raiment of the upper middle classes.

A second road to prosperity was to leave the working class altogether and become a professional or a businessman. Though few ordinary shoeworkers were able to succeed at this, a substantial number of the more favorably situated wage earners who dwelled in the charmed circle of prosperity were able to spin off from the working class by converting real estate, savings, or credit into capital. They purchased a house and sold it at a profit, or built an addition to their house to sell groceries, or rented rooms from a large manufacturer, installed a few sewing machines, hired half-a-dozen women to operate them, and contracted with a larger manufacturer for specialty stitching. At this point they would begin to call themselves manufacturers and start to think of a wage increase as an infraction of the immutable law of supply and demand.

At the upper reaches of prosperity were a very well-to-do band of bankers, merchants, and industrialists who skirted the regions of opulence but did not possess quite enough wealth to be part of the truly big money. They built homes that stood as mansions according to the standards of the local community, but lacked the baronial grandeur of the palaces built by the likes of Frick and Vanderbilt.

Only a tiny handful of the small group at the top in Lynn qualified for entry into the ranks of *opulence*. Since the shoe industry was locally owned by industrialists rather than financiers, and since capital outlays were small in comparison to rails, steel, and oil, the profits from the industry did not reach the *rentier* scale of big city investment banking (which is why the robber barons stayed away). Only an occasional John B. Alley or Simon Bubier were permitted to deck themselves out in the full regalia of their class. Of course, to the ordinary shoeworker caught between grinding poverty on one side and only somewhat less poverty on the other, the differences between five servants and ten, or between twenty rooms and forty were distinctions of little account.

7

MILITANTS

Direction action on the economic front has been the hallmark of the American industrial worker from the great railroad strikes of 1887 to the autoworkers sitdown of 1937.[1] These and other classic episodes of class conflict—Pullman, Ludlow, Lawrence—established the rank-and-file tradition of hard-nosed combat in pursuit of recognition, shorter hours, higher wages, and better working conditions. The tradition might be called "militant pragmatism." To be sure, the militancy of the American worker was conditioned partly by the open-shop, antiunion policies of American businessmen, whose use of the iron-clad oath, the yellow-dog contract, blacklisting, espionage, strike-breakers, Pinkertons, and thugs pushed workers time and again up against the wall. But, in the end, the aggressive spirit arose in the worker who knew exactly where the wall was and who could say "this far, and no farther."

Thus an inquiry into the behavior of the American working class leads to an inquiry into American character, and this inevitably leads to the subject of individualism. Since the eighteenth century, primary source materials have resounded to the vibrations of that iron string. American men of letters extol it; travelers from Europe encounter it; statistical studies of mobility confirm it. So pervasive has individualism been in American life that it is tempting to think of it as an original American invention, but, of course, such is not the case. Individualism was invented in Europe, and only after it was developed by the European middle classes as the social expression of bourgeois forms of property ownership in the seventeenth and eighteenth centuries was it imported to the New World. There it found an extremely favorable environment in the burgeoning marketplace economy and took firm root in the competitive operations of Pennsylvania wheat farmers, Virginia tobacco planters, Yankee shopkeepers, and urban merchants from Boston to Charleston. These bustling businessmen were breaking down an old pattern of communal decision making and replacing it with private resource management, just as they were abandoning the social constraints of feudal ranks and degrees and erecting a new social order based on the individual pursuit of wealth. They believed that this form of property should govern political affairs and enshrined their belief in the federal Constitution.

The spread of individualism to propertyless people awaited the rise of industrial capitalism. The old forms of bond labor did not survive in the context of a free market for labor, and as the slave auction and the contract of indenture gave way to the industrial wage bargain between employer and employee, individualism went democratic. With few exceptions, laboring men and women saw themselves not as one rank in a hierarchy of ranks but as individuals coequal with everyone else.[2] They belonged to no master; they lived and worked where they chose; they had a hand in shaping their own destinies. Every time a working person changed jobs, left town, or voted for the party of his choice, the belief in individualism was confirmed.

It should be clear that militancy is not simply a reflex of exploitation. Exploitation breeds opposition, but the form and intensity of working-class opposition to capitalism was determined by the special mixture of forces in each national environment. The United States represented the purest form of capitalism in the world; that is why individualism and egalitarianism went further there than anywhere else, and that, in turn, is why working people who drank so deeply of these waters were so quick to express their hostility to inequality and authoritarianism in the management of American industry.

The very historical conditions that gave rise to individualism created a class system in which individualism became the basis for collective action of one class against another. In any marketplace transaction, buyers and sellers have opposing interests. As buyers of labor, manufacturers had a common interest among themselves which was opposed to the common interest of workers, as sellers. If the wage bargain between manufacturers and workers had been mutually beneficial, then the conflict of interest would have been historically insignificant. But the bargain was unequal, and when working people compared their lot in life with the rich, or watched police break a strike, or experienced a speed-up in production, they felt compelled to take collective action in the form of negotiating committees, trade unions, strikes, and political campaigns. In the context of industrial capitalism, "I" became "we," and the intense spirit of individualism was transformed into militant collective action.

Knights and Daughters of St. Crispin

The Knights of St. Crispin exemplify the paradoxical transformation of individualism into collective action. Eight years after the Great Strike, five years after the first full-fledged factories, three years after the Civil War, Lynn shoemakers founded Unity Lodge, and a second lodge was established not long thereafter. The same thing was happening in dozens of other towns, and the Knights of St. Crispin soon grew to be the nation's largest trade union. Some Crispin orators claimed a membership of more than 100,000, though historians of the order estimate no more than one-half that number, and it is always wise to observe the caution that the hard core of union activists who consistently paid their dues was considerably smaller still.[3] Nonetheless, the Crispins had accomplished the mighty feat of signing up one-third, perhaps even one-half, of all the men in American shoe manufacturing.[4] In Lynn, more than one-half of the resident shoeworkers pledged themselves to the new order. The dues book of Unity Lodge registered a tally of nearly 2,000 names, to which must be added several hundred from Lynn's second lodge so that the combined total was easily more than one-half the 3,737 men listed as shoemakers in the census of 1870.[5]

The rise of the Crispins was an upwelling upon an upsurge. In all sections of the country, in the various trades, and among the different races and nationalities that worked in industry, the labor movement was gaining strength. Black workers in Baltimore, printers in Chicago, German cigar makers in New York, and hundreds of other groups founded local lodges, citywide trade assemblies, national trade unions, labor newspapers, eight-hour leagues, sections of the International Workingmen's Association, and the National Labor Union. The historian who has best catalogued this surge of activism, David Montgomery, believes that "a larger proportion of the industrial labor force enrolled in trade unions during the years immediately preceding the depression of 1873 than in any other period of the nineteenth century."[6] The Knights of St. Crispin were among the most active of the activists and among the most militant in a period of rising militancy. Lynn Crispins put their city in its customary place at the leading edge of the American labor movement, just where it had been in the workingmen's organizations of 1829–30 and 1844–45, and just where it would be again when the Knights of Labor (KOL) swept the country in 1885–86. (Only once was Lynn on its own; the strike of 1860 carried buoyant shoemakers ahead of most other workers, but otherwise the tides in Lynn ran in the same direction as the rest of the country.) In this regard, Lynn's history typifies the history of American labor in the nineteenth century.

In another regard, however, it was unusual, for the Knights of St. Crispin was one of the few successful organizations of *factory* workers.[7] The explanation for this lies not in the fact that most shoeworkers were American-born and, therefore, more inclined to stand up for their rights (as the nativist argument went at the time) but rather in the fact that working people salvaged the tradition of Equal Rights from the social wreckage of the factory system.

Factory workers in the shoe industry were able to organize because most of them had been shoemakers in prefactory days. This gave shoeworkers a common identity through a continuity of shared ideas and experiences. They remembered the self-reliance of the artisan and recalled the time when the tasks of shoemaking intimately intermingled with the tasks of family and community life: when the journeyman was husband to the binder, father to the young helper, neighbor to the shoemaker family next door; a time when the binder was at once shoemaker and homemaker, arranging time for each task according to the needs of the day; a time when the journeyman was both shoemaker and householder, whose daily activity followed the intertwining rhythms of both roles. Among the kith and kin of the neighborhood, shoemaker families borrowed and lent, gave and received, grieved and celebrated with one another. Searching within this fine mesh of community relationships, who could say where life left off and labor began?

Then the factories came to their communities like bulldozers, and shoemakers experienced a massive disruption in their way of life. They saw the ecology of the mill town displace the ecology of the artisan community. They saw job separated from home, workplace from neighborhood, labor from life. Now they were subjected each day to the tasks and rhythms of the production line, to the will of the owner, and to a denial of any identity on the job other than as laster, stitcher, heeler, or packer. To add insult to injury, they were still not paid a living wage.

They knew they deserved more than this. As they talked among themselves about wage trimming, churlish foremen, and arbitrary rules, anger flashed from one to another, carried along on the energy of mutual support and common feeling, the sort of trust that results when people recall their past together. "Do you remember before the War how the shoemakers went on strike?" asked one. "Yes," replied another, thinking back to the strike of 1860, "we chose officers, issued circulars and sent them to the manufacturers, praying them to give us our old prices and desist from a course which must starve us and our families; but our prayer was treated with scorn and contempt. We could do nothing but fight it out as best we could, and the strike continued until the first of May."[8] This is the stuff of which traditions are made: the recreation of the past in the present, the reverberating memory of choosing officers, organizing a strike, and fighting it out.

Artisan protest inspired factory protest. Artisan organization engendered organization among factory workers. The Mutual Benefit Society of Journeymen Cordwainers and the Mechanics Association left a legacy that became the Knights of St. Crispin. The legacy contained not only the *experience* of organizing but also the stubborn conviction that a worker had as much *right* to organize as anybody else. Acting on this belief, Crispins petitioned the Massachusetts legislature for a charter of incorporation, and in Lynn, Crispins denounced manufacturers for their interference with personal liberty when they attempted to lock out union members. In 1872 a Lynn mass meeting damned the lockout as "tyrannical" and damned the manufacturers for offering terms that amounted to "a complete sacrifice of self-respect." The meeting vowed to "assert and maintain at every cost and every hazard our right to belong to and participate in any organization, social, industrial, religious, political or beneficiary."[9]

(The idea that trade union organization among nineteenth-century factory workers, unskilled as well as skilled, was predicated on artisan resistance to capitalism in the industry could be tested by further studies of particular industries like ready-made clothing, food processing, and machinery, all of which had a factory system but no trade union to compare with the Knights of St. Crispin.)

The Knights of St. Crispin had a sister. Women shoeworkers in Lynn organized the Daughters of St. Crispin in 1869. The general causes of the organization were much the same as those discussed above, and, in addition, binders were the first group of workers to encounter factory methods when stitching shops were opened in the 1850s, and they were the first to protest. Women struck in 1860 because they suffered directly from the loss of jobs and from depression wages after 1857. With their own grievances and their own tradition of protest, workingwomen deepened the roots of the labor movement in the community. They ensured that labor would not be divided along sexual lines and thereby contributed heavily to trade unionism in Lynn.

The Daughters of St. Crispin was centered in Massachusetts, but the order spread to nine states from Maine to California. The membership in the Lynn lodge amounted to one-quarter of the local female work force, and additional hundreds of women participated in another labor organization friendly to the Crispins called the Working Women's Associates. Although these organizations worked closely with the Knights of St. Crispin, they were not just ladies' auxiliaries. In the summer of 1871, for instance, when the men had a satisfactory union agreement, women were organizing to combat new and unjust "encroachments on our rights." On an August evening, several hundred Daughters gathered together to protest a proposed condition of employment which would have required them to stay at their jobs for a minimum of three months and to deposit $5 from their first paycheck with the payroll office, to be forfeited if they left before the time was up. Bowing to the protest, the manufacturers quietly abandoned the scheme for a while, but a year later, still plagued by high labor turnover, they tried it again, and again they provoked a storm of protest. Nine hundred shoeworkers unanimously endorsed a set of resolutions that decried this attempt at robbery and bondage. The mass meeting resolved:

That we will accept no terms whatever, either with regard to a reduction of prices, notices to quit, or forfeiture of wages.

That while we utterly ignore the spirit of selfishness and illiberality which prompted the late action of our would-be oppressors, we will not hesitate to resist, in a proper manner, the unjust encroachments upon our rights.

In the next resolution, women proposed to "desist from our work," and this threat of a strike was enough to force the manufacturers to back down a second time.[10]

Beyond the world of work, it is not clear from Lynn's example whether the artisan tradition promoted sexual equality in politics, in the home, or in other social arrangements. Though feminists from outside the city, like Boston's Jeannie Collins, sometimes spoke in Lynn, and though every female trade unionist was in some sense a feminist, there was apparently no local group agitating on women's issues. In a city with the effervescent radicalism of Lynn, that is something of a surprise. It is not clear what workingwomen or the wives of workingmen thought about Mary Baker Eddy, the founder of Christian Science, who made her home in the city. Nor is there anything revealing in the fact that one of Lynn's native daughters was Lydia Pinkham, a businesswoman whose products for feminine hygiene were known to women throughout the country. There is evidence that the activism of women workers did not fully disrupt older patterns of deference to male leadership: women customarily accorded a man a spot as vice-chairman of their meetings, which would betoken simply an effort to unify the actions of male and female workers, except that men never reciprocated the honor.

Yet even if their action was limited to the economic front, and if they did not show much interest in political equality or social equality in the areas of homemaking and lovemaking, women workers harried the middle-class cult of True Womanhood into the lace curtain parlors and French revival sitting rooms of the business homes on Ocean Street.

UnCommons

The main task of interpreting the Knights of St. Crispin for twentieth-century scholars fell to John Commons and his followers, notably, the author of a monograph on the Crispins, Don Lescohier.[11] The Commons' team must be credited with a monumental and invaluable contribution: their research and interpretations in the field of American labor history underwrote all subsequent investigation. But virtually everything they said in the particular case of the Knights of St. Crispin is worthless. Their view rests on two propositions: first, that the Crispins were old-fashioned artisans, and second, that the union's primary aim was to fight off the influx of unskilled green hands. Both propositions are wrong. In the first place, Crispins were modern industrial employees drawn more heavily from the new factories than from the shops of old, as we have seen from the quantitative evidence presented earlier. In the second place, the primary aim of the union was to fight the employers for recognition and improved wages, hours, and conditions; the issue of green hands was never a central question either at the national or local level or in any major Crispin strike.[12]

The Commons' interpretation could be excused the first mistake on grounds of insufficient evidence, but the second is a more serious matter of bogus evidence adduced in support of a questionable theory of industrial relations. Commons articulated the theory in his long 1907 article "American Shoemakers, 1648–1895: A Sketch of Industrial Evolution,"[13] in which he outlined seven historical stages of production, from the simple stage of itinerant craftsmen through the complex and highly developed factory system. Presiding over the progression from lower to higher stages was the omnipotent, impersonal power of the market. The essential dynamic of the marketplace was the war of all against all. However, people entered the marketplace through different doors according to their different economic functions. Some individuals bought labor, others sold. In each functional unit, people shared an overriding common interest, and they could unite to form what Commons called a "bargaining class" for collective bargaining with other classes. A trade union was simply labor's legitimate bargaining agent. It haggled with an employer over wages just the way a manufacturer haggled with a wholesaler, a wholesaler with a retailer, a retailer with a consumer. Economic history was largely a series of struggles among bargaining classes "to strengthen this bargaining power of one element against another, showing their results in the movement of prices, values and rates, whether for commodities, land, stocks, bonds, interest or wages. It is the emergence of these various struggles involved in the emergence of bargaining classes that we see when we follow the extension of markets."[14]

Whatever merits Commons' theory may have in elucidating the trials of prefactory artisan shoemakers, the history of the artisan encounter with the factory system, as we have seen, tends to prove the theory wrong. Evidence compels one to ask what is the merit in a theory that regards the power of industrial employees on the same plane as their employers, as if the ownership of property in a marketplace economy did not confer power on the owners? What is the value in a view which regards the wage bargain between employers and employees as essentially the same thing as the price bargain between a manufacturer and a merchant, and the same as the terms of a loan between a manufacturer and a banker? But where is there an example of a manufacturer settling a dispute with a merchant by kicking the merchant out of his home, and when has a manufacturer bargained for better terms with the bank by sending Pinkertons to shoot up the board meeting? What in American history is the businessmen's counterpart of the workers' experience at Ludlow? When has an American corporation been destroyed by federal troops the way the American Railway Union was destroyed in the Pullman strike? Merchants, manufacturers, and bankers have been callous and ruthless with one another's fortunes and reputations, but the denial of food and shelter and bullet bargaining have been reserved for disputes between those who sell their labor and those who buy it.

Commons sought a place in classical economics for the labor movement. He hoped to legitimate collective bargaining by bringing it under the aegis of Adam Smith. In the same effort, he was hoping to rescue the labor movement from the clutches of Marxian socialism. The effort to refute Marx was a steady undercurrent in his writing. He relegated the Marxian categories of surplus value and the mode of production to the status of "secondary factors, results, not causes." He denied the reality of class conflict and exploitation, at least for American history, on the grounds that the ownership of the means of production and the income gap between owners and wage earners were simply a reflex of the market. "Instead of 'exploitation,' growing out of the nature of production, our industrial evolution shows certain evils of competition imposed by an 'unfair' menace." Since Marx was wrong to assert that ownership was the source of oppression, Commons held that appropriation of the means of production was no answer to the laborers' needs. "Instead, therefore, of an idealistic remedy sought for in common ownership, the practical remedy always actually sought out has been the elimination of the competitive menace through a protective organization or protective legislation."[15]

Commons' history of American shoemakers, his attack on Marxism, his development of the notion of "bargaining classes," indeed, the whole of his intellectual contribution were intended to take class conflict out of the arena of irreconcilable struggle and transfer it to the bargaining table, where some compromise could be worked out. He argued that both sides would gain in the transfer: workers, by peacefully winning material improvements, owners, by securing the existing distribution of property. If this required some change in the status quo, the ultimate end was conservative: "Recognition of unions through collective bargaining would protect business and the nation against politics, radicalism and communism, by placing a conservative labor movement in the strategic position."[16]

Like so many middle-class labor reformers before him and like so many Progressives of his own day, Commons' overriding objective was to achieve social harmony without disturbing basic property relations. He outlined his position in "Economists and Class Partnership" and presented it to the 1899 session of the American Economic Association, an organization founded by Commons' teacher and mentor Richard T. Ely. "Recognition of social classes," he contended, "means self government based on legalized justice between classes." Such recognition should take place in politics, as well as economics, where bona fide labor leaders should be brought into the process of decision making. "What is needed is a representative assembly which will bring together these leaders with the leaders of all other classes, so that they can make similar compromises in politics." In a grand proposal that harks back to the foundation of representative government in the United States, Commons proposed a national assembly of delegates from the various social interests. Labor would choose men like Gompers and Debs, business would pick such captains of industry as Morgan and Rockefeller, and likewise farmers, and even economists would choose their own representatives.[17]

Taken as a whole, Commons' ideas were a restatement of classical liberalism in the context of industrial and corporate capitalism. His emphasis on the primacy of the marketplace restated the economic doctrines of Adam Smith; his view of politics as a field for compromise between contending economic interests reiterated the Madisonian philosophy of the *Federalist* # 10, which spoke of "a landed interest, a manufacturing interest, a mercantile interest, a moneyed interest, with many lesser interests" as the basis of politics.[18]

In Commons' national assembly of bargaining classes there would be no question of the basic rights of ownership. The framework of a marketplace economy was assumed; only the relative advantage within it was up for discussion. With this conservative aim in mind, Commons assiduously promoted liberal reforms through his teaching and academic empire building at the University of Wisconsin, his voluminous writing in both popular and scholarly publications, and his practical work on such agencies of class partnership as the Industrial Commission of Wisconsin, the U.S. Commission on Industrial Relations, and the National Civic Federation. Commons never separated his scholarship from his activism and was a living embodiment of John Dewey's concept of "instrumentalism," the notion that ideas are plans of action. The scholar provided grist for the reformer's mill.[19]

Commons shuttled back and forth between the labor movement and the Progressive movement. To the middle-class Progressives, he advocated collective bargaining as the surest means of resolving industrial strife and promoted the type of bread-and-butter unionism best represented by Samuel Gompers. To the labor movement, he preached the evil of revolutionary unionism of the sort represented by the IWW and urged acceptance of the employing class as a permanent and legitimate interest group. As an ambassador of reform, Commons traveled widely in labor and Progressive circles, enlisting in Robert La Follette's campaign to bring honest government to the state of Wisconsin, supporting the German socialists in Milwaukee in a project to improve the efficiency of municipal government, and serving as a member of Woodrow Wilson's Commission on Industrial Relations.[20]

The consistency in these travels was his faith that America's industrial problems could be solved at the bargaining table where third parties like himself could offer their expertise to help resolve disputes peaceably and thereby serve the mutual interest of both sides while promoting the welfare of the general public. Though he gained a reputation as an advocate of labor, his basic ideas were in full accord with the philosophy of corporate liberalism. Like the leading proponent of that philosophy, Herbert Croly, Commons advocated the large-scale organization of both capital and labor, distinguished between good and bad unionism, as between good and bad capitalists, and proposed that technical experts working for the government oversee disputes among private economic interests. A self-conscious opponent of revolution, Commons was an efficiency expert in finessing class struggle. His influence on the field of labor history is a fact of history and can not be discounted, but historians must recognize and weigh carefully the scholarly prejudices of his personal political orientation.

Strike!

The early dynamism of Crispin recruiting gave the local organization confidence in its power, and, in 1870, the union raised its first challenge to the factory owners. Controversy developed during the summer layover when owners proposed to reduce the customary wage for heavy fall shoes. Workers were willing to accept a slight reduction, but not as much as the owners wanted, and so the union called the first in a long series of strikes. The young organization met the test of battle, emerging after three weeks with a victory on every issue. On the question of wages, they took what they demanded, not what the owners offered. On the question of union recognition, the Crispins sustained the principle of no reprisals for striking members, and they won their wage demands through collective bargaining.[21]

Never before had shoemakers won so much. The discontented artisans of the 1840s had created a voluntary trade association and launched a newspaper, but in terms of wage increases and recognition they got nothing. The shoemakers who struck in 1860 held out for six weeks but won none of their demands. For several decades workers had been talking Equal Rights, but not until 1870 did they feel they had reached a moment of equality. The treasurer of the Crispins, L. C. Legro, told how he stood up to Samuel Bubier, the wealthiest resident of Lynn, the largest shoe manufacturer in Massachusetts, and perhaps the largest in the country. As befitting such a paragon of industry and a first citizen of the community, Bubier directed Legro to form a committee of workers and appear before the manufacturers' Board of Trade. Legro refused and instead retorted "that our organization must be recognized by theirs—that we must be treated as equals." Bubier went back to the Board of Trade with this demand, and the Board assented. The result was a series of three meetings between committees of five Crispins and five manufacturers, chaired jointly by the heads of each group. Out of the meetings came a mutual agreement on a list of wages to be in force for one year. The Crispins' victory created a jubilant mood among workers. One Crispin relishing the feeling of equal recognition with the bosses, said, "I don't think there has been a time for years when the feeling was so good between employers and employed as it is now, and has been since the contract was made."[22]

The outcome was a complete turnabout from the strike of 1860. Then, the industry had been depressed, orders were scarce, and manufacturers were desperate to keep the few customers they had, so they sent materials to out-of-town scabs, imported out-of-town police to protect the flow of materials, and did all they could to "defeat and disgrace" the strikers. Now, the industry was booming, orders were piling up, outworkers had become factory workers, so why shouldn't the manufacturers come to terms with the men and women on strike? Lured by the vision of business prosperity and driven by the unity among Crispin ranks, manufacturers set aside their open-shop principles of individual contract and settled with the union. The strike and the settlement went beyond the common form of labor struggle over wages in the nineteenth century; instead of posting wage rates and then trying to restrain fellow workers from going into a shop that paid less (a method that could be effective for labor aristocrats whose skill monopoly gave them some marketplace power), Crispins refused to work until a contract covering their collective labor had been signed.[23] The settlement included all types of workers (except the cutters, who held aloof from the conflict). It catapulted Gilded Age shoe factory workers into the era of industrial unionism.

Crispins did not know it then, but their movement had reached its zenith; after 1870 the power of the union began to decline. Although the agreement on wages was adopted by the same process of collective bargaining the following summer, that was the last formal agreement Lynn would see for many years. The manufacturers soon decided they had had enough of the union; recognition and union wage scales were becoming too expensive; the Knights of St. Crispin had to be destroyed. One by one manufacturers cut wages, refused to discuss the cuts with union representatives, and responded to the next Crispin strike in 1872 with a lockout. They declared "it is for the best interests of the city of Lynn that every manufacturer manage his own business, irrespective of any organization." Fifty manufacturers, including the largest owners, signed an agreement not to hire any worker "subject to, or under the control of, any organization claiming the power to interfere with any contract between employer and employee."[24]

The strike ended four weeks after it began with a victory for the owners. Citywide collective baragining was gone, some Crispins were blacklisted, and the men had to accept the wage cut. However, the lockout against Crispin members was not effective; most union members got their old jobs back, and labor relations simply returned to the point where they stood prior to 1870, with grievances left in the hands of Crispin shop committees.[25]

After the strike of 1872 the organization limped along on a declining membership base and surrendered the lodge charter, so that for most of 1873 and 1874 there was apparently no citywide union activity. But the interregnum ended in 1875 with the resumption of the charter. Remembering the beating they had taken in 1872, leaders who reconstituted the organization expressed a wariness of the strike tactic, looking upon it only as a "desperate remedy." The local executive Board of Arbitration instead endorsed the principle of negotiated settlement, and, functioning as an outside labor mediator in shop disputes, brought about numerous compromise settlements. In 1875 and 1876 most of the disputes occurred over wages, though in a few instances the issue was the discharge of a fellow employee. In a few cases, contingents of the Daughters of St. Crispin turned out against their bosses.[26]

During the "year of violence" (1877), Lynn was peaceful. A local editorial on the violence that occurred in the great national rail strikes saw nothing but "madness" in the destruction of property, and contrasted this with the peaceful behavior of the Lynn Crispins. The paper felt the Board of Arbitration promoted a "community of interest." However, the illusion of common interest was shattered the following year when Lynn experienced another bitter strike. The perennial wage dispute arose at the start of the spring season, when manufacturers tried to cut the wage for the lighter spring work and workers resisted. The Board of Arbitration attempted to reestablish the citywide bargaining of predepression years by drawing up a bill of wages shortly before Christmas 1877 and inviting the manufacturers to appoint a committee to discuss it. A few manufacturers appeared at the Board's meeting room, but they did not speak for the whole group, and by the first of the year walkouts were in progress at about half-a-dozen shops.[27]

The manufacturers took up the challenge by vowing once again to destroy the Crispin organization. Rallying to the battle cry "control our own shops," manufacturers began posting an ironclad oath to the effect that every employee had to "acknowledge his independence of any interference in any matter between himself and his employer." Then at the beginning of February, some of the manufacturers decided to resume full production with scab labor. They issued a call for new workers in the local papers and set up a network of committees to recruit the new hands and find lodging and jobs for them in Lynn.[28]

Strikers appealed for support through a broadside addressed to the "shoemakers of Massachusetts"; they asked for financial help, "but

above all things," they pleaded, "keep away from Lynn." Their call
was to little avail, and skeleton scab crews got the factories back in
production. A few of the hated strikebreakers were roughed up, and
soon it become common for detachments of city police to escort scabs
to and from the factories. Some manufacturers then settled with their
old employees by toning down slightly the terms of the ironclad oath;
they said they did not object to union membership, only to union
"interference." In other words, it was all right to be in the union as
long as it never did anything. Thus by one means or another the strike
ended in favor of the manufacturers.[29]

The Crispin challenge was beaten back not because shoeworkers
lacked a will to fight, or because they were weak in numbers, but
because they were up against an opponent who was simply stronger
than they were. Entrenched in the marketplace, fortified by the laws
and customs of private property, enjoying the advantages of political
incumbents, the factory owners needed only to act in the name of
law and order to call out the police, force strikers to give way to
strikebreakers, and put the factories back in operation. Their victory
was based on class power—their ownership of the principal economic
resources; their control over jobs, income, and, ultimately, survival;
and their support from the state. Of course, the factory owners themselves liked to think of their supremacy as an immutable fact of
nature and economic law, as in the following example of fierce, iron-
willed business conservatism:

> Business, whatever dreamy enthusiasts may say to the contrary,
> can never be honestly conducted on sentimental principles. The laws
> which govern it are fixed, and can no more be violated, with any
> permanent benefit to the community or nation, than the movements
> of the planets could be improved by man, allowing that restless tink-
> erer the power to practice on them. What is given to one is always
> taken from another, and morbid humanity towards any particular
> class can hardly be gratified without injustice to another.[30]

Storm the Fort

The Knights of St. Crispin was defeated in 1878, but not destroyed.
The next generation of shoeworkers drew upon its fraternal inspira-

tion, borrowed its rituals and organizational forms, and built upon the on-going work of Crispin shop committees in plant grievances and local walkouts. One group of shoeworkers, the lasters, founded the Lasters' Protective Union (LPU) in the midst of Crispin defeat to carry on Crispin traditions. Lasters epitomized the continuity in the generations of shoemakers, because they still made shoes by hand, tugging and pulling uppers around a last with needle-nosed pincers. No doubt an unusually high proportion of lasters had been artisans, and because the number of ex-artisans out of work was so large, lasters' wages were depressed. They had the experience of skilled workers, yet the market position of the unskilled. Lacking the secure, well-paying jobs they felt they deserved, these underpaid labor aristocrats turned their talents and ambitions to collective action and became the tough spine of trade unionism in the shoe industry.[31]

During the strike of 1878 they established their union. The LPU stubbornly carried on through thick and thin until 1895, when it joined with a remnant of the Knights of Labor and another organization of shoeworkers to form the Boot and Shoe Workers Union. During its seventeen-year life span, membership in the Lynn local, which was the main branch of the LPU, ranged from a few hundred to upwards of one thousand. The LPU maintained friendly relations with the Knights of St. Crispin and its successor, the Knights of Labor. Organized under the auspices of Unity Lodge, the LPU shared meeting grounds, members, and philosophy with the KOSC. In 1885, in the midst of the nationwide renaissance of trade unionism, the Lynn *Knight of Labor* warmly praised the LPU as "the parent organization that has raised so many dutiful children."[32]

The number of dutiful children multiplied rapidly to thirty-four distinct labor associations affiliated with the Knights of Labor in Lynn. Brothers assembled in such lodges as the Morocco Finishers (which had antecedents going back to 1860), the Boot and Shoe Cutters (for the first time cutters joined the labor movement), the Helping Hand Assembly (a combination of several trades which included some Black workers), and Unity Lodge (a revival of the old Crispin outfit). Sisters assembled in the Daughters of Labor and the Ladies Stitching Association. Counting all the KOL assemblies plus the Lasters' Protective Union, the labor movement could muster more than 10,000 members in Lynn at a time when the total number of working people in the city was not much above 15,000.[33]

This claim to have enrolled two-thirds of the labor force would be utterly unbelievable (organized labor enrols about about one-fourth today) were it not for the evidence that labor exerted such great influence in all spheres of life. In politics, the party of working-men was in office more than it was out. In social life, fairs and picnics drew thousands of participants and were community celebrations reminiscent of the 1860 strike parades. Before one such picnic, members of the Heelers Assembly, KOL, gathered at union headquarters and paraded through town behind a big brass band. This parade followed on the heels of the lasters' summer festival, which saw hundreds of families leave Lynn by train and travel to Walden Pond where men and boys competed for $300 in prizes that went to the winners of foot races, oar boat races, a scull race, a sack race, and a one-mile run. With a Boston band playing music, there was dancing in a large hall all afternoon. High spirited and recalcitrant, lasters picnicked on Monday to give themselves an extra day off from work. In the cultural life of the city, the various KOL lodges provided fraternity and sorority to their members, and 2000 subscribers read the *Knight of Labor*.[34]

The Knights encompassed both Irish and Yankees, the two main ethnic groups in the city. Judging from the names of prizewinners at the picnics, heelers contained roughly equal numbers from each group, while the lasters were mostly Yankee, and the morocco finishers were mostly Irish. Regardless of the Pope's condemnation of the Knights of Labor, Irish workers were quite prominent in the organization. Both immigrants and first generation Irish-Americans, like Grand Master Workman Terence Powderly, joined the Knights in droves and occupied leadership positions. Since Irishmen were often in the lower paying unskilled jobs (three-fifths of the laborers in Lynn were Irish immigrants), the ethnic makeup of the union reflected its class base as a mass organization of all who labored. The KOL in Lynn was truly One Big Union.[35]

Just as the KOSC built upon the experience of its forerunners, so the KOL further developed the trade union practice of the KOSC. This was most apparent in the area of arbitration, a term which was loosely applied to many methods of settling industrial disputes, but which in Lynn meant either negotiation between employer and employee representatives or policing the agreements that resulted from these negotiations. In the first case, one or more Knights met with an equal number of employer representatives and selected the same number of third parties; this team heard the proposals from both sides and reached a verdict in each dispute; the process was designed to be like the deliberations of a jury rather than the adversary proceedings of modern collective bargaining. Then the labor and management representatives carried the verdict back to their respective organizations and tried to win approval. This sometimes put the KOL representatives in conflict with members of affiliated assemblies; at one point in 1886, cutters and stitchers were reported to be "warring with the Board of Arbitration," and at a few other points, the KOL negotiators refused to support shop grievances.[36]

The preference of the KOL for negotiated settlement did not mean the union opposed strikes as such. The Lynn *Knight of Labor* cautioned against strikes for trivial reasons, but when a fundamental issue of the rights and liberties of a wage worker was at stake, then a strike was in order. Thus the KOL backed a strike lasting several weeks against a major Lynn manufacturer who hired scabs to operate one of his factories in Maine. The strike ended with a complete KOL victory; not only was the manufacturer compelled to take back all his union employees, but his invitation to settle the matter in his offices was refused, and instead he had to trudge over to union headquarters to sign the agreement ending the strike.[37]

With every upsurge of trade unionism, labor presses would roll. The first labor paper in Lynn was the *Awl,* a weekly platform in the 1840s for Equal Rights. Its successors included the *New England Mechanic,* voice of the generation who carried out the strike in 1860, the *Little Giant,* a Democratic paper which bore the marks of labor's influence, the *Vindicator,* a journal of trade unionism and social reform founded in the Greenback-labor atmosphere of the late 1870s but which steered clear of politics, and the *Knight of Labor,* a mirror of the labor movement of the 1880s.[38] Although four decades separated the *Awl* from the *Knight of Labor,* the similarities between the two were remarkable. Both defined the labor question as a problem of the total regeneration of society; both saw the worker as someone with cultural, social, and political concerns, as well as straight economic interests. Thus both journals endorsed temperance, denounced money power and monopolization of the land, defended the ballot as a weapon of reform, entertained their readers with moralistic fiction, and, in addition to all of this, featured columns on the state of the shoe industry and the progress of organization among the laboring classes. The *Awl* and the *Knight of Labor* were two pages out of the same book of Equal Rights.

In Lynn as in the nation the strength of the Knights of Labor was in the way they organized working people as whole human beings and members of a community, not simply industrial employees. They broke down sexual, ethnic, trade, and skill barriers in an attempt to mobilize men and women, Irish and Yankee, skilled and unskilled in a union of all the toilers. Far from being an old-fashioned bunch of muddleheads (as some historians have suggested), they were quite sophisticated in their strategy and tactics and demonstrated both prudence and militancy.[39] They failed to sustain a high level of organization because the institutional framework of the union was inadequate to the demands placed upon it. The tremendous growth of grass roots enthusiasm simply overreached the capacities of the organization. Neither was the American Federation of Labor up to— or even interested in—the task of organizing workers on a mass basis, with the result that most of the major industrial battles before World War II ended in defeats for workers. To measure the KOL unfavorably against the endurance of the AFL is to confuse survival with success.

After the Knights of Labor, the aims and philosophy of the labor movement split into two main branches: pure and simple trade unionism and socialism. Each in its way went beyond the Equal Rights tradition, the first because it organized around the job to build tough, longlasting unions that fought for the self-interest of particular groups of employees; the second because it developed a more rigorous analysis of the exercise of class power in industrial capitalist society.

So the Knights were the culmination of a half century of labor history. They agreed with the oldtime artisan that the producing classes are the source of all wealth and that the laborer is entitled to a fair share of the fruits of his toil. They stood with the working-men of the 1830s and 1840s in demanding a sound public currency freed from the clutches of a money aristocracy and in demanding an end to monopolization of the soil. Like their predecessors in the Eight-Hour Leagues and Ten-Hour Associations, they knew that a shortened workday was the necessary precondition for the moral and intellectual elevation of labor, especially now as industrial discipline was intensified. They saw in the numerous examples of cooperative production that individual self-reliance and mutual support could be harmonized best in workshops that were managed by workers them-selves. They learned from the experience of trade unionists like the Knights of St. Crispin that strikes could be very costly, and, where-ever possible, that arbitration should be the method of resolving industrial disputes. The Knights of Labor was the largest labor ori-ganization in nineteenth-century America because it encompassed so much of the prior history of labor. It was as if all the branches on labor's Tree of Liberty bloomed forth in one great flowering of Equal Rights. With their words reverberating across a century of American culture, working people in the 1880s sang the popular anthem of their movement:

> Storm the fort, ye Knights of Labor,
> Battle for your cause;
> Equal rights for every neighbor,
> Down with tyrant laws.

8

POLITICIANS

The industrial working class came into being during the greatest upheaval in American history. Its very existence marked the profound changes wrought by the Industrial Revolution, as factories and railroads overturned old community traditions. Its uneasy birth occurred in the turmoil of Civil War, when the federal Union burst asunder, the dominant classes lunged at each other's throats, lives and property turned to blood and rubble, and an entire network of property rights in chattel slaves perished in the conflict. As witnesses to the holocaust, industrial workers knew the capaciy for great deeds of a people imbued with crusading righteousness and felt the terrible power of the sword's might in crushing an enemy. What, then, was to prevent the emerging industrial working class from turning its traumatic lesson in violent warfare against its opponents at home?

As the material in the previous chapter indicates, the spector of working-class discontent materialized often enough between 1860 and 1890 to justify the haunted nightmares of men of property that workers might someday rise up to overturn the existing order. However, this ultimate fear was not realized, largely because the intensity with which workers pursued pragmatic economic aims was not carried over into their political activities. Their radicalism was not the equal of their militancy. Whereas the American economic system engendered bitter class conflicts, American politics, for reasons which will become clear as the discussion unfolds, tended to generate mechanisms for resolving those conflicts.

War and Peace

The foremost mechanism of this kind in nineteenth-century history was the Civil War itself. At the beginning of the war, Lynn was deeply and bitterly divided as a result of the Great Strike of 1860,[1] which had impelled the defeated strikers to organize a Workingmen's party and take control of city government.[2] The war, however, over-came this division by uniting workers with their bosses in a common struggle against slave owners. Just at the time when the factory system was fastening its hold on the city, just when awareness of class antagonism was sharpening, attention was diverted away from the conflict between capital and labor to the conflict between free labor and slavery. Workingmen who had been cool to Republican ideas and candidates in the past now warmed up to the slogans of "free soil, free labor, and free men" and supported the Republican president. The Equal Rights philosophy, which had been pushed by the rise of industrial capitalism and the Great Strike toward a thoroughgoing critique of capital, was reunited with an ideology of property ownership.

Partisan political activity virtually ceased in Lynn for the duration of the war. During these years the evils of capitalism seemed to be washed away in the greater sins of slavery, as workers were infused with patriotism for the Union, devotion to its cause, and respect for its leaders and heroes. The Workingmen's mayor observed that "the year 1861 will ever be memorable," not because his election marked the first victory of a labor ticket in the city's history, but because it marked the start of the Civil War. The suffocating embrace of wartime unity did not end when the war ended; with attenuated impact, it extended into the next decade when partisan activity resumed in full force. In 1872 the national head of the Knights of St. Crispin told a Lynn audience why he supported the Republican ticket of Grant and Wilson (a former shoe manufacturer): not only did the Republican convention accept his proposal for a plank recognizing the rights of labor, but when he recalled his wartime experience with all its suffering for the old flag, he "could not shake hands over the bloody chasm with the unrepentent rebels who now support Greeley." When Grant died in 1885, the Lynn *Knight of Labor* eulogized him as "the grandest citizen the nation ever knew."[3]

In foreclosing debate on the effects of the factory system during the crucial decade of industrial conversion, the war stunted the growth of ideas opposed to the regime of the factory owners.[4] In giving businessmen free reign of the city, the war provided a crushing setback to the development of confidence among workers in their own capacity to govern. Even though labor mayors would be elected in the future, they would not imagine themselves making fundamental changes in the way the city or the economic system was run. They lacked the equivalent assurance of the manufacturers in making revolution. Moreover, the war experience helped persuade the members of the newly emerging working class that the state, even when controlled by the owners, functioned in the interests of the operatives.

The contention that the war limited workers' political options and channeled their beliefs away from radicalism implies that radical politics would have been more widespread without the war. It is impossible to say with certainty just how the politics of the emerging working class would have been different without the war (as it is impossible to prove any counterfactual assumption), but the existing facts are consistent with alternative outcomes. The historical record before the war and after shows a tendency toward independent political action in the recurrent sproutings of numerous Labor Reform and Workingmen's parties in which the influence of Equal Rights assured an antimonopoly, if not a socialist, critique of capitalism. Moreover, the Republican party was a minority party when it won the presidency, and, without the war to consolidate its position, the field would have been thrown open to a host of other factions. The 1860s may have become an extension of the disarray of the 1850s, and, in such a fluid situation, the increasing impact of Industrial Revolution might have brought about a tough, durable national party of labor. Without the experience of fighting and dying for the Union, industrial workers may have been more inclined to see businessmen as their political enemies and to see the state as a hostile institution. At any rate, it is essential to keep such historical alternatives in mind, to interpret events as consequences of other events, and to avoid the fallacy of regarding whatever happened as the sole and inevitable conclusion to the logic of events.

The existence of a more radical potential among workers was revealed in the breakup of the wartime alliance under the twin impact of a great upsurge of trade unionism and a revival of independent political action. These symbiotic movements were represented nationally by the National Labor Union and the National Labor Reform party, and locally by the Knights of St. Crispin and a branch of the

Labor Reform party. Although Crispin rules excluded partisan politics from the lodge room, and despite the fact that many shoeworkers
counted themselves Republicans or Democrats, the Labor Reform
effort in Massachusetts was essentially the political wing of the KOSC.
Crispin grievances brought it into being, Crispin officers performed
the day-to-day organizing tasks, and rank and file Crispins provided
the staple supply of votes. The state legislature was responsible for
catalyzing this effort when it rejected the union's petition for incorporation in 1869. In a matter of months, Labor Reformers fielded
a large slate of candidates, elected a dozen to the state house, and
returned next year with Wendell Phillips as their nominee for governor. Phillips captured 15 percent of the statewide vote, faring poorly
in textile centers like Lawrence and Newburyport, but doing quite
well in Crispin strongholds like Lynn, where he won a large plurality.[5]

The man in charge of getting out the vote in Lynn was George P.
Sanderson, chairman of the Labor Reform club, KOSC officer,
former strike leader in 1860, and future mayor of Lynn on the
Workingmen's ticket.[6] On every level from neighborhood to nation,
trade union organizing and political reform went hand in hand; in
fact, as Sanderson shows, the same hand that rapped the gavel at a
political convention shook hands with lodge brothers and carried on
correspondence with the national trade union office. Therefore, it is
a mistake to assert that politics and trade unionism were mutually
antagonistic activities conducted by separate groups of people, an
interpretation commonly put forth by historians in the tradition of
John Commons, but recently countered effectively by David Montgomery.[7]

The Labor Reform program rested on the Equal Rights principle
that labor is the source of all wealth. This was the first resolution of
the first party convention in the state, but its meaning was not as
clear as its importance. Middle-class reformers associated with the
party, such as its well-to-do candidate for governor, E. M. Chamber-
lain, took it to mean that labor and capital were mutually dependent
and equally entitled to the benefits of legislation, such as the right to
incorporate. But the principle had a more radical meaning as well:
since labor was the source of wealth, laborers had a just claim to the
wealth they produced. This idea lurked behind two other resolutions

at the founding convention: a demand for free transportation and communication and an endorsement of cooperation (which was coupled with the demand that the state issue no charters of incorporation unless employees were to share in the profits).[8]

Crispins took a direct interest in cooperation. S. P. Cummings had called the above Labor Reform convention to order, and two Lynn Crispins, one a Knight, the other a Daughter, were chosen as vice-presidents of the session that endorsed cooperation. The third national convention of the KOSC adopted a committee report which recommended the use of union funds to finance cooperatives. The report asked, "If labor produces all the wealth of a country, why should it not claim ownership?" Joint ownership, the report affirmed, was a just dessert for the producing classes and a practical remedy for the woes of wage earners.

We claim, that although the masses have advanced towards independence, they will never be completely free from vassalage until they have thrown off the system of working for hire. Men working for wages are, in a greater or less degree, in the bonds of serfdom. The demand and supply of labor makes them the football of circumstances. Today, independent to all appearance; tomorrow, the veriest slave, begging for work, that he may earn a crust to sustain a miserable existence. We cannot expect to overcome this law of demand and supply; yet we believe, that in proportion as a man becomes his own capitalist, in the same degree does he become independent of this law. How all men can become their own capitalist, is a question already decided by political economists. The answer is—*cooperation*.[9]

The practical achievements of cooperation stood in inverse proportion to the imagined results. Three or four ventures begun in Lynn were unable to become independent of the ruthless dictates of the law of supply and demand and perished within a few years, just like the shoemaker cooperatives of the 1840s. Their existence testifies to the rudiments of an anticapitalist mentality among both artisans and factory workers; their disappearance testifies to the crushing power of the capitalist marketplace and the need to overcome wage-serfdom through other methods.

The machinations of presidential politics chopped the National Labor Reform party to bits in 1872, and in Massachusetts Ben Butler swallowed the pieces. Colorful and outspoken, Butler was not one to ride the fence; instead he rode all sides, depending on where he could best organize on his own behalf. After several years as a Radical Republican in the congressional seat formerly held by John B. Alley, he became a Greenback Democrat, once he had reached the conclusion "that I could not be governor in the Republican Party." Butler's close association with Alley and his ownership of a textile factory might have given him a reputation as a businessman's politician, but Butler was a maverick who was very popular with labor. He appealed to the antimonopoly sentiments of labor voters with rhetorical attacks on the banking system and support for greenbacks, and he entertained them with humorous stories about his opponents. One opponent told a labor audience in Lynn that he could understand their interests, having done manual labor: "I assure you, fellow-citizens, I was as dirty as any of you." Quick to sense the insult, Butler turned it to his own advantage by affirming that, as far as he was concerned, it was only necessary to be "a respectable, well-clad, decent American citizen" to be the equal of the Lynn shoemakers. Lynn voters returned the compliment by supporting the Butler-Republican ticket for a number of years and then switching to Butler-Greenback in 1878.[10]

The Workingmen's Party

Butlerism and Greenbackism set the stage for a local Workingmen's party that was thrust into the scene by the shoe strike of 1878. Unlike all its forerunners in Lynn, this Workingmen's party enjoyed both success and long life, dominating city politics for a dozen years, and sending a native son and "true friend of labor," Henery B. Lovering, to Congress. Since the Workingmen ended the reign of Republican shoe manufacturers and began a new labor era, the triumph of the party was something of a turning point in the city's history. But, as will soon become clear, the change brought more in the way of a boost in morale to labor's self-esteem than practical solutions to labor's social problems. It would be more accurate to characterize 1878 as a turning point about which the city's history failed to turn.

In the essential dynamics of events, 1878 was 1860 revisited.

Replaying key episodes of the Great Strike, crowds of 1878 strikers clashed with squads of police, and small-scale violence erupted on at least three occasions. In one incident an angry knot of strikers surrounded a scab and roughed him up, though the intention of the strikers was to intimidate, not harm, since they had armed themselves with nothing more dangerous than snowballs. They had tossed a few of these missiles in the scab's direction before police arrived to break up the crowd, arrest a snowball thrower, and fend off an attempt to rescue the captive. The arrest added vengeance to the strikers' feeling of hostility. Later in the day, with no police standing by, the same scab was waylaid again, and this time his assailants left him lying unconscious on the sidewalk. Like the strike leadership in 1860, the Knights of St. Crispin condemned such acts of violence as violations of the spirit of the strike, and like the city administration in 1860, the mayor and Board of Aldermen met in emergency session and voted 5 to 3 to beef up the regular police force with 100 special deputies to patrol the manufacturing districts and escort strikebreakers to work.[11]

To Mayor Samuel Bubier, police protection for strikebreakers was nothing more than equal protection of the law. But to Crispin strikers it was a gross violation of Equal Rights, a slander on the reputation of the vast majority of respectable strikers, and a perversion of the public trust. Crispins perceived an unholy league of mayor, marshal, and manufacturers united in hostile acts of provocation and intimidation with the aim of enforcing the lockout against Crispin employees and destroying the union. Crispins knew exactly what they had to do: go to the polls, defeat the present administration, remove the city marshal, and thereby break up the evil combination among their enemies.

The campaign pitted George Sanderson, a long-time Crispin, against Mayor Bubier. The lines of battle during the bitter contest appeared to duplicate the strike: a party of Workingmen faced the defenders of capital, employees squared off against employers, the producing classes confronted the possessing classes. The two main contestants had fought each other before; Sanderson cast one of the three votes against Bubier's request to augment the police force during the strike of 1878, and eighteen years earlier the two men had stood on opposite sides in the Great Strike. Indeed, in a touch of supreme irony, Sanderson had been in Bubier's employ at that time, and now the humble son of toil and want was contesting his onetime oppressor for the community's highest honor. They fought on only one issue— the police. The same issue had propelled the Workingmen's movement of 1860 to victory, and 1878 was no different: Sanderson trounced Bubier 2919 to 1154, with 744 votes going to a third candidate.[12]

Once the Workingmen had avenged their strike defeat, they abandoned their battle lines and ceased to pose as the representatives of an aggrieved class. Images of class struggle dissolved in the gray vapors of Sanderson's inaugural address. He smoothed over the craggy edges of class feeling by imitating the rhetorical style of his business predecessors, in all its florid oratorical pomposity. The performance was so convincing it prompted an opposition newspaper to praise the speech for its sound sense and to congratulate Sanderson for transcending his narrow campaign appeal to "that class called 'workingmen.' "[13] The new administration emulated the political culture of its opponents instead of creating a new working-class style of its own. It emphasized continuity with the past rather than change for the future. It sought entry into the political system, only to become confined within it.

Some Workingmen who did daily battle in the factories criticized the party's style of accommodation. The style was on display at the city's 250th anniversary celebration, held a few months after the new administration took office. In a typical show of social harmony, Sanderson sat among leading businessmen from the community on the speakers stand and at the banquet table, no doubt relishing the exquisite feeling of equality with men who were once his superiors. While rubbing elbows with the well-to-do, Sanderson completely forgot about his labor supporters. As one embittered workingman pointed out, labor was left off the list of invited guests and ignored by the celebrities in the round of toasts, yet labor taxpayers would be called upon to foot the bill. "Does it relieve the burden of labor that the 'bloated bondholders' should be invited guests to a banquet that costs the city six dollars per plate, and not give the 'white slave who pays all the taxes' even a smell?"[14] The references to slavery and bondholding identify the writer as a vigilant sentry of antimonopoly and suggest that the critical spirit of Equal Rights was not altogether snuffed out by success at the polls. As we will see later on, such criticism sparked a more radical vision of working-class politics.

Next to winning the election, the major accomplishment of the Workingmen's party was firing the hated city marshal whose zealous protection of strikebreakers was the cause that brought the party into being. Finding a replacement, however, was a more complicated affair, and, in the end, Sanderson appointed a compromise police chief who had been deputy marshal during the strike, but who had not been closely identified with the manufacturers. Sanderson had to accept the second spot in the department for his first choice, the chairman of the Crispin Board of Arbitration and a prominent strike leader, but he probably won effective control of the police through his wholesale dismissal of regular officers and the appointment of friends and relatives to take their places.[15] Thus for the first time since the department was put on a professional footing in the 1860s, control of the police was no longer securely in the hands of the factory owners, and that was the one memorable accomplishment of the Workingmen's administration. It would be a dozen years before local police were used again against workers in a labor dispute.

Beyond winning the election and purging the police department, the Workingmen's party had no objectives. It did not enact a program of municipal reform because it had no such program. It did not begin a thorough overhaul of city government to suit the needs of working people because it did not perceive the political interests of workers as fundamentally different from other social groups. It did not do for labor what the Republican party had done for manufacturers. Instead, Workingmen infiltrated the structure of government established by the Republicans and carried out business as usual. Even the offices they occupied were located inside a Republican structure; as has been shown, the City Hall had been constructed in 1867 as a tribute to the growing wealth and stature of the shoe manufacturers. If Sanderson and the Workingmen had historical counterparts, they were George Hood and his Democratic supporters, who in 1850 gave up their opposition to the city form of government once they had installed Hood in the mayor's office. They were in perfect agreement with the Workingmen's party that popular grievances could be settled by "properly exercising the privilege of the franchise and substituting honest and capable men for those holding public office."[16]

The position of the Lynn Workingmen's party was indistinguishable from the national policy of the Knights of St. Crispin, who resolved in their convention of the same year that "we believe in a *government of the people,* and that the *people,* in a day not far distant, will place upon the statute-book just laws, which will right the wrongs of labor." The resolution identified Crispins as staunch supporters of the existing political system who saw the specter of communism in social disorder and proclaimed "our abhorrence of 'Communism' and our firm adherence to law and order." How much of this was heartfelt conviction and how much was just public relations propaganda is open to debate, but whatever the balance in motivation, the effect was to link the most politically active workers with middle-class opinion on this question.[17]

For all its rhetorical identification with Labor, the Workingmen's party represented the intersection of two classes, not the interests of one. On the one hand, it carried the economic grievances of industrial workers into the political system, and, on the other, it carried the middle-class premises of the system into the working class. The nature of the party as a vehicle of interclass communication was evident both in its ideas and its candidates.[18]

In terms of ideas, the party arose in the Greenback milieu of the late 1870s. It championed the demands for soft money and lower interest rates and attacked the banking system as a set of monopolizing institutions whose stranglehold on currency and credit favored big capitalists over laborers and small businessmen. With the depression of the 1870s festering through its fifth year, the Lynn Greenback Club, George P. Sanderson presiding, arranged a debate on currency and banking reform which featured ex-congressman John B. Alley taking the side of hard money and ex-mayor James N. Buffum, member of a small business family with a history of ardent abolitionism, taking the side of soft money and taking Alley to task for his great wealth. Buffum became a loyal Workingman.[19]

Another telltale mark of middle-class influence was the irrepressible urge of party leaders to clothe themselves in the garb of middle-class "respectability." This was revealed in their search for public sympathy among the local middle class during the strike of 1878. Strike leaders formally tendered a resolution of thanks to a pair of ministers "for their noble efforts on our behalf, as expressed in their pupits on Sunday last." They must have been desperate for support, because the best either of the good reverends could claim for the Crispins was that a worker was entitled to a living wage sufficient to maintain "respectability, to clothe his family and send his children to school, and appear in the house of worship on the Sabbath." In addition, to ask for a living wage in a spirt of mutual respect was "as compatible with scripture as Masonry, Odd Fellowship, or organized capital." Otherwise, the clergymen found much to condemn in Crispinism: "Its persecution and usurpation of authority, as exemplified in preventing men from working and hooting them through the streets, have no Gospel sanction." One minister who said he got a "morbid, dreary feeling" whenever he fell to thinking about industrial relations, condemned the harassment of scabs and the breaking of factory windows as violations of social harmony, and warned workers to stay within the bounds of the existing distribution of property and power: "There cannot be an equal distribution of capital; some men are bound to be rich and some poor. From Communism and mob law may we be delivered."[20]

Strikers must have been divided in their feelings toward these spiritual deliverers. Although the local Crispin lodge issued its own denunciation of strike violence, and the national Crispin convention had condemned communism and mob law (which it equated), some strikers continued to harass scabs. While KOSC officers fretted over their standing in the community and readied their apologies, their brothers and sisters of a more desperate temper vented their anger on those who would deny them a livelihood. Many workers took a middle ground, holding their own tempers, but also withholding criticism of those whose anger exploded. No doubt, feelings of all three types went to make up the source of passion and energy that propelled the Workingmen's party to its triumph in the fall elections. No matter what their opinions on harassment, shoe workers were united in outrage against the city's use of police to break the strike— that was universally perceived as an enemy action and in all parts of the city became the basis of electoral solidarity. Nonetheless, there is also no doubt that the leadership, program, and achievements of the party represented *areas of agreement between workers and middle-class reformers* rather than the areas of agreement within the working class. The Workingmen's party was not a party of the proletariat.

Having shown solicitude for both labor and middle-class voters, the Workingmen's party was overwhelmingly reelected the next fall. Its popularity was enhanced by a reduction in the city's property tax rate, a move which was most beneficial to middle-class property owners, but which also eased the financial burden on the 15-20 percent of shoeworkers who owned their own homes. The reelection victory enabled the new party to consolidate its organization, stabilize its patronage appointments, and weld together Democrats and Greenbackers to form an urban political machine. Thus when Sanderson retired after his second term, the party was able to elect one of his appointees to succeed him.[21]

The heir was Henry B. Lovering, a man with all the credentials for a Workingmen's endorsement. He was a Civil War veteran who could demonstrate valiant service by pointing to his artificial left leg, and an ex-shoemaker who could prove his devotion to the cause of labor by citing his service on the first Crispin Board of Arbitration. Above all he was a professional politician, and after two terms as mayor of Lynn, he moved on to take the congressional seat once held by his associate Ben Butler, while Butler stayed in Massachusetts to satisfy his craving to be governor. With Lovering in Congress and Butler in the State House, Workingmen hardly minded losing the race for mayor in Lynn the next two years in a row.[22]

When they won the mayor's office again in 1885, the great nationwide upsurge in unionism associated with the Knights of Labor was well under way. With unions winning concessions from the manufacturers and with Workingmen's candidates winning elections, labor was having a heyday of success. Lynn's *Knight of Labor* basked in the confidence that the Knights, "who of course embrace the majority of Lynn's voters," could choose whatever political leadership they wished. The newspaper's offhanded assurance that a majority of voters belonged to the Knights of Labor was based on the simple fact that there were more Knights than voters. Allowing for exaggerated membership claims and for the failure of many voters to vote, the paper's attitude was not unreasonable, and, of course, the real proof was in the vote count, which gave Workingmen a clear victory in the mayor's race over a Republican manufacturer and a thumping majority (19 to 11) on the Common Council.[23]

Once again the main issue was the police, only this time the shoe was on the other foot. Manufacturers and some middle-class reformers wanted to oust the police chief, while the labor movement defended him. A patronage appointee of the first Workingmen's administration, Chief Alexander had been promoted to the top spot at the request of the Knights of Labor and was popular with labor for the same reasons he was unpopular with the manufacturers. During a turnout against one of the city's biggest firms, strikers tacked a protest banner near the factory to warn off other workers, and Alexander let the banner fly. A grateful supporter wrote a letter to the *Knight of Labor* in which he lionized the Chief as

one of the workingmen from the shops, and his sympathies are naturally with those who are struggling for a better condition of things for themselves and families. They know that in case of a strike, though all laws will be enforced, and the rights of all respected, he will never play the tyrant, or be the lick spittle of capital, and arrest a toiler in the arbitrary manner certain manufacturers would like the police force to do, and as they intend to do it if they can get rid of the influence of the Knights of Labor in the police department.[24]

Confident of their vitality and acting with a sense of historical momentum, Lynn workers swelled the ranks of the country's buoyant labor movement, which was expanding into economic and political realms abandoned for over a decade since the demise of the NLU. Watching these events unfold, Friedrich Engels wrote that the burgeoning union membership, plus the increasing appeal of workingmen's parties, were nothing less than "the first levies *en masse* of the great revolutionary war." In a famous passage, he contrasted the more tedious development of a self-acting working class in Europe with the rapid development in America: "On the more favored soil of America, where no medieval ruins bar the way, where history begins with the elements of modern bourgeois society as evolved in the seventeenth century, the working class has passed through these two stages of its development within ten months."[25] A considerable portion of bourgeois opinion in the United States agreed with Engels' analysis. Imagining the armies of discontent already on the march, business, pulpit, press, and farm reacted hysterically to the Haymarket bomb as the first event in the great revolutionary war.

The American labor movement fulfilled neither the great hopes of its friends nor the great fears of its enemies. It put several armies into the field, one behind the Knights of Labor, another behind the Federation of Organized Trades and Labor Unions, and others behind the issue of the eight-hour day, Henry George, Chicago anarchists, New York socialists, and a host of workingmen's parties from coast to coast. But this mass mobilization exceeded the capacity of the movement to organize the troops into a disciplined fighting force. Part of the reason for this failure lies in the meager resources of the still young and inexperienced trade union movement. Another part lies in the disorganizing effect of competing institutions, especially the two major political parties. And a third part lies in the limits of Equal Rights. So optimistic about the potential for reform, so sure of the basic goodness of the political system, so pleased with success, Equal Rights was unable to look beyond victory at the polls toward programs that would infringe upon the rights of property and effectively redistribute wealth to bring about the equality it so passionately desired. By the time the bomb exploded the past was wearing thin. The artisan radicalism of Equal Rights was no longer able to carry a working-class load, and the movement it inspired collapsed under its own weight.

Beyond Equal Rights

The Tree of Liberty, planted in the American Revolution and nourished by generations of farmers, mechanics, and industrial workers, spread its branches beside the institutions of industrial capitalism and for six decades after 1830 gave forth the lush fruit of egalitarian agitation: antimonopoly, fair wage, right to organize, cooperation, free soil, free labor. The fruit of Equal Rights satisfied the artisan taste for tart, radical criticisms of the new order and nourished the militant protests of the first generation of factory workers, as well. But ultimately, the Tree of Liberty died in the poisoned soil of industrialism, its withered fruit no longer satisfying to the second generation of factory workers, who demanded more complete, or at least more immediate satisfaction of their wants. The demise of Equal Rights opened the way for new forms of working-class political action; while some workers developed an appetite for the pure and simple rewards of officeholding, others felt a deeper hunger for radical changes in the political system.

In Lynn, the pork-barrel temptations of pure- and-simpleism lured most working-class voters back to the two regular parties. As the Knights of Labor declined and the Workingmen's party proved incapable of improving the daily lot of its supporters, the shortcomings of these organizations convinced a majority of politically active workers that their needs were not likely to be served worse by Republicans or Democrats. In fact, the last time a Workingman won the mayor's race, he was also supported by both Republican and Democratic organizations, a situation that gave labor independents horrible nightmares. The candidate combined ancient Yankee ancestry (he claimed descent from the first white person born in Lynn 250 years earlier) with modern Irish alliances (in state and national elections he worked for the Democrats, increasingly a party of Irishmen).[26]

This strange, three-headed fusionist's dream occupied the mayor's office in 1890 when the city once again was convulsed by another of its hard-fought strikes. Apart from the fact that the strike occurred in the tanning factories, the events of 1890 began with a replay of 1878. As in the earlier conflict, factory owners attempted to break the strike by importing scabs, and a zealous, law-and-order police chief arrested several strikers who had intimidated and harassed the outsiders. At this point, however, the chief went beyond all custom and precedent to arrest strike leaders on conspiracy charges, though they had nothing to do with the harassment. Representing a much smaller segment of the community than the shoeworkers, the leaders of the tanning workers were more exposed to this kind of union busting tactic, and factory owners, no doubt, counted on occupational divisions among the city's wage earners to prevent a public outcry. In this the owners were mistaken, for a large part of the labor movement came to the defense of strike leaders. In the next elections, labor leaders jacked up the sagging apparatus of the Workingmen's party, cut loose from the two regular organizations, threw over the mayor who had permitted his chief of police to run amuck, and put up a candidate committed to appointing a new chief.[27]

Four times between 1860 and 1890 the labor movement ran its own candidate on the police issue. The first three times the candidate won; the last time he lost. The defeat in 1890 was the last political offensive of the Workingmen's party, the closing episode in an era of labor reform that reached back to the first workingmen's party of the 1830s.

At the same time, the result was hardly a total defeat for the labor movement. Although the nominal candidate of labor suffered defeat, his Republican opponent boasted a strong labor background of his own: thirty years as a veteran shoemaker, and active membership in the Knights of Labor. True to his working-class origins, and respectful of the size of the labor vote, he lost little time in firing the objectionable chief of police.[28] With enemies like that, why did workers need friends like the Workingmen? Moreover, the Republican party, with its ties to state and national party patronage, had more to offer than a localized organization like the Workingmen, which had no such mechanism of its own and had to scurry about to catch crumbs falling from the Democratic groaning board. And finally, the limited accomplishments of the Workingmen's administrations hardly earned the undying support of working-class voters. With friends like the Workingmen, workers were still in need of friends.

The labor movement never regained the drive and cohesion of the 1880s, and, accordingly, the politics of labor fell into disarray. Labor voters ran helter-skelter among the two major parties and several minor organizations, and the disorganized state of affairs gave the Republican party its first opportunity since the Civil War to consolidate the dominant position in city politics, though its triumph had far less to do with the special appeal of Republican principles than with the spread of pure- and-simpleism. The same attraction for practical politics was evident in the overwhelming rejection of William Jennings Bryan, the old-fashioned candidate of the "producing classes." As far as Lynn was concerned his campaign came ten years too late, for the voters sent the Great Commoner down to defeat by a margin of almost 2 to 1.[29] To be sure, Bryan's defeat represented revenge for Democratic depression and mistrust of midwestern manners, as well as the rejection of the old-style reform mentality, but there is little doubt that a Bryan candidacy occurring when the Knights of Labor reigned in Lynn would have swept to victory.

While the majority of working-class voters returned to the folds of the regular parties, a minority remained outside to give voice to a newfound proletarian radicalism. Those who contended the worker was entitled to the full fruit of his toil, who took Equal Rights to its radically egalitarian conclusion, who defined the Republican and Democratic parties as capitalist institutions, and who fulminated over the failures of the Workingmen's party, spoke with a rhetoric of conflict, not compromise, praised a culture of toil, not pomp, and proclaimed a political program of economic and social change, not just a changing of the guard at city hall.

The new departure in radicalism bore an ambivalent relation to the old tradition of Equal Rights: it was a direct offspring of the old tradition, but something quite different from the parent. Antimonopoly became anticapitalism, cooperation became collective ownership, the producing classes became the working class, independent political action became socialism. Proletarian radicalism was the child of Equal Rights, but the artisan parent, caught across a generation gap, could not have acknowledged the ideas of its offspring as its own.

Yet the lineage was clearly revealed in the demand of the *Knight of Labor* for the federal government to take possession of the railroads and run them for the benefit of the people "instead of letting them be run for the benefit of a few capitalistic rogues." Workingmen could accomplish such feats only by cutting loose from all past party affiliations and by voting for men selected from their own ranks. How foolish it was, the *Knight* scolded, for workingmen "to spend their time in denouncing the capitalist and when election time comes go to the polls and vote for the men selected by the capitalists." Casting a glance over its shoulder at the recent Haymarket affair, the *Knight* turned on the Democrats and Republicans with bitter satire to condemn those politicians who wooed workers at election time after denouncing them the rest of the year as anarchists and law breakers. It sneered at this deceitful hypocrisy and challenged workingmen not to be "the dupe of these knavish politicians and their heelers from the barroom to the pulpit."[30]

Shrapnel from the explosion in Chicago's Haymarket Square embedded itself in sections of the labor movement all across the country, severely wounding the Equal Rights tradition. At first the Lynn *Knight of Labor* tried to ignore the explosion altogether, but the insistent din of national hysteria compelled the paper to come to grips with the bomb at the end of May 1886, three weeks after the event. Making the assumption that a violent revolutionary had committed the act (though it has never been established whether the bombing was an anarchist *attentat,* a police provocation, or some lunatic's revenge), the *Knight* condemned the violence and lashed out at Lynn manufacturers for trying to "place the follies of those unmerciful bomb throwers of Chicago on the shoulders of the Knights of Labor." "Socialists and dynamiters," the paper declared, "had no place in the Knights organization." Wounded, riled, and fighting on the defensive, the *Knight of Labor,* nonetheless, did not become panic stricken. It kept its senses and tried to explain the causes of violence by a rational analysis of the social and political injustices that lay behind it. Without such evils, the *Knight* reasoned, there would have been no bombing, and those men responsible for injustice shared the responsibility for the violent protest against it. Through the smoke of Haymarket, the *Knight* saw the logic of revolution, though it was not yet prepared to abandon reform.

It must be remembered that in communities where social and political evils prevail there exists a cause for disorder and defiance of law and those who engage in unlawful conflicts are less guilty than those who have had it in their power to root out evils and establish justice, and who have failed to do so. There would have been no French revolution if the people had not been goaded to it by oppression. Let us be warned in time. Reform is better than revolution. Let us have reform.[31]

Reform, however, was not forthcoming, which is exactly why some workers who saw the logic of revolution began to search for new paths beyond Equal Rights.

As the party of labor reform blended back into the parties of tradition, small clusters of radical voters attached to a wide variety of party labels appeared in local and national elections. The first such grouping appeared in 1889 when disenchanted Workingmen formed the Independent Labor party and ran a candidate for mayor against the nominee of the Workingmen, who was also a fusion candidate of both Republican and Democratic organizations. By 1892 the Independent Labor ticket had disappeared, but its place was taken by the People's party, which continued to offer candidates until 1896, and which got more votes in Lynn than any other breakaway party: at its peak popularity the People's mayoral candidate won almost one-fifth of the votes. Most of the People's support came from radicalized workers, but class-conscious wage earners also had an opportunity to vote Socialist Labor party. In 1894, the SLP fielded a full slate of candidates for local offices, though it did not garner many votes and never enjoyed as much influence in local politics as in the labor movement (as we shall see in a moment). By the end of the decade the People's party had vanished in a fit of suicidal fusion with the Democrats, McKinley was still the favorite of Lynn majorities, and the few hundred socialist votes were divided between the SLP and the Social Democracy. This new Socialist party consistently did better than its rival (even in 1900 when the SLP candidate for president was a Lynn native son), but it never duplicated the success of the Socialist organizations in the sister shoe towns of Haverhill and Brockton.[32]

For Massachusetts shoeworkers, socialism at the pools was largely a function of socialism in the Boot and Shoe Workers Union. The BSWU originated in 1895 when three separate unions in the industry amalgamated: the Knights of Labor National Trade Assembly 216; the Boot and Shoe Workers International Union, affiliated with the AFL; and the Lasters Protective Union, the tough old spine of trade unionism in Lynn, also AFL affiliated. Socialism permeated the new organization. Its president, James Tobin, was a member of the Socialist Labor party, its general secretary, Horace Eaton, held socialist opinions, and both AFL affiliates had gone on record in favor of the famous Plank 10 of the 1894 Political Program, which called for collective ownership of the means of production. The

BSWU wrote Plank 10 into its constitution by calling for "the collective ownership by the people of all means of production, distribution, communication and exchange."[33]

In cities where the BSWU was strong, it delivered the vote to socialist candidates, first to the SLP and increasingly after 1898 to the Social Democratic (Socialist) party. In Haverhill, where the BSWU and the Socialist party were headquartered in the same building, labor votes in successive elections sent ex-shoeworker James Carey to the city council, the mayor's office, and the state legislature. In Brockton, shoeworkers elected seven Socialist members of the BSWU to the city council in 1902. In Lynn, however, the BSWU floundered from the start, suffered a crippling schism in 1898 when the Lasters withdrew, rankled the city's labor movement by mobilizing scabs to break a strike of cutters in 1903, cheated socialist insurgents out of a legitimate victory for top leadership in 1906, and felt Lynn's revenge in 1909 when the city became a sanctuary for a rival union, the United Shoeworkers of America.[34] Thus around the turn of the century, just as socialists were registering significant electoral gains in the areas of BSWU strength, shoeworkers in Lynn were rejecting BSWU leadership in both politics and economics. With the city's labor movement splintered into hostile factions of BSWU stalwarts, BSWU insurgents, rebel Lasters, and a few Knights of Labor (not to mention the other trades and industries, notably the rising contingent of electrical workers at General Electric), the city's labor movement lacked the inner cohesion necessary to mobilize workers on behalf of a united socialist party. So instead, labor votes fell into the clutches of the two "capitalist" parties.

Socialist votes did not measure the extent of radical ideas among the city's workers, nor did disapproval of the BSWU mean opposition to socialism. In the first place, the national leadership of the BSWU adopted the conservative position of Sam Gompers; indeed, from 1895 to 1905 Tobin retraced Gompers' steps from socialism to anti-socialism. The dissident lasters were socialists who opposed this political regression, just as they opposed the drift toward more autocratic control of the BSWU by the central administration, and accordingly, Lynn shoeworkers organized several locals of the American Labor Union, a socialist rival to the AFL.[35] Second, radicalism

among shoeworkers was not confined to people who voted the socialist tickets, but extended to many nonvoting, militant direct-actionists
of the Wobbly type. Indeed, at least one body of Lynn shoeworkers
conducted discussions with Joseph Ettor of the Industrial Workers
of the World over the possibility of affiliation, and it would not be
long before the shoe industry would be nurturing anarchists like
Nicolla Sacco. Given the opportunity to cast a vote for a cohesive
socialist organization, most Lynn shoeworkers might have done as
their brothers did in other shoe towns, though more impetuous radicals would have refused to have anything to do with a party of
"Slow-cialists."

Politics as a Safety Valve

Political parties were ladders to success. Ever since the establishment of a party system in the days of Andrew Jackson, a man dis-
satisfied with the status of his present occupation could become a
professional politician, and if his talents were suited to the job, he
could spend the rest of his life in elective and appointive offices. If
anything in American life was open to an individual of industry and
ambition, it was party politics, a fact which made the composite
backgrounds of political leaders closer to a social cross section of the
population than the background of business leaders.

Lynn's political leaders were drawn from all major social groupings (save the most dispossessed), although at different periods the
center of gravity for recruitment rested at different points in the social
structure. Before 1878, scratching a politician was likely to uncover
a successful businessman who fashioned himself after such local
luminaries as George Hood, the first mayor, or Congressman John B.
Alley. After 1878, the scratch was more likely to reveal a man who
might best be described as an "ex-worker." [36] Commonly of working-
class origin, he might have become an ice dealer (essentially a team-
ster who owned a horse and wagon and hired an assistant), a superintendent in a factory (really a glorified foreman who was as much
a part of labor as of management), or a small businessman like a
grocer or sign painter (who were latter-day artisans or shopkeepers
far removed from the upper regions of industrial capital).

The progenitor of the ex-worker politician was George Sanderson. Son of a small-town clergyman, Sanderson migrated from the out-work regions of Maine to Lynn in time to join the Great Strike of 1860 and to help run the Crispin strikes of the next decade. Locked out of the shoe factories after 1872, he tried carpentry, helped organize a shoemaking cooperative that survived for three years, and finally took a job in a factory as a production supervisor. With no great occupational success to speak of, Sanderson turned to politics as his avenue of ambition, and after a decade in Labor Reform, city politics, and Greenbackism, he finally reached the mayor's office, where, at last, he could be satisfied he had worked his way back up to the level of prominence and esteem enjoyed by the minister's family in a small New England town.[37]

Sanderson set a pattern for his successors. Of the ten men who occupied the mayor's office from 1878 to 1894 (there is biographical information on nine), only one was a leading businessman, but six were ex-workers, men with strong labor backgrounds, who had become agents, salesmen, small businessmen, and the like. Of the others who had no working-class connections, one was a lawyer, the other a gardener.[38] Though there is less biographical data on members of the Common Council, the available information reveals a preponderance of workers and small businessmen, while the city's preeminent business leaders, the factory owners, hardly showed their faces. For example, the city council elected at the height of the Workingmen's movement contained one shoe manufacturer out of twenty-six councilors that can be identified; the remainder were divided almost equally between workers and small businessmen. Among the thirteen workers, six were labor aristocrats (cutters and foremen), and among the ten businessmen, the largest contingent (six) were grocers. The two remaining members were clerical.[39] The picture that emerges is a political leadership drawn from the social strata that formed where the middle class and the working class intersected. Just as the worker politicians came from occupational levels where they enjoyed enough income and security to enter the economic cycle of prosperity, so the businessmen were not far removed from the condition of the labor aristocrats.

The social origin of the leaders is consistent with the middle-class limits imposed on reform ideas that circulated in local political councils and reinforces the view of the Republican, Democratic, and Workingmen's parties as institutions of class integration, rather than as vehicles of class conflict. However, it should be stressed that the leaders' social situation did *not* determine their ideas and program, and was, in fact, consistent with other political views. The choice among different views was circumscribed by the social situation, but the choice was made by a particular sequence of historical events. The Marxian idea of society's material base determining its ideological superstructure can best be applied to the long sweep of events and should not be forced into such narrow confines as these.[40]

Local politics provided a convincing demonstration to wage earners that men from their ranks could rise to the highest position of honor in their community, and this experience tended to reinforce a belief in the legitimacy of the existing political system. Electoral victory was a crucial force in shaping working-class consciousness because it occurred when the Civil War effect was wearing off and when workers were showing disbelief in the concept of America as a land of opportunity. The idea that any individual could rise on the strength of his own talent and industry had long been worshipped by countless aspiring entrepreneurs, praised by endless numbers of rising landowners, glamorized by the '49ers rushing for gold, idealized in Abraham Lincoln, mythologized by Horatio Alger. No doubt, some wage earners were also entranced by the idea, and, in true Equal Rights fashion, condemned monopoly in land and finance as the chief enemy of opportunity for all. However, in the mind of most wage earners as the Industrial Revolution ground on, the lengthening shadows of monopoly loomed larger than the sun of golden opportunity.

Among New England shoeworkers the belief in individual opportunity was virtually eclipsed by the factory system. They demonstrated their rejection of individualist notions of success by organizing the Knights of St. Crispin, the Lasters' Protective Union, and the Knights of Labor to *fight collectively for improvements in their condition as wage earners*. The very existence of such unions—mass-based organizations that enrolled a majority in their trades—testified to the widespread belief that individual effort was futile, and the militancy of these unions testified to the belief that collective action of all wage earners was the only way things would get better for each one.

The overriding objective was a living wage, and although some expected to turn their wages into a "competence," they knew that a house to live in and money for old age were not means of production but means of subsistence. They saw the factory system squatting squarely across the path to ownership of the means of production. Shoeworkers told the Massachusetts Bureau of the Statistics of Labor that the high cost of plant and machinery made it more difficult than it once was for a manual worker to become a manufacturer. Not only did it take larger capital resources to become an owner, but a smaller proportion of factory workers possessed even minimal resources: 15 percent of male factory workers in 1870 held $500 or more, compared to 25 percent of male shoemakers in 1860.[41] Even though some workers improved their standing by getting into better paying nonmanual occupations (including the ex-worker mayors), and even though some improved their condition by scrimping and saving, the overwhelming number of shoeworkers knew they could not count on paths of individual mobility to reach prosperity or higher status. They were not expectant capitalists, would-be entrepreneurs, or future frontier farmers, but self-conscious wage earners. Most did not expect to rise *above* their class, but to rise *with* it (in a general improvement of the condition of labor) or to rise *within* it (by moving up to better paying factory jobs and by putting aside small savings).

The relation between social mobility and working-class consciousness has been the subject of considerable study ever since Frederick Jackson Turner proposed the agrarian frontier as a safety valve for industrial discontent. Though Turner's original claim has not withstood subsequent attacks and revisions (see Chapter 2), the idea of mobility as an outlet for discontent retains a powerful voice in recent interpretations, notably the influential study of *Social Mobility in Industrial Society* by S. M. Lipset and R. Bendix. The authors argue that a widespread belief in America as a land of opportunity helped to sustain "the acceptance of the social and political order by the lower classes." They dub this belief "ideological equalitarianism" and identify it as a special expression of American political culture, not a direct expression of the actual rate of mobility. They assert that Europe and America have similar rates of mobility from nonmanual to manual occupations, but European workers reject ideological equalitarianism, while American workers accept it.[42] Is their assertion valid? Certainly not as far as American shoemakers are concerned. Having rejected ideological equalitarianism after a few years in the factories, shoeworkers could not very well use it to bolster their faith in the existing social and political order. Since these were not European workers (only a small minority were immigrants), this sociological assertion will have to find supporting historical evidence somewhere else.

Another influential exploration of mobility as a safety valve is Stephan Thernstrom's *Poverty and Progress.* The book appeared at the frontiers of scholarship a decade ago as a pioneering application of quantitative methods to the study of mobility in the urban working class. It took Lipset and Bendix to task for probing only in the area of occupational mobility, and it used census manuscripts and savings deposit records to forge ahead into the area of property ownership. It reached the conclusion that few of the Irish laborers of Newburyport, Massachusetts, were able to rise outside the ranks of manual labor but that many were able to move up within the ranks by taking skilled jobs and acquiring a small nest egg. In sum, Thernstrom concluded there was an inner frontier of mobility within the working class.[43]

Founded on sophisticated questioning and creative methodology, the conclusion was still a revision, not a rejection, of the old-fashioned, land-of-opportunity view of America. The conclusion certainly had some merit (the data, after all, showed that even the most impoverished workers in one industrial city could find a path to material possessions), but it was fragile because the group was so small and may have been biased toward the more successful individuals. Moreover, the crucial question arises of what workers themselves thought about their experience: did their little bits and pieces of success convince them that the existing social and political order was worthy of their allegiance? Unfortunately, the Irish laborers of Newburyport offered virtually no evidence on this question— no labor press, no independent political action, no records of trade union debates. Thus Thernstrom considerably overstepped the bounds of evidence when he answered yes to the question and argued that this group of Irish workers joined a Lockean consensus of Anglo-American values and accepted Horatio Alger as "a primary symbol of the American political tradition." [44] This opinion is composed of one part pure speculation, one part consensus historiography, and no part of the actual ideas of Newburyport's laborers. It reveals the dangers in trying to speak on behalf of "the inarticulate."

In nearby Lynn, articulate, activist Irish shoe and leather workers joined Yankees in flatly rejecting the myth of success. Irish and Yankee workers jointly wrote a long history of trade unionism, contributed to the militancy of the Crispins, supported the reform ideas of the Knights of Labor, looked for labor candidates when they went to the polls, and resisted strikebreaking by local police.

Every mass action, every collective expression of opinion identifies Horatio Alger as an outcast in the minds of Lynn workers. They put their hopes for material improvement elsewhere, and instead of rising clerks and successful businessmen, they adopted aspiring politicians like U. S. Grant, Ben Butler, and the ex-worker mayors of their city as their positive symbols of the American political tradition. As long as labor could run friends like Sanderson against enemies like Bubier and win, as long as the party system provided rewards to workers in the form of career opportunities and patronage jobs, as long as it offered some tangible benefits to working-class voters like the removal of an antilabor police chief, the political system was not likely to appear to most wage earners as the instrument of an oppressive ruling class. Electoral politics, not faith in occupational success or property ownership, was the main safety valve of working-class discontent.

CONCLUSION
EQUAL RIGHTS AND BEYOND

Taking a suggestion from the definition of fire as a rapid oxidation, the Industrial Revolution can be succinctly defined as rapid capital accumulation. Just as oxidation precedes fire, the process of capitalist accumulation precedes industrialization. Long before the first railroads and factories were built, entrepreneurs who valued gain for its own sake and approached the world through a rationalist frame of mind were accustomed to pursue private profits in a worldwide marketplace. Their daily dealings in the affairs of trade produced a distinctive style of behavior, which we might glimpse by making an imaginary visit to a place where the denizens of the marketplace gathered together. Bypassing wharves, warehouses, and counting houses, we choose for our visit a community tavern located in any North American seaboard city sometime after the middle of the eighteenth century.

As we step from the glare of the afternoon sun into the main room of the tavern, it seems as if we have descended below decks into the timbered darkness of a merchant vessel. We have a brief moment to adjust to the dim yellow light of dripping candles suffused through a grey tinge of pipe smoke before a crew of men from a nearby countinghouse tumble through the door behind us seeking some refreshment away from the tally sheets of the day's receipts and disbursements. While they quaff a dram of rum or sip East India tea sweetened with West India sugar, we overhear them chortling about the news of some adversary's reversal, joking about their own trivial embarrassments, and talking about the prospects for trade in tropical commodities like molasses, tobacco, and slaves. One of the men mentions his need for capital to undertake a venture in this area—he wishes to outfit an African slaver—and it is not long before he has found his credit within these close circles of business friendship. A bargain is struck, hands are clasped, smiles spread across jovial faces, and a packet of snuff is passed around to seal the bargain. But one man's loan is another man's debt, and what if, on the day the note falls due, the borrower cannot come up with the money? Will the lender demand his pound of flesh? And is the thin brown stream of tobacco juice that slips from the corner of one man's mouth a sign to us of a bourgeois gentleman drooling over profits?

If wishes were horses, then the capitalist economy of eighteenth-century America would have ridden a steep, upward curve of economic growth. But the Yankee desire for gain depicted in this tavern scene was held in check by economic underdevelopment, so that the drooling gentleman could not expect to obtain all that he wanted. Unless he was an unusually wealthy entrepreneur with ties to one of the great commercial houses of Europe and perhaps connections to the landed aristocracy, his ambition was closely bounded by pre-industrial technological limits on productivity, which ensured that new accumulations of wealth would be slow and modest. The process of accumulation was especially hampered in North America because its Indian inhabitants had built up nothing comparable to the treasures of Central and South America for the European settlers to plunder. Compelled to start over from scratch, the whites were avaricious enough to traffic in human flesh or to wink at the traffic, and the profits of slave labor built up many substantial estates. But taking their cumulative weight, the accumulations of wealth in British North America were puny compared to the princely fortunes of the Old World.[1]

As a consequence, class relations outside the regions of plantation slavery were characterized by a blurring of the distinctions between ruler and ruled. This has often been attributed to relatively widespread land ownership in rural areas and the existence of a large class of petty proprietors, but perhaps more important was the fact that even when someone acquired vast tracts of land, he did not automatically obtain lordly control over substantial capital resources or large bodies of dependent cultivators. Because of the scarcities of capital and labor, his great landholdings did not generate great wealth. Unlike the plantation economy of the South (where greed, climate, and cash crops had combined to produce the distinctive castes and classes of a slave society),[2] commercial and family farming regions of the middle and northern states were poised between the inequalities of the aristocratic past and the inequalities of the capitalistic future.

These observations provide a brief overview of the context in which the United States embarked on the Industrial Revolution and in which our case study of that process begins. There was nothing in the late eighteenth-century town of Lynn or in its contacts with other American communities to compare with the range of inequality or the ravages of class conflicts coursing through revolutionary Europe. True, in the 1770s Lynn residents had loosed their wrath against the legal, political, and military agents of the English upper classes, but the American Revolution left a weak legacy of internal class conflict. Within Lynn itself, artisans (including the special artisan group of shoemakers), petty shopkeepers, and farmers coexisted in a round of mutually dependent economic exchanges—shoes went for cloth, cloth for flour, flour for shoes. Even the relations between Lynn and Boston (where one or two fashionable homes displayed more servants, silks, and porcelains than could be found in all of Lynn) did not reveal marked features of inequality. The Boston merchants who cargoed Lynn shoes did not exploit the labor of Lynn farmer shoemakers the way English merchant-capitalists exploited rural weavers under the putting-out system.

This is not to say that eighteenth-century Lynn existed within a classless or a "one-class" society,[3] but class influences were mitigated by the limits on wealth alluded to above and by the fact that the household basis of production in both agriculture and industry tended to prevent solidarities from developing among people of similar condition. If some social and religious disputes had overtones of conflict between different types of property, nonetheless, the single most important event—the one that aroused the community to violence against British domination—brought different social interests in the community together. Moreover, the village completed the transfer from farming to manufacturing without displacing the household as the fulcrum of the community's social balance.

Industrial capitalism released the energy that upset that balance.

Beginning slowly, almost imperceptibly, after the War of 1812 and growing in intensity during the 1830s, changes in the shoe industry transformed Lynn from a small artisan village into a bustling manufacturing town that bristled with social discontent. Once, the basic production decisions had been made by master artisans who owned means of production and labored at the bench. Now, decisions were made increasingly by manufacturers who performed no labor at all and whose control derived exclusively from ownership of property, raw materials, and finished products. Once, ordinary journeymen and binders worked under the tutelage of a master and were often dependents in the master's household. Now ordinary shoemakers were on their own, free to sell their labor to the highest bidder. Once, Lynn's shoe industry had been contained within the borders of the community. Now, manufacturers hired shoemakers hither and yon in a search for cheap labor designed to ensure that the wage bargain would not be struck on the seller's terms. Once, informal credit and accounting methods characterized the industry. Now, it was double entry bookkeeping, careful calculations of wage costs, and scrupulous attention to the terms of a loan. The sum total of these changes was a division of the community into two separate groups of people, one of which hired the labor of the other in order to reap a vastly greater gain for itself.

The rise of industrial capitalism was predicated on the development of institutions through which owners wielded power over production. The most important was the central shop. Larger than an old artisan ten-footer and smaller than a factory, the central shop was the manufacturer's command post, serving as a warehouse for raw materials, a workshop for leather cutters, a distribution center for the domestic system (most shoeworkers still worked at home), and a countinghouse. From his position overlooking the routes of trade, the manufacturer directed the flow of people and products to and from the marketplace. He was fortified by capital resources drawn from a local bank chartered in 1814, which gave him sufficient liquid capital to advance wages to more than 100 permanent employees, thereby undermining the status of journeymen and binders and eliminating the master altogether. And since the manufacturer was now able to hire so many people to make so many shoes, he was also able to accumulate wealth in sums that would have been impossible half a century before. The influence of the old restraint was waning fast. The old equalities were being pushed aside. The eighteenth-century balance was tipping to one side.

Yet the triumph of industrial capital was not complete. As long as binders and journeymen were able to hold their position in the household, labor still exercised a certain independent authority in the process of production and was able to withstand some of the pressures exerted by capital. The manufacturer could rant and rave when a binder did not make a shoe exactly to specifications and when the journeyman did not bring in the finished product on time, but there was little the owner could do to bring his employees to heel, especially in periods of expansion when he scrambled to hire all the additional people he could get. Thus beleagured defenders of thousands of little household forts were able to fend off the attacks on the status of the producing classes until the eve of the Civil War. Though they suffered great losses, they were not overrun.

Not until the factories. The factory system gave the manufacturers a weapon far more potent than the central shop for organizing production to suit their interests. The new system proved itself superior to the old by tripling the productivity of labor in the industry between 1860 and 1870, a compelling economic advantage which finally overwhelmed the old order. Faceless economic forces rounded up the household producers by the hundreds and herded them into the factories to take their places in the whirring world of belts and gears, sewing machines and steam engines.

With the triumph of capital in the economy, the owning class sought to extend its sway beyond industry into politics. The political ascendancy of industrial capitalism in Lynn coincided with its ascendancy in the nation at large during the Civil War.[4] While the Union armies restored the southern states bit by bit to the national market and Republican politicians enacted the economic legislation demanded by industrial investors, the shoe manufacturers of Lynn took the opportunity to transform the town of Lynn into a city that operated in accordance with the factory principles of efficiency and discipline. Capitalizing on the wartime popularity of the new Republican party, Republican manufacturers who had established the party in Lynn won control of city government and then embarked on a program of thoroughgoing reform. They modernized the city's water system and created a professional, steam-powered fire department to protect their new investments against fire. Following the military model of rigid discipline, they reformed the police department to protect their properties against theft and their streets from disorder. They extended their leadership into the realm of culture by building an ornate city hall to symbolize their prosperity. Never before had so many significant changes been carried out so swiftly by a single group in the community. Thus by the depression of the 1870s, with labor stripped of all property shares in the means of production, with the factories piling up unprecedented accumulations of capital, with slavery defeated, and with the owners of capital grasping the reins of political power, the revolutionary epoch of industrialization drew to a close.

The focus thus far has been on the class that triumphed with industrialization. But in the same period another class originated and rose alongside the first. The two classes encountered one another in the marketplace as buyers and sellers of labor, though the bargain they struck was decidedly in favor of the buyers. In the early stages of industrialization, this favoritism was reflected in a simple equation: one's gain was the other's loss. Even later on when the laborers' impoverishment had ceased to be the precondition for the industrialists' enrichment, the gains of the former were always overwhelmed by the far greater gains of the latter. Given this unequal condition, wage earners have always sought to improve their terms, and in certain circumstances they have sought to change the system that made the bargain unequal in the first place.

The shoemakers of Lynn normally stood at the forefront of such efforts. Their resistance to business domination was more persistent and pervasive, their control over community folkways more effective, and their militancy more notorious than workers in several other nearby New England communities that have received intensive study.[5] This is not to say that Lynn workers were exceptional in offering resistance; one need only point to other communities where labor's impact was as strong as in Lynn, including several mining and manufacturing communities in the industrial belt from New Jersey to the Great Lakes that have also received intensive study.[6] Rather, to cite the special intensity of Lynn's labor movement is to ask what were the conditions that enabled its working population to keep the pot boiling, while conditions in certain other places kept it only lukewarm?

We will begin with the specific circumstances of Lynn's history and proceed to some general conclusions about the causes of mass opposition to industrial capitalism in the nineteenth century. It is said that history does not repeat itself, but the history of Lynn between 1860 and 1890 contradicts that axiom, because a certain sequence of events that occurred first in 1860 recurred with uncanny similarity in 1878 and again in 1890, giving the researcher reading the local newspapers a strong feeling of déjà vu. Each time there were three steps in the sequence: (1) a strike occurred, (2) bringing out the police, (3) causing the strikers to mount a political campaign to unseat the incumbent officials and dismiss the police chief. Each strike was of major proportions, and every time the police tried to break the strike their intervention caused such widespread outrage that it became the sole issue in the ensuing local elections and resulted in the firing of all three city marshals. There was almost a fourth recurrence of the same sequence in 1885 when a strike again raised the issue of police intervention, but this time a Workingmen's party controlled city government and the marshal had been nominated to his post by the city's largest labor organization, so there was no intervention and no subsequent campaign for political vengeance.

What does this striking pattern tell us about labor history? It points to the presence of a strong popular tradition of resistance to authority and defense of the Liberty Tree. The tradition provided both the emotional inspiration and the organizational tools people needed to mobilize against an infringement of their liberties, in this case, their rights to join a labor organization, to withhold their labor power, and to obtain an equal voice in setting wages, hours, and working conditions. The strength of the tradition is indicated by the fact that it survived defeat. Each of these strikes resulted in a setback to the local labor movement, for which the firing of the city marshal was only partial compensation, yet the memory of struggle outlived the experience of defeat. Thus, to reverse Santayana's famous dictum, those who know their own history are fortunate enough to be able to repeat it.

The tradition of resistance to established authority encompassed a wide range of groups including feminists, abolitionists, come-outers, communitarians, and frontiersmen, but it exercised its greatest impact in Lynn's history through labor's version of the tradition, that is, the philosophy and practice of Equal Rights. Again it is worthwhile to consider some special aspects of local history. Beginning in the 1830s, shoemakers expressed distrust of the large central shop owners, whom they regarded as a clique of would-be overlords. To reassert their equal status in the community as freeborn household producers subject to no master, shoemakers organized the first labor societies and proposed the first strike in the community's history. The next decade produced another journeymen's society and the *Awl,* the first labor newspaper. The 1850s saw another society, another newspaper, and in 1860 the first actual strike. Though the strike centered in Lynn, it also involved thousands of men and women in dozens of other communities and was by all accounts the largest single episode of labor protest in American history before the Civil War.

It occurred during the conversion to factory methods—that is, after binding was mechanized but before full-scale factories had been set up to manufacture the whole shoe. For this reason it was a crucial pivot for Equal Rights, enabling the tradition to pass easily from artisans to industrial workers. The consequence was the Knights of St. Crispin and its counterpart among women, The Daughters of St. Crispin. Both were militant, factory-based, industrial unions. Equal Rights culminated in the 1880s, when the majority of the city's labor force enrolled either in the Lasters' Protective Union or in one of the more than thirty assemblies affiliated with the Knights of Labor. The majority of labor voters supported a Workingmen's party in its frequent successes at the polls and combined with voters in other communities to elect a friend of labor to Congress. Through picnics, fairs, and entertainments, the labor movement captured the leisure-time interests of thousands of residents, and in the *Knight of Labor* it reincarnated the Equal Rights philosophy of the *Awl* for hundreds of readers. Whereas the labor movement did not interfere with fundamental rights of property ownership, it had some success in reining in the urge of business toward authoritarian control. Therefore, in assessing the character of the Gilded Age, while recognition must be paid to the supremacy of business in the political economy of the nation at large, facile generalizations about the popular acceptance of business leadership at all levels of life and notions of America as a middle-class society do not square with examples like Lynn, or with other centers of Crispin activity, or with other industrial communities from coast to coast where labor maintained a similarly extensive influence.

Apart from confirming an interpretation of this period put forth most persuasively by Herbert Gutman, what general conclusions can be drawn from the vitality of the Equal Rights tradition in Lynn?[7] Without attempting to propose a set of laws to explain labor activism, the following propositions offer some insight into the subject. First, the labor movement in the city was a community affair, not simply the private concern of men clustered together in separate occupational groups. This was partly the result of the fact that Lynn was a one-industry town, but more important was the fact that both sexes worked in the industry. Wives and daughters did not wonder in confusion or resentment why their husbands and sons complained about the boss—they had the same complaints themselves. Family members talked to each other about the same subjects in the same language, and the whole family went into a strike together. In the street theater of a strike, young children watched as most of the adults from both sexes they looked to as role models paraded by in protest against industrial oppression.

Second, the militancy of the factory worker is hard to imagine without the legacy of artisan protest against the encroachments of capital into the sphere of production. The importance of the artisan influence is confirmed by comparing New England's two major industries, shoes and textiles. The latter lacked a mass organization comparable to the shoeworker unions, its strikes were not as well fought, and its communities displayed far less of the political, and cultural influences described above. To account for these facts, some interpreters have pointed to the high proportion of women operatives, whose "docility" was supposed to have made them averse to protest, or to the increasing proportion of Irish, whose poverty and religious conservatism resulted in the same thing. However, these explanations will not stand up under comparative analysis with the shoe industry, where women of the same Yankee farm background as the textile operatives engaged in protest, and where Irish workers presumably of the same background were more heavily represented in the union than in the labor force. With these sexual and ethnic factors out of the way, a sharp contrast appears in the fact that the textile industry in New England began at the factory stage, having gone through no prior development under a domestic system. Consequently, labor had no opportunity to establish its household independence, to create prefactory customs in the work process, or to develop the means to resist industrial capitalism as an encroachment on established patterns of work and life. The presence of all these conditions in the shoe industry appears to make the difference between an aggressive and a defensive labor movement.

A third conclusion points to the origins of the shoemakers' commitment to equality in the republican community of the late eighteenth century well before the impact of industrial capitalism. When a laboring man achieved the rank of householder (that is, became a married adult with property, entitled to obedience from wives, children, and other dependents), he took up a position in the functional life of the community, which was bounded, it may be recalled, by relatively moderate distinctions between the poorest and the wealthiest householder. Since a large portion of the early labor force in shoe manufacturing was recruited from these eighteenth-century householders, the values of a republican social order were built into the shoe industry from its very beginnings. When the rise of the central shop stretched the boundaries of wealth and created a new distinction between householders who labored and those who owned property but did not labor, these values were threatened, and their reassertion in the 1830s launched the tradition of Equal Rights.

The sustained expression of mass opposition to industrial capitalism that we have seen in Lynn poses another problem in interpretation: what prevented the discontent of the dispossessed from assuming the shape of a revolution against bourgeois society? As all but the most blindly optimistic could see, the new social order generated intense pressures among the have-nots for an improvement in their condition. Anxious conservatives compared this pressure to the force of compressed steam and warned that social controls comparable to the iron restraints of boiler and cylinder were necessary to keep the wheels of society turning smoothly. Surely pressures as great as these required some outlet, some safety valve to let off the steam should the levels of discontent become dangerously high.

Countless popular philosophers found the safety valve in the western frontier, a discovery formally patented by Frederick Jackson Turner. Nowadays, Turner's original patent is outmoded because it does not fit the facts, but in several revised versions (for example, open land made Americans a "people of plenty," labor scarcity relative to land made for high wages in industry) it is still pending. In one recent version, propounded most effectively by Stephan Thernstrom, the opportunities for wage earners to acquire property and raise their occupational level constituted the safety valve, and, in more general terms, mobility was the inner frontier of industrial society.[8]

We might evaluate this mobility/frontier thesis by taking different types of mobility in turn—geographical, occupational, and property. Concerning *geographical* mobility, it has been argued that high turnover among a community's working population significantly impedes class organization and consciousness because it interferes with the necessarily lengthy process of developing bonds of solidarity among friends and neighbors.[9] There is much to be said for the point that trust is difficult to develop within a group when its members are changing constantly, but this should not be carried too far. A high overall rate of population turnover is consistent with the long-term persistence in the community of a stable core of wage earners around whom floaters and other migrants coalesce. Such was the case in Lynn, where a high turnover (on the order of half the male shoemakers disappeared within ten years)[10] masked the existence of a virtually permanent minority who played the key role in organizing discontent. Moreover, mobility promotes a social, as opposed to a personal, view of one's situation because it exposes a person to others whose sufferings are like his own. It may, therefore, foster an awareness of common class interests. Movement from job to job, town to town, boss to boss may confirm the view that all bosses are fundamentally alike and that there must be some nefarious system behind the scenes that makes the same evil creature reappear in so many different places. In these terms, geographical mobility figures prom-

inently in the biographies of class conscious American workers, epitomized by the Wobblies, who learned through experience on the tramp
in different industries in different towns that the employer was not an
individual but a class enemy.[11]

Turning to the subject of *property* mobility, there is no more ven-
erable cliché about the United States than the notion that it offers its
lower classes a chance to get rich. It is but a short step to the conclusion that the worker who acquires wealth is not likely to turn
against the system that has rewarded him and that others who see his
example will be inclined to blame themselves, rather than the social
order, if they do not get ahead. Another safety valve. The success of
this argument depends on the convincing demonstration of two
things: first, it must be shown that it is possible for significant numbers of the poor to find their way to at least some wealth, if not to become rich; and second, that the combination of the actual rates of
improvement with the perceptions of those rates by the poor resulted
in a feeling that the improvement which took place was enough. Without the first point, the second cannot be shown. Without the second
point, the first is meaningless, as far as the safety valve hypothesis is
concerned.

The closest thing to an inventory of individual wealth in the nineteenth century is the record of real and personal property ownership
contained in the census manuscripts of the middle decades of the century. After the pioneering application of these records to the frontier
thesis by Merle Curti, they have since been used in urban and working-class studies.[12] Because the local census contained a built-in
bias toward the more stable members of the community, who tended
to be more favored in terms of property ownership, and because an
acquisition may have meant an individual finally acceded to the wealth
of the older generation and did not actually rise on his own, conclusions from these records must be drawn with care. Nonetheless, it is
apparent that the paths to property were by no means closed to the
poor, including low-wage, common laborers and factory operatives.
Certainly, the evidence from Lynn demonstrates that some factory
workers were able to acquire a competence (defined as a nest egg or
a piece of real estate worth at least $500, a little more than the an-
nual income of a male shoemaker).

Yet even if the factories did not foreclose all opportunities, they ensured that the improvement registered by some would be swamped by the much greater increase in the number without property. And since many of these propertyless workers came to Lynn from the family farms of rural New England, they may very well have lost access to family property in the course of their migration. The result in the equation of property mobility was a net loss, a fact which impelled workers to protest against their degraded condition. The form and intensity of their protest were shaped by the Equal Rights tradition, including the shoeworkers' rather high estimation of their own dignity and worth, which produced the conviction that the gains of the few were insufficient for the mass and inspired the exaggerated claim that the factories made it impossible for a worker to buy a home or set aside savings. For the Yankee in the shoe trade the feeling of being proletarianized was an accurate mirror of economic reality, and so it might seem that the critical factor in shaping their beliefs was the actual rate itself. Yet cultural factors were equally critical. Witness the example of the Irish shoemakers, a group who had very likely improved their condition after the flight from famine-ridden Ireland, but who also concluded that their gains were not enough and became active trade unionists.

The mobility/frontier argument concerning *occupational* mobility holds that a man who raises his status or gains some freedom from the dictates of a boss by changing jobs is a man who is not likely to feel trapped on the bottom of society; moreover, those who do feel trapped will envy the man on the move, seek to emulate his success, and, if they fail, blame themselves. Frustration and discontent will be diminished, and, where these feelings exist, they will not find expression in collective protest. As in the case of property mobility, a successful statement of the argument must demonstrate both the existence of actual opportunity for individuals to rise and the acceptance of the actual opportunities as sufficient, thereby making collective protest unwarranted. For the study of occupational mobility, the census manuscripts, supplemented by city directories have proved to be indispensable in performing mass career-line analysis.

The resulting picture is a contrast between considerable movement and considerably less success. Concerning movement, the swift circulation of individuals among different occupations is easily explained as an economic premise of industrial capitalism. In the rational cost calculations of the marketplace, individuals become interchangeable parts, so that one is let go when he is no longer needed and when demand resumes, another is hired to replace him. In the meantime, the first must find another job, often in a different occupation. But for the purposes of testing the safety valve hypothesis, the only really important movement is up and down the occupational hierarchy. "Up" has usually been defined as a white-collar or nonmanual job, "down" as blue-collar or manual, and the chief concern of researchers has been the extent to which manual workers could move "up" to nonmanual jobs. (For a critique of the normative implications of this terminology, see Chapter 6.)

Statistical studies have repeatedly found that significant numbers of nonmanual workers and their sons moved up, and although some of these moved back down, the number was not as great.[13] The evidence from Lynn confirms this finding, although like other community studies, it is based on the careers of men who stayed in one place for long periods of time and may be biased toward those who were in a more favored position. Among an entire group of shoeworkers who spent twenty years in the city, a minority never left their original occupation. Among the majority who changed occupations, far more moved up than down or across, and a substantial minority (though less than 20 percent) moved up to stay. The fact that one of every two or three shoemaker families could point to someone in the family who had become a petty manufacturer, a small shopkeeper, or a clerk was proof enough that upward mobility was a widespread and clearly evident feature of working-class experience.

But that does not prove that most workers relied on individual mobility to get ahead. On the contrary, the overwhelming evidence from Lynn is that the city's industrial workers looked mainly to collective action to improve their condition. Despite the fact that some workers were gaining status and income by moving into nonmanual occupations and some others who remained workers were able to acquire a competence, most wage earners sought to rise with their class. That is clearly demonstrated by the strength of the labor movement from the Knights of St. Crispin through the Knights of Labor to the

United Shoeworkers of America. Indeed, the mobility/frontier thesis
can be turned upside down to argue that the gains made by some individuals only whetted the appetite of those left behind for more.
Since they remained wage earners, their rising expectations could only
be satisfied by an improvement in their condition as workers. Given
the existence of a marketplace in which they sold their labor, the logical recourse was to do exactly what they did—combine among themselves to sell their labor collectively under terms that were more
favorable than any single worker could have won by himself. Clearly,
the safety valve was not doing what it was supposed to; it was not
siphoning off discontent or preventing collective protest.

A final word might be added about the overall linkage between
social fluidity and class consciousness. There is, no doubt, something
to be said for the idea that fluidity between classes tends to drain
away group consciousness. When an ordinary worker made a success
of a small business or took a job in management, he left behind a
host of friends, brothers, nieces, and cousins who could look upon his
example and reflect that the world was not divided into two species
of human beings who had nothing in common. But this view could not
become a popular article of faith until it had passed through cultural,
ideological, and political mechanisms whose cumulative effect could
either thwart or reinforce the original tendency. In the United States
the effect was to reinforce it. The network of interclass exchange and
communication created by social fluidity became the social base for
the two major and most of the minor political parties in the nineteenth
century, including those that styled themselves "workingmen's." The
parties' appeals to the "little guy" or the "ordinary American" encompassed both wage earners and small employers and eschewed a
class appeal to the working class alone. Thus there was a certain
correspondence between the message of the political parties that
America was a classless society and the social experience of interclass
fluidity: this much can be granted.

But what has *not* been granted is just as important. Social fluidity
does not exercise the determining role in shaping political ideas and
certainly does not preclude the development of class consciousness.
High levels of interclass mobility accompanied the Industrial Revolution wherever it took place, yet in certain European countries, no-

tably France and Germany, a pronounced class consciousness developed among wage earners. In other words, the friends and relatives left behind by the mobile individual regarded themselves as the decisive group in society and regarded the departed one as an outsider, either a traitor to his class or an ally, but not one of them. The argument has been made that levels of mobility in America were sufficiently higher than those in Europe to account for the difference in consciousness, but in the face of opposing contentions, the point is not yet convincing.[14] All in all, the mobility/frontier thesis, while offering a vital perspective on social experience, appears to be of secondary importance in explaining working-class action and belief, particularly on the subject of class consciousness.

What, then is primary?

Reducing an answer to the minimum essentials, the establishment of political democracy in the early stages of America's Industrial Revolution gave wage earners a vested interest in the existing political system before they felt the worst effects of industrial capitalism.

This answer is a deliberate simplification designed to place certain fundamental points on the agenda for discussion, not to offer a magic formula for resolving them. We might begin with the subject of industrial capitalism. Since inequality, exploitation, and social conflict are inherent in the economics of industrial capitalism, it might be tempting to conclude that some automatic reflex in the mind of the industrial worker produces an awareness of the class causes of these experiences. Such an explanation, however, is unsatisfactory, for it ignores the fact that substantial numbers of real working people have rejected class analysis. Taking this reality into account, a revised version of the argument describes workers who do not think in class terms as suffering from "false consciousness." This stopgap revision allows one to preserve the original economic interpretation, but in writing off the dominant mentality of the American labor movement as "false," it is not likely to take us very far in understanding the historical roots of that mentality, so it, too, is unsatisfactory.

A more tenable position is one which accords economic processes an important, but not an all-important, role in the formation of consciousness. The nineteenth-century capitalist marketplace and the industrial workplace were two primary schools of hard knocks which gave workers basic cultural instructions in ideas, values, and beliefs. By the examples of employer intransigence and bullet bargaining they were taught the tactics of bare-knuckled direct action that appear in the hard-fought strikes and episodes of labor's violent revenge that are so frequent in American history. Such experiences were traumatic reminders of the basic issues at stake and defined the lower limits of the worker's social awareness. Because of these limits, any set of ideas based on an assumption that power, opportunity, and rights are equally distributed has been rejected out of hand as pure nonsense.

However, American wage earners can hardly be described as committed doctrinaires of class struggle. Taking tough-as-nails stands on economic battlefields is not the same thing as radical class consciousness. Consequently, it is necessary to probe elsewhere to discover why economic militancy did not broaden out to become widespread political radicalism despite pressures in that direction. Moving to the point on the agenda that deals with political democracy, it is advisable at the outset to clear away some possible misconceptions. First, I am using the term "democracy" to connote "popular democracy," as opposed to "property democracy" which is best termed "republicanism." Second, suggesting that political democracy existed by the end of Jackson's presidency, I do not mean to imply that democracy characterized economic or social relations, nor that political decisions were actually made by consent of the governed. One need only add up the numbers the population excluded by reasons of sex and race to reach the quick conclusion that democracy was still the province of privileged minority. Yet the fact remains that the principles of popular sovereignty, equality before the law, basic civil rights, manhood suffrage, and popular participation were firmly established.

Originating in the bourgeois milieu of the eighteenth century, political democracy came into its own in the United States during the transition from the commercial to the industrial phase of capitalism. From the first murmurings of democratic sentiments during the American Revolution to the bellows of vox populi during the Jacksonian period, the demands for democracy usually arose among small property owners—farmers, artisans, and shopkeepers. Elements from this class of petty capitalists joined with elements among the slavemasters and certain of the commercial gentry in a revolutionary movement to defeat monarchy and aristocracy and banish these enemies of the republican government from the new nation. Freed from the constraints of the feudal past, republicanism grew into democracy well within the lifetime of a person born during the Revolution.

While these political changes were taking place, the economic leadership of agriculture and commerce was being challenged by industry, and in 1820s and 1830s an industrial working class was just beginning to emerge. This coincidence in the timing of events had profound consequences for the development of class consciousness. By the end of the 1830s the basic democratic objectives that might have been raised later on as class demands of industrial workers had already been won through the agitation of petty property owners. Thus in its formative years the American working class could identify with the achievements of bourgeois political economy and could claim the Declaration of Independence and the Bill of Rights as its own heritage.

The contrast with the timing of events in the Old World helps to emphasize this point. The modern European working class emerged when republicanism—let alone democracy—was still a thing of the future. In fighting simultaneous battles for political emancipation and economic improvement, they concluded that the state was an instrument of their oppression controlled by hostile social and economic interest. Thus the seed of a widespread class consciousness was planted early in the history of Europe's Industrial Revolution, and as it grew to maturity along with the industrial working class, it was well watered by the remembrance of bloody class conflicts during the epoch of the French Revolution.

Yet it would be a mistake to conclude on the basis of this comparison that American wage earners were conservative defenders of the status quo. The confrontation between their democratic sensibilities and the new inequalities of employer and employee produced a critique of American society that called for the elimination of the baneful influences of slavery and monopoly. Blending with the ideas of agrarian and utopian reform for a thorough restructuring of society, this critique of the threats to liberty in the land of liberty, while not expressed in class terms, represented the radical potential of democratic ideas. One can imagine a sequence of events in which the radical beliefs of wage earners in the 1830s and 1840s encountered the intensifying ravages of industrial capitalism in a series of increasingly abrasive and brutal contacts and were finally transformed into the conviction that workers must win control of the state, through violence if necessary, and confiscate the property that was the source of their employers' power. The fact that tens of thousands of people had actually gone through this development by the end of the century suggests that the sequence is not wholly imaginary.

But equally revealing is the fact that most wage earners did not travel this road. In assessing the reasons for this, it is difficult to avoid the conclusion that an entire generation was sidetracked in the 1860s because of the Civil War. Northern wage earners who rallied to the Union cause—the overwhelming number did—played out a version of the events described above, except that their class enemy was the southern slavemaster, while their employers became their allies in a violent movement to confiscate the property in slaves which was the vital source of the slavemaster's power. This traumatic experience gave the young industrial working class its memorable vision of class struggle. Wage earners perceived the slave power as an expanding economic interest with aggressive political designs whose treasonous secession was made doubly obnoxious by its alien imitations of aristocratic culture. They feared that this monstrous influence had taken over the federal government by winning control of the presidency directly through Democratic doughfaces, by dominating the Supreme Court through Chief Justice Taney and his decision on Dred Scott, and by manipulating Congress through the sort of wire pulling that passed the Kansas-Nebraska Act. Thus the pivotal political event of the nineteenth century and the greatest influence in popular culture for several generations to come ended with the worker convinced that the chief enemy of liberty had been vanquished by those who believed in free soil and free labor.

Once again, timing was crucial. The 1860s were the turning point of the Industrial Revolution, a period that saw the economic and political ascendancy of industrial capitalism and the full emergence of an industrial working class ready to organize national trade unions, like the KOSC and other constituents of the NLU, and to unleash an insurrectionary spirit, as in the great strikes of 1877. At a time when scores of industrial communities like Lynn were seething with resistance to industrialism, national politics were preoccupied with the issues of war and reconstruction. Economic and social issues arose, such as factory reform, the hours of labor, the distribution of wealth, and cheap money, but they were crowded off the center stage of debate by issues of military strategy, presidential impeachment, racial adjustment, and reconstituting the Union. Workers who had fought and bled in the war were vitally interested in these matters and did not have to be hoodwinked into paying attention by devious employers. Since workers did not pursue a clear-cut position on reconstruction, and since they soon reapportioned their loyalties among two major and several minor political parties, the net effect was to channel their thinking away from an analysis that would have defined the political system as an inherently hostile set of institutions.

Thus a special configuration of events having to do with the inter-class character of the American Revolution, the radical, antimonopoly critique of capitalism, and the nationalist impact of the Civil War established among nineteenth century-workers an orientation away from class consciousness and toward a view of labor as one interest group in a pluralist society. Just as class consciousness laid the psychological foundation for the ideological acceptance of socialism, so the interest group mentality laid the foundation for the ideological acceptance of what has been called "laborism." The distinction between class consciousness and group awareness was noted by the one labor leader who did more than any other to steer the American labor movement away from collectivism embodied in the famous Plank 10 and toward pure and simple trade unionism. Sam Gompers drew a contrast between *Klassenbewustzein,* that is, intellectual awareness of labor's oppression as a class, and *Klassengefühl,* the sympathetic understanding and fellow feeling among those who labor for a living. He argued that the latter was common among American workers, while the former was atypical.[15] Although Gompers' analysis may have been biased because of his vested interest in pure and simple trade unionism, nevertheless his view accords well with the persistent minority status of socialist and labor parties within the working class and the consistent failure, not only of the craft-dominated AFL but of most twentieth-century industrial unions, to propose a program that would abolish the wage system, take control of investment out of the hands of private capital, and equalize the distribution of income.

Yet we must be careful not to explain the weaknesses of socialism in such a way that discounts socialist influence altogether. Some historians have conjured up an imaginary environment so hostile to socialism that real socialist groups could hardly have existed at all. In a strange reversal of critical analysis, they have de-reified reality into a theoretical impossibility. Writers like Daniel Bell see the socialist movement as a phantasmagoria, something that may dwell *in* the world but is not *of* it.[16] Others have taken the equally absurd view that the United States has always been a middle-class society in which workers shared in an all-American consensus around middle-class values.[17] A more sophisticated explanation of the relative weakness of American socialism was offered by Selig Perlman, the most perceptive of the Wisconsin-School historians.[18] Unlike the vulgarized argument that socialism was a foreign ideology or that it was just plain "un-American," Perlman offered reasons to demonstrate why socialism did not succeed: these included widespread opportunity to get ahead, the free gift of the ballot, ethnic hostilities, the adaptability of the major parties, and the antimonopoly philosophy. Each of these points is valid enough taken on its own terms, and the cumulative impact is impressive, but Perlman was also eager to show why the triumph of laborism was *inevitable*, or, in his words, why socialism was not "fitted" to the American environment. As a former Russian socialist he had believed that proletarian revolution was preordained, and under the influence of John Commons, he simply reversed the outcome without relinquishing the notion of its inevitability. This is where he strayed from the true path of historical analysis, pursuing what might be called the "ontological fallacy." The fallacy is to regard what *was* as what *had to be*. If the outcome of a particular series of events was inevitable from the outset, then there were never any logical alternative outcomes, and, hence, no causes. Such reasoning from being to events is the antithesis of historical reasoning, which proceeds from events to being.

To criticize the notion of historical inevitability, however, is not to say that anything can happen. Events take place within an inherited context which sets the terms and conditions for any particular epoch. Thus the class feeling of the nineteenth-century industrial worker was based on the existence of a working class and, therefore, was something that the eighteenth-century household journeyman could not have experienced. In the same vein, social and economic thought in the nineteenth century was compelled to come to terms with the inequality inherent in industrial capitalism. Though there was no compulsion to explain it in class terms, no significant analysis could ignore it. Ideas are free to roam widely about the historical landscape, but there are limits beyond which a set of ideas cannot go and still remain relevant to social and economic realities.

Social inequality was like a tether on the tradition of Equal Rights, continually bringing it up short and forcing it to reexamine the root causes of the wage earner's plight. The result was a persistent radical impulse that became increasingly class conscious toward the end of the nineteenth century and laid the foundation for the socialist altern-ative to laborism. Whether workers who expressed this impulse favored the Wobbly form of direct action, the parliamentary methods of the Socialist party, or some other strategy of revolution, they be-came convinced that equality was an impossibility without the over-throw of the class in power and the establishment of a classless society. They came out of the Equal Rights tradition, but unlike their brothers and sisters who only desired "more," they demanded *awl* or nothing! In the words of the old shoemakers' song,

> *Stick* to the *last,* brave cordwainers!
> In the *end,* you'll *awl* be gainers!

APPENDIXES

BIBLIOGRAPHY

NOTES

INDEX

APPENDIX A

Tables on Population, Output, and Employment

TABLE 7. Population, Percent Decennial Increase, and Output (in Pairs of Shoes), 1765–1880.

Year	Population	Decennial increase percent	Output
1765	2,198	—	—
1768	—	—	80,000
1788	—	—	100,000
1789	—	—	175,000
1790	2,291	—	150,000
1796	—	—	400,000
1800	2,837	24	—
1802	—	—	400,000
1810	(4,087)	44	1,000,000
1820	4,515	(10)	—
1826	5,341	—	—
1830	6,138	36	—
1831	—	—	1,675,781
1832	—	—	1,482,167
1835	8,419	—	2,205,384
1837	9,323	—	2,546,149
1840	9,367	53	—
1845	—	—	2,412,722
1850	14,257	52	4,478,700
1855	15,713	—	4,637,797
1860	19,083	(34)	5,652,000
1865	20,747	—	5,359,821
1870	28,233	48	11,251,800
1875	32,600	—	11,678,880
1880	38,274	36	13,000,000

Source: Population. 1765: Lewis and Newhall, *History* I, 585; *1790–1880*: U.S. Census for each decade; *1810*: the figure in parentheses is the assumed population of the area covered by Lynn in 1820, after the separation of Lynnfield and Saugus. The reduction is 22 percent, the proportion these two towns would have had in an unreduced Lynn, 1820; *1835*: James R. Newhall, *Essex Memorial*, pp. 140–155; *1837*: John W. Barber, *Historical Collections*, p. 197; *1855*: Frances DeWitt, *Abstract of the Census . . . 1855*, p. 139; *1863*: Oliver Warner, *Abstract of the Census . . . 1865*, p. 64; *1875*: Wright, *Census, . . . 1875*, I, 351.

Percent Decennial Increase. Only the increase between federal census years is recorded. The percentage increases for 1820 and 1860 are in parentheses because the geographical boundaries changed in each preceding decade: between 1810 and 1820, Lynn lost Saugus and Lynnfield; between 1850 and 1860, Lynn lost Swampscott and Nahant. Therefore, the percentage understates the true rate of increase in population.

Output. 1768: Boston *Palladium,* Feb. 6, 1827; *1788:* J. P. Brissot de Warville, *New Travels in the United States of America, 1788,* p. 362; *1789:* Washington,*Diaries,* IV, 40; *1790:* Coxe, *View,* p. 266; *1796:* Duc de la Rochefoucauld, *Travels,* p. 13; *1802:* Morse, *American Gazetteer,* "Lynn" (Boston, 1810), no page; *1810:* Lewis and Newhall, *History,* I, 371; *1831:* Lummus, *Directory,* p. 14; *1832:* McLane, "Documents Relative to Manufacturers," pp. 224–237; *1835:* Newhall, *Essex Memorial,* pp. 140–155; *1837:* Barber, *Historical Collections,* p. 197; *1845:* Palfrey, *Statistics,* pp. 8–38; *1850* and *1860:* Calculations from raw data in U.S. Census manuscripts for Lynn products of industry; *1855:* DeWitt, *Information,* pp. 139–142; *1865:* Warner, *Information,* pp. 158–161; *1870:* Reporter, Jan. 14, 1871; *1875:* Reporter, Jan. 8, 1876; *1880:* U.S. Tenth Census, XVIII, 249, reports a value of nearly $17,000,000, and estimating $1.30 as the average price in 1880, the result is about 13,000,000 pairs.

TABLE 8. Shoe Employment, Overall and Resident, 1831–1900.

Year	Total	Overall Male	Overall Female	Total	Resident Male	Resident Female
1831	3,516	1,741	1,755	—	—	—
1832	3,207	1,448	1,759	—	—	—
1835	2,350	—	—	—	—	—
1837	5,185	2,631	2,554	—	—	—
1845	5,930	2,721	3,209	—	1,514	—
1850	10,383	3,876	6,507	—	1,872	—
1855	11,021	4,545	6,476	—	—	—
1860	9,806	5,881	3,925	—	2,569	—
1865	10,968	6,984	4,984	—	—	—
1870	—	—	—	—	3,737	—
1875	9,011	5,844	3,167	5,798	4,029	1,769
1878	—	—	—	5,871	4,040	1,831
1880	10,679	7,284	3,391	8,300	5,661	2,639
1885	—	—	—	9,474	6,112	3,362
1890	12,478	7,961	4,456	—	—	—
1900	10,082	—	—	—	—	—

Source: 1831: Lummus, *Directory,* p. 14; *1832:* McLane, "Documents Relative to Manufactures," pp. 224–237; *1835*: Newhall, *Essex Memorial*, pp. 140–155; *1837*: Barber, *Historical Collections*, p. 197; *1845*: Palfrey, *Statistics*, pp. 8–38; *1850*: overall—calculations from U.S., Seventh Census manuscripts for Lynn products of industry; resident—Shattuck, *Report*, p. 504; *1855*: *News*, Sept. 14, 1855 (the state census for 1855, Dewitt, *Information*, pp. 139–142, incorrectly printed the total employment as the number of females); *1860*: overall and resident—calculations from U.S. Eighth Census manuscripts; *1865*: Warner, *Information*, pp. 158–161; *1870*: calculations from U.S. Ninth Census manuscripts; *1875*: Wright, *Census, 1875*, II, 391, 611, for overall; *Census, 1875*, I, 500–501, for resident; *1878*: Bureau of Labor, *Ninth Annual Report*, pp. 225–226; *1880*: overall—U.S., Tenth Census, XVIII, 249; resident, U.S., Tenth Census, I, 885; *1885*: Wright, *Census, 1885*, I, pt. 2, pp. 126–131; *1890*: U.S., Eleventh Census, V, 314–320; *1900:* U.S., Twelfth Census, VIII, pt. 2, pp. 390–391.

APPENDIX B
Research Methods

The census manuscripts provided a wealth of information on career lines, property ownership, and family patterns that was otherwise unavailable; but that information lay buried under its own bulk. Recording the names of several thousand individuals, searching for their names in later census tracts, and compiling meaningful statistics was a complicated and tedious job, to say the least. It would have been impossible without the use of electronic data processing. The assistance of two individuals on this task was invaluable. Steve Watt wrote a special computer program for the project and helped shape the whole format of the census research; Katy Dawley improved the research methods and helped in the painstaking chores of collecting, sorting, and cleaning up the data.

Electronic data processing facilitated certain steps in the research process, but enormous amounts of human labor time were required to set up the computer for its split-second calculations. Like the McKay stitcher, the computer saved labor time at only one step along the way. Otherwise, it seemed to multiply the work instead of decreasing it; before the information was ready to be read into the computer, it was necessary to transcribe names by hand from the manuscripts, write a coding system and a program, transfer coded data to punch cards, carefully go through each card for keypunch mistakes, correct the errors on a new card, and replace it in the deck. Then after a few seconds of data processing at about the speed of light, the human organism returned and slowly organized the leafy printout sheets, scrutinized the data for errors, rewrote and resubmitted certain instructions, and finally, with the traditional pen and paper, translated the results into significant statistics and intelligible prose. All this consumed hundreds of hours in the lives of three people, who understood considerably more about the tedium of tending machinery than they did before they began.

When people call an electronic calculator a "brain" and marvel at how fast it "thinks," they are praising and mocking it at the same time; it is truly wonderful that a machine can think, but everyone knows it can't. That combination of respect for its capabilities and recognition of its limits is the right attitude to cultivate when applying the computer to history. Twentieth-century wonders like the computer do not fit well into the technologies of earlier eras. Whereas they count things with brilliant precision, the quantitive source material from the past is often irregular and imprecise. Whereas computers do not make mathematical mistakes, they can make accurate tabulations of inaccurate statistics. One example of this problem is the task at hand—the application of the computer to the nine-teenth-century census manuscripts. Since the census enumerators of the last century normally missed somewhere between 5 and 10 percent of the urban population, the information available to the computer is of limited accuracy to begin with. Thus much of the sophisticated statistical para-phernalia available to the modern researcher is out of place in earlier time periods. The output of a computer is only as good as its input. To bombard nineteenth-century census data with standard deviations, regression analy-sis, probability factors, and the like is to risk twentieth-century techno-logical overkill.

Still, the census was more complete than the other main source on population and residence, the city directories. Comparing portions of the census listings of 1860 and the Lynn city directory of the same year re-vealed the many omissions from the directories, especially of younger men, while the census omitted comparatively few names found in the directo-ries. This finding is consistent with Peter Knights' observations for Boston in the same years.

Questions about the nature of masses of people cannot be answered without massive statistical information, and so our statistical investigation of Lynn's industrial work force began, cognizant of the limits of such methods, but hopeful of discovering solid information about the social character of the city's industrial workers as the city's main industry was revolutionized by the factory system. The census of 1860 was selected as the base year, since virtually all the male shoemakers still worked either in their homes or in central shops. The census of 1870 was selected as the companion, since by that time the factory system was an accomplished fact, affecting virtually all of the workers in one way or another.

Following is a description of the five major steps in compiling the sta-tistics.

1. The name of each male shoemaker listed in the Lynn census manu-scripts of 1860 was recorded, along with accompanying information about him. The same thing was done for sons of shoemakers ten years and older. The information included twelve items for each person: (a) an identifica-tion number based on the household number in the census and family and individual numbers assigned by the researcher, (b) ward of residence, (c) occupation, (d) value of real property (all property values from the manu-scripts were rounded off to the nearest $100), (e) value of personal prop-erty, (f) age, (g) birthplace by state, if New England, and otherwise by country, (h) wife's occupation, (i) number of children in the family, (j) number of children at work, (k) father's occupation, and finally, (l) value of total property held by the individual's parents.

2. Each piece of information was coded and all the information for each man was punched on a computer data card. Using all the cards, an alphabetical list of the 1860 shoemakers, including sons, was prepared to

facilitate the search for these individuals in the 1870 census manuscripts. Of 3057 names from 1860, 1657 turned up in 1870. (This included 134 sons under twenty years old who had established careers, lived with their fathers, but who had not originally been counted in 1860.) Information from the manuscripts was taken for each person and included the following nine items: (a) ward of residence, (b) occupation, (c) real property, (d) personal property, (e) marital status, (f) birthplace of father, foreign or native, (g) citizenship, (h) parent's property, and (i) father's occupation.

3. The listing of 1860 shoemakers was also checked against two sets of names connected to trade union activity. The first set was compiled from newspapers and included nearly 100 leaders of the 1860 strike. The second was a list of the Knights of St. Crispin in Lynn taken from a union dues book which contained over 2000 names. (Of the 1152 shoemakers who bridged 1860 and 1870, 32 were strike leaders and 248 were Crispins. The data cards were punched accordingly.)

4. The study was extended another decade by searching for the names of the stable shoemakers in the 1880 city directory. The directory was chosen in preference to the census manuscripts because its listings were alphabetical, a fact which greatly reduced the search time. The only item of information recovered and transferred to the data card was occupation. Directories commonly listed fewer men than the census tracts, but their omission applied chiefly to younger men, and since most of the original 1860 group were over thirty the error in the recovery rate was very slight. The findings for 1880 apply to all 1860 shoemakers and their older sons who stayed the twenty years. Had all the younger sons been included in the study, the rate of movement into nonmanual occupations would have shifted downward somewhat. About 9 percent (96 of 1061) of the people present in both 1860 and 1880 were not present in 1870. Many of these moved out of the city and then back; others were missed by the 1870 census, by the researcher, or represent two people with the same name.

5. Separate information was compiled for all *new* male shoeworkers in 1870. Their names were not taken, but otherwise the items repeated the information taken in step 2. In addition, age and birthplace were recorded for each man. Then during the process of transcribing information from the census, individual names were checked in the membership list of Knights of St. Crispin. There were 746 new shoemakers on the Crispin list. Altogether, eleven items were coded and punched on data cards. The great majority of the new shoeworkers in 1870 were also new residents of Lynn, though a small portion had lived in the city in 1860 but were not shoemakers then. There were 2585 new men "mobile" in Lynn shoemaking in 1870, and they combined with the 1152 "stable" shoemakers to make up the total resident work force of 3737 men.

APPENDIX C
The Ward 4 Factor

There were two systematic errors in the Lynn census manuscripts for 1870. One was a tendency not to report small amounts of property. This showed up as an aberration in the distribution of property holders, with the number of holders unmistakably understated at the level of $100. Perhaps the census enumerators were told not to be very concerned about such small amounts and to record the person at $0. To overcome the error, the categories of $0 and $100 have been combined.

The second error was a systematic understatement of the number of factory workers in Ward 4, one of the large, innercity wards. Although enumerators in other parts of the city made full use of the three main designations for shoeworkers ("shoemaker," "cutter," and "works in shoe factory"), the Ward 4 enumerators shied away from the factory designation. Or perhaps the enumerators used the three categories, but a careless clerk created the error in transcribing their findings. Whatever the reason, the error was glaring. Whereas the raw data assigned Ward 4 about the same small proportion of factory workers as the outlying, semi-pastoral wards, in fact Ward 4 was full of factory workers. It was the center of the business district and the location of the largest bank, the main railroad station, and the largest shoe factories. It had more shoeworkers than any other ward, the largest immigrant and out-of-state migrant population, the largest number of boardinghouse residents and the highest population density

To correct the error it was necessary to convert numerically a portion of the nonfactory workers ("shoemakers") to factory workers ("works in shoe factory"). The most effective approach was to determine the proportions in these two categories from a comparable ward in the city and apply the proportions to the raw data for Ward 4. In all respects, the neighboring Ward 5 was most like Ward 4 in its social and economic characteristics. It was second in all the things in which Ward 4 was first— total shoemakers, foreign-born residents, number of factories. To make the conversion factor as accurate as possible, the "mobile" and the "stable" shoemakers were separated and different proportions of factory and nonfactory workers found for each group. Leaving aside the cutters, the "stable" shoemakers in Ward 5 contained 63 percent factory workers (122 of 194) and 37 percent nonfactory workers (72 of 194). Applying these percentages to the 171 "stable" shoeworkers in Ward 4, the result was 108 factory workers and 63 nonfactory workers. The uncorrected figures were 41 and 130, respectively, a shift of 67. Turning to the "mobile" shoe-

workers the proportion of factory workers in Ward 5 was much higher—
94 percent (587 of 623). Applying this percentage to the 831 "mobile"
workers in Ward 4, the result was 781 factory workers. The raw data
showed a meager 19, so the difference was 762. The combined difference
of the "mobile" and "stable" groups was 67 + 762 = 829. The results for
the shoeworkers in the city as a whole are shown in Table 9.

**TABLE 9. Shoemakers in 1870, Data Correction for Ward 4
Error.**

Category	Mobile			Stable			Total		
	Raw	(Change)	Correct	Raw	(Change)	Correct	Raw	(Change)	Correct
Factory	1169	+ (762) =	1931	437	+ (67) =	504	1606	+ (829) =	2435
Nonfactory	1257	− (762) =	495	570	− (67) =	503	1827	− (829) =	998
Cutters	—	—	159	—	—	145	—	—	304
Total	—	—	2585	—	—	1152	—	—	3737

Source: U.S., Ninth Census manuscripts for Lynn.

It is essential to keep in mind that although the new percentages are
quite accurate, the actual numbers are only approximate. There is always
a certain risk in using approximate figures, but the compelling reason to
correct the data anyway is that not to correct it would be to guarantee
inaccuracy.

Once we have corrected the proportions of factory and nonfactory
workers, we can also reestimate the differences between these two groups
concerning nativity and property ownership. In the case of nativity, the
shift of Ward 4 shoemakers from the nonfactory to the factory category
results in an increase in the proportion of factory workers born in New
Hampshire and Maine and a decrease in the proportion of those born in
Massachusetts. Nonfactory proportions, of course, changed in just the
opposite directions. Little change occurred either in the proportions of
those born elsewhere in the United States or in the proportion of foreign-
born. In percentage terms, the proportion of factory workers born in New
England (exclusive of Massachusetts) increased from a raw figure of 17
percent to a corrected figure of 23 percent, while the proportion of Massachusetts-born decreased from a raw 62 percent to a corrected 56 percent.
The proportion of nonfactory workers born in New England (exclusive of
Massachusetts) decreased from 23 percent to 16 percent, while the proportion born in Massachusetts increased from 55 percent to 61 percent.
The corrected percentages appear in Chapter 5, Table 3.

In the area of property ownership the most important thing to recognize is that the Ward 4 correction almost certainly widens the gap between factory and nonfactory workers by subtracting propertyless workers from the nonfactory category and adding them to the factory category. Since the exact breakdown of property ownership by ward was not obtained, the actual calculations of this change have not been performed, so that the figures reported in Chapter 6, Table 4, actually understate the proportion of factory workers without property. Finally, the Ward 4 factor affects only the distributions of factory and nonfactory workers. Neither cutters nor the combined totals for the entire group of 3737 shoemakers are affected at all.

BIBLIOGRAPHY

Note on the Sources

The basic research rides on two main axles, the federal census manuscripts for Lynn and the local newspapers. Beginning in 1850 the census gathered a wealth of social and economic data that is unavailable in other sources and that offers an intimate, in-depth view of basic social processes. The more traditional source, the newspapers, provides overviews of these processes and captures them in crisis events, such as strikes. The most useful newspapers for prefactory Lynn were the *Awl*, published by and for artisans, and the *Lynn News,* a more general organ of community life. The *Lynn Reporter* represented the views of the manufacturers and is most useful for the period of industrial conversion. The *Knight of Labor* was the organ of wage earners in the 1880s; in style and ideas, it was a virtual reincarnation of the *Awl*.

Supplementing the census tracts, the published results of both state and federal census returns provide a series of statistics on population, employment, and production that makes it possible to interpret the significance of the manuscript data. The state industrial surveys of 1837, 1845, 1855, and 1865, along with Carroll Wright's *Census of Massachusetts* in 1875, were actually more beneficial than the federal census reports, which did not begin serious industrial research until 1850 and lagged behind Massachusetts in statistical sophistication for the entire period. Massachusetts also led the way in studying the labor force with the creation of the Bureau of the Statistics of Labor in 1869, whose annual reports are useful for both state and local history. The annual *Documents* of the city of Lynn are the basic source for changes in public life; the inaugural addresses of the mayors, the reports of the city marshals, and the reports of the committee on accounts are especially revealing.

David N. Johnson's *Sketches of Lynn* is not only an excellent view of the changes in Lynn from 1830 to 1880 but also a perceptive study of the process of industrialization. Offering fewer insights into the pattern of events, the two-volume *History of Lynn,* by Alonzo Lewis and James R. Newhall, still provides a great deal of essential information on the community. These books supplement the newspapers and both are of much higher quality and significance than the usual efforts in local history. The dues books of the Lasters' Protective Union and the Knights of St. Crispin enabled the author to determine the social background of a thousand trade unionists.

Any study involving shoemakers owes a major debt to John Commons, who not only made valuable investigations into the shoe industry himself but stimulated several other scholars to pursue the topic. Following Commons' lead, Blanche Hazard produced the basic work in the field, *The Organization of the Boot and Shoe Industry in Massachusetts before 1875*. As a model for research on the community level into major social processes, Oscar Handlin's *Boston's Immigrants* stands unsurpassed. In addition, Stephan Thernstrom's *Poverty and Progress* provided initial guidance and inspiration for the study of social mobility.

I. Manuscripts

Attwill, Richard I. Scrapbook, no date. Lynn Public Library.

Boyce, Jonathan. Ledger, 1793–1812. Lynn Historical Society.

Breed, Aaron. Account book, 1810–1816. Lynn Historical Society.

Breed, Amos F. Account book, 1760–1772. Lynn Historical Society.

Breed, James, Jr. Account book, 1798–1810. Lynn Historical Society.

Buffum, Israel. Ledger, 1806–1810. Lynn Historical Society.

Burrill, John. Account book, 1819–1820. Lynn Historical Society.

Chase, Nathan D. Scrapbook, no date. Lynn Public Library.

Collins, Nathaniel. Account book, 1785–1825. Lynn Historical Society.

Collins, Nehemiah. Account book, 1756–1777. Lynn Historical Society.

Hill, Ivory B. Diary, Northwood, N. H., 1857. New Hampshire Historical Society.

Johnson, David N. Scrapbook, no date. Lynn Public Library.

Keene, George W. Ledger, 1845–1853. Lynn Historical Society.

Lasters' Protective Union. Dues Books, Lynn, 1868–1878. 2 vols. Baker Library, Harvard University.

Nichols, John B. Scrapbook, no date. Lynn Public Library.

Purinton, James. Account book, 1758–1760. Lynn Historical Society.

Robinson, Christopher. Ledger B, 1853-55. Lynn Historical Society.

Rogers, George W. Scrapbook, no date. Lynn Public Library.

Shoe manufacturer, anonymous. Ledger, 1830–1831. Lynn Historical Society.

Sovereigns of Industry. Miscellaneous papers, Labor History Collection, Wisconsin Historical Society.

Tarbox, Nathaniel, and Nathaniel Tarbox, Jr. Account book, 1774–1824. Lynn Historical Society.

Tilton, Jeremiah D. Diary, Deerfield, N. H., 1840–1850. New Hampshire Historical Society.

United States Census. Manuscripts, Lynn, 1850, 1860, 1870. Massachusetts Archives.

United States Census. Manuscripts, Northwood, N. H., 1850, 1860, 1870, and Pittsfield, N. H., 1860. Population schedules in National Archives. Products of industry in New Hampshire state library.

Valuations of Towns, 1771. Lynn valuations in Massachusetts Archives, vol. 133.

II. Newspapers

Unless otherwise noted, newspapers were published in Lynn.

The Awl, 1844–1845.
Bay State, 1850, 1860–1863.
Boston Gazette (Boston), Oct. 21, 1764.
Boston Palladium (Boston), Feb. 6, 1827.
The Engine, March 10, 1838.
Essex County Whig, 1844.
Knight of Labor, 1885–1886.
Little Giant, Jan. 15, Feb. 26, Oct. 29, 1870.
Lynn Evening News, 1900.
Lynn Focus, 1837.
Lynn Freeman, 1841–1843.
Lynn Item, 1886.
Lynn Mirror, 1825–1860.
Lynn News, 1825–1828.
Lynn Record, 1837–1839.
Lynn Reporter, 1863–1879.
Lynn Transcript, 1872–1879, 1886–1894.
Lynn Weekly Times, 1896–1900.
New Hampshire Statesman (Concord, N. H.), 1858–1860.
Saturday Union, 1885, 1886.
The Pioneer, 1845–1849.
True Workingman, 1845.
The Vindicator, October – December, 1878.

III. Public Documents

De Bow, J. D. B. *Statistical View of the United States.* Washington, 1854.
De Witt, Francis. *Statistical Information Relating to Industry in Massachusetts . . . 1855.* Boston, 1856.
———*Abstract of the Census of . . . Massachusetts . . . for 1855.* Boston, 1857.
General Statutes of the Commonwealth of Massachusetts. Boston, 1860.
Index to Occupations: Alphabetical and Classified. Dept. of Commerce, Bureau of the Census. Washington, 1915.
Lynn, City of, *City Documents.* Published annually, Lynn, 1849–1881. Volumes included the annual inaugural address of the mayor and annual reports of the auditor.

McLane, Lewis. "Documents Relative to the Manufactures in the United States," *House Document,* 22 Cong., 1 sess., no. 308, 2 vols. Washington, 1833.

Massachusetts Bureau of the Statistics of Labor. *Annual Report.* Published annually in Boston, 1870–1881.

Palfrey, John G. *Statistics of the Condition . . . of Industry in Massachusetts.* Boston, 1846.

United States Census
Sixth Census, 1840. *Compendium of the . . . United States.* Washington, 1841.
Seventh Census, 1850. Washington, 1853.
Eighth Census, *Population of the United States in 1860.* Washington, 1864.
Eighth Census, *Manufacturers of the United States in 1860.* Washington, 1865.
Ninth Census, 1870, I, III. Washington, 1872.
Tenth Census, 1880, I, II, XVIII, XX. Washington, 1882.
Eleventh Census, 1890, II, IV, V. Washington, 1892.
Twelfth Census, 1900, II, VIII, pt. 2, IX, pt. 3. Washington, 1902.

Warner, Oliver. *Abstract of the Census of Massachusetts, 1865 . . .* Boston, 1867.

Wright, Carroll D. *The Census of Massachusetts, 1875.* 2 vols. Boston, 1876.

——*The Census of Massachusetts, 1885.* 2 vols. Boston, 1887.

IV. Sources on Lynn

Abstract of the Arguments . . . for a Rail-Road . . . Boston, 1846.

Alley, John B. *Principles and Purposes of the Republican Party.* Pamphlet of a speech in the House of Representatives, April 30, 1860. No city.

——*State of the Union.* Pamphlet of a speech in the House of Representatives, Jan. 23, 1862. No city.

Bassett, Hannah. *Memoir of Hannah Bassett, with Extracts from her Diary.* Lynn, 1860.

Bassett, William. *Proceedings of the Society of Friends in the Case of William Bassett.* Worcester, Mass., 1840.

Celebration of the 275th Anniversary of the First Church of Christ. Lynn, 1907.

City Directory. Lynn, 1832, 1842, 1851, 1854, 1856, 1858, 1860, and annually thereafter.

The City Hall of Lynn . . . 1867. Lynn, 1869.

Clapp, Henry, Jr. *The Pioneer, or Leaves from an Editor's Portfolio.* Lynn, 1846.

Clark, William. *Discourse on the Formation and Progress of the First Methodist Episcopal Church in Lynn.* Boston, 1859.

Cook, Joseph. *Outlines of Music Hall Lectures on Factory Reform.* Boston, 1871.

Felt, Charles W. *The Eastern Railroad of Massachusetts.* Boston, 1874.

Gannon, Fred. *The Ways of a Worker.* Salem, 1918.

History of Ward 4 Union Recruiting Association of Lynn, 1864–1865. Lynn, 1881.

Johnson, Samuel. *A Ministry in Free Religion.* Boston, 1870.

——*Lectures, Essays, and Sermons.* Boston, 1883.

Knights of St. Crispin. *Constitution of the International Grand Lodge.* No city, 1869.

——*Constitution and By-Laws of Eureka Lodge . . . of Marlboro, Massachusetts.* Boston, 1869.

——*Proceedings of the International Grand Lodge . . .* Boston, 1869. Proceedings for 1870 published under the same title in Milwaukee, and for 1872 in New York.

——*Ritual of the Order of the Knights of St. Crispin.* Milwaukee, 1870.

Lasters' Protective Union. *Constitution of the Lasters' Protective Union of America.* Lynn, 1886. Constitutions under the same title also published in Lynn, 1889, and 1892.

Nason, George W. *Minute-Men of '61; History and Complete Roster of the Massachusetts Regiments.* Boston, Smith and McCance, 1910.

Newhall, James R. *Proceedings in Lynn, Massachusetts, June 17, 1879 . . .* Lynn, 1880.

Philbrick, Samuel. *Facts and Observations . . . in the Society of Friends.* Boston, 1823.

Porter, James. *Three Lectures on Come-Outism.* Boston, 1844.

"Reasons and Facts Against the Pending Charter," Broadside. Lynn, April 15, 1850.

Remonstrance of the Eastern Railroad Company against the Establisment of Parallel Rail Roads. No city, Feb. 20, 1847.

Report of the Town Committee Upon the City Charter. Lynn, 1849.

Semi-Centennial of Incorporation. Lynn, 1900.

Spear, J.M. *Address before the Universalist Anti-Slavery Convention . . . in Lynn.* Waltham, Mass., 1840.

Stetson, Caleb. *A Sermon Preached at the Ordination of John Pierpont, Jr. . . . 1843.* Lynn, 1843.

Trial of Benjamin Shaw . . . for Riots and Disturbances of Public Worship . . . Salem, 1822.

Washington Total Abstinence Society. *First Annual Report 1842.* Lynn, 1842.

Wetherell, Ellen F. *After the Battle, or a Lesson from the Lynn Strike.* Lynn, 1903.

Workingmen's Advocate. *A Plan for Assisting Workingmen . . . to Easily Obtain Houses* . . . Lynn, 1880.

V. Historical Works on Lynn

Burrill, Ellen Mudge. *Essex Trust Company.* Lynn, 1914.
Boot and Shoe Recorder, Lynn Centennial Number, XXI. Boston, Aug. 10, 1892.
A Century of Service, Lynn Institution for Savings. No city. 1926.
Cumbler, Jonathan. "Continuity and Disruption: Working Class Community in Lynn and Fall River, Massachusetts, 1880–1950," unpub. diss., Univ. of Michigan, 1974.
——"Labor, Capital, and Community: The Struggle for Power," *Labor History*, 15 (Summer 1974), 395–415.
Faler, Paul. "Workingmen, Mechanics, and Social Change: Lynn, Massachusetts, 1800–1860," unpub. diss., University of Wisconsin, 1971.
Fenno, Henry. *Our Police: The Official History of the Police Department of the City of Lynn.* Lynn, 1895.
Hawkes, Nathan M. *An Historical Address Delivered before Bay State Lodge . . . 1894.* Lynn, 1894.
Hobbs, Clarence W. *Lynn and Surroundings.* Lynn, 1886.
Johnson, David N. *Sketches of Lynn, or the Changes of Fifty Years.* Lynn, 1880.
Lewis, Alonzo, and James R. Newhall. *History of Lynn.* 2 vols. Lynn, 1897, ed.
Lynn Five Cents Savings Bank, 75th Anniversary. No city. 1930.
Lynn Public Library, and Lynn Historical Society. *Lynn, 100 Years a City.* Lynn, 1950.
Mangan, J.J. *The Story of Lynn Newspapers.* Lynn, 1910.
Martin, George H. *The Unfolding of Religious Faith in Lynn.* Lynn, 1912.
Meredith, William. *An Account of the 51st Anniversary of the Boston Street Methodist Episcopal Church.* Lynn, 1904.
Mount Carmel Lodge. *One Hundred Years.* Lynn, 1905.
Newhall, James R. *Centennial Memorial of Lynn.* Lynn, 1876.
Newhall, John B. "Early Lewis, Broad and Nahant Streets," *Lynn Historical Society Register for 1906.* Lynn, 1907.
Pinkham, Arthur, and Frank Bruce. *Men, and Money at the National City Bank* . . . . Lynn, 1929.
Sanderson, Howard K. *Lynn in the Revolution.* Boston, W.B. Clark, 1909.
Semi-centennial of the National City Bank of Lynn, Massachusetts. No city. 1904.
Tapley, Henry F. "An Old New England Town as Seen by Joseph Lye, Cordwainer," *Register of the Lynn Historical Society*, XIX. Lynn, 1916.
Tracy, Cyrus. *The City Hall of Lynn* . . . . Lynn, 1869.

Usher, Edward Preston. *A Memorial Sketch of Roland Greene Usher 1823–1895*. Boston, 1895.
Walthal, Howard. "Abolitionism in Lynn, Massachusetts: A Case Study in the Origin and Development of Anti-Slavery Sentiment (1820–1860)," unpub. honors thesis, Harvard University, 1964.

VI. Nineteenth-Century Works

Baldwin, Simeon. *Life and Letters of Simeon Baldwin*. New Haven, Conn., The Tuttle, Morehouse and Taylor Co., 1918.
Barber, John W. *Historical Collections*. Worcester, Mass., 1841.
Bishop, J. Leander. *History of American Manufactures from 1608 to1860*. Originally Philadelphia. Reprints of Economic Classics, New York, Augustus M. Kelley, 1966.
Bragdon, Joseph H. *Seaboard Towns: Or the Traveller's Guide Book From Boston to Portland*. Newburyport, Mass., 1857.
Brissot de Warville, J. P. *New Travels in the United States of America, 1788*. Trans. Mara Socceanu Vamos and Durand Echeverria; ed. Durand Echeverria. Cambridge, Mass., Harvard Univ. Press, 1964.
Bryant, Seth. *Shoe and Leather Trade of the Last Hundred Years*. Boston, 1891.
Butler, Benjamin F. *Butler's Book*. Boston, 1892.
Coxe, Trench. *A View of the United States of America*. Philadelphia, 1794.
——*A Series of Tables on the Several Branches of American Manufactures*. Philadelphia, 1813.
Dow, George F. *Two Centuries of Travel in Essex Co., Mass.* Topsfield, Mass., Topsfield Historical Society, 1921.
Ely, Richard T. *The Labor Movement in America*. New York, 1886.
Foster, Frank K. "Shoemakers in the Movement," *The Labor Movement: The Problem of Today*, ed. George E. McNeill. Boston, 1887.
Freedley, E. T. *Philadelphia and Its Manufactures*. Philadelphia, 1859.
Hamilton, Alexander. *Papers on Public Credit, Commerce, and Finance*, ed. Samuel McKee, Jr. New York, Liberal Arts Press, 1957.
Haverhill Board of Trade. *Haverhill, Massachusetts, an Industrial and Commercial Center*. Haverhill, 1889.
Hobart, Benjamin. *History of the Town of Abington*. Boston, 1866.
Hurd, D. Hamilton. *History of Essex County, Massachusetts*. Philadelphia, 1888.
Martin, Edgar W. *The Standard of Living in 1860*. Chicago, Univ. of Chicago Press, 1942.
Martineau, Harriet. *Society in America*. 2 vols. London, 1837.
Morse, Jedidiah. *The American Gazetteer*. Boston, 1810.

Nason, Rev. Elias. *A Gazetteer of te State of Massachusetts.* Boston, 1878.

La Rochefoucauld Liancourt, duc de. *Travels Through the United States of North America . . .* London, 1799.

Newhall, James R. *Essex Memorial for 1836: Embracing a Register for the County.* Salem, 1836.

Phillips, Wendell. Speech of Dec. 7, 1871, in Swinton, John, *Striking for Life.* Westport, Conn., 1970. Originally 1894.

Pitkin, Timothy. *A Statistical View of the Commerce of the United States of America.* Hartford, Conn., 1816.

Prince, J. *A Wreath for St. Crispin: Being Sketches of Eminent Shoemakers.* Boston, 1848.

Rice and Hutchings. *Retrospect, 1866–1916.* Cambridge, Mass., The University Press, 1916.

Roads, Samuel, Jr. *The History and Traditions of Marblehead.* Boston, 1880.

Shattuck, Lemuel. "Annual Report of the Board of Health of Lynn," *Report of a General Plan for the Promotion of Public and Personal Health.* Boston, 1850.

VII. General Historical Works

Abbott, Edith. *Women in Industry: A Study in American Economic History.* New York, D. Appleton & Co., 1910.

Bailyn, Bernard. *The New England Merchants in the Seventeenth Century.* Cambridge, Mass., Harvard University Press, 1955.

Bedford, Henry. *Socialism and the Workers in Massachusetts, 1886–1912.* Amherst, Mass., University of Massachusetts Press, 1966.

Bell, Daniel. *Marxian Socialism in the United States.* Princeton, N.J., Princeton University Press, 1967.

Biographical Directory of the American Congress, 1774–1961. Washington, D.C., U.S. Government Printing Office, 1961.

Blakey, Roy G., and Gladys C. *The Federal Income Tax.* New York, Longmans, 1940.

Bordua, David J., ed. *The Police: Six Sociological Essays.* New York, J. Wiley, 1967.

Bücher, Carl. *Industrial Evolution.* New York, A. M. Kelley reprint, 1968.

Bushman, Richard. *From Puritan to Yankee: Character and the Social Order in Connecticut, 1690–1765.* Cambridge, Mass., Harvard University Press, 1967.

Cole, Donald. *Immigrant City: Lawrence, Massachusetts, 1845–1921.* Chapel Hill, N.C., University of North Carolina Press, 1963.

Commons, John R. "American Shoemakers, 1648–1895: A Sketch of Industrial Evolution," *Quarterly Journal of Economics*, 24 (November 1909), 39–84.

——*Labor and Administration*. New York, A. M Kelley reprint, 1964.

——et al. *History of Labour in the United States*, 4 vols. New York, The Macmillan Company, 1918–1935.

Darling, Arthur B. *Political Changes in Massachusetts 1828–1848: A Study of Liberal Movements in Politics*. New Haven, Yale University Press, 1925.

Demos, John. *A Little Commonwealth: Family Life in Plymouth Colony*. New York, Oxford University Press, 1970.

Foner, Philip. *Business and Slavery: The New York Merchants and the Irrepressible Conflict*. Chapel Hill, University of North Carolina Press, 1941.

——*History of the Labor Movement in the United States*. 4 vols. New York, International Publishers, 1947–1965.

Frisch, Michael H. *Town into City: Springfield, Massachusetts, and the Meaning of Community 1840–1880*. Cambridge, Harvard University Press, 1972.

Galster, A. E. *The Labor Movement in the Shoe Industry, with Special Reference to Philadelphia*. New York, Ronald Press Company, 1924.

Ginger, Ray. "Labor in a Massachusetts Cotton Mill, 1853–1860," *Business History Review*, 28 (March 1954), 67–91.

Gompers, Samuel. *Seventy Years of Life and Labor: An Autobiography*. New York, Dutton & Company, 1925.

Green, Constance M. *Holyoke, Massachusetts, A Case History of the Industrial Revolution in America*. New Haven, Yale University Press, 1939.

Grob, Gerald N. "The Knights of Labor and the Trade Unions 1878–1886," *Journal of Economic History*, 18 (June 1958), 176–192.

——*Workers and Utopia: A Study of Ideological Conflict in the American Labor Movement*. Evanston, Northwestern University Press, 1961.

Gutman, Herbert. "Class, Status, and Community Power in Nineteenth Century American Industrial Cities—Paterson, New Jersey: A Case Study," in *The Age of Industrialism in America*, Frederick Jaher, ed. New York, Free Press, 1968.

——"Industrial Workers Struggle for Power," in *The Gilded Age: A Reappraisal*, ed. H. Wayne Morgan. Syracuse, Syracuse University Press, 1970.

Hall, John P. "The Knights of St. Crispin in Massachusetts, 1869–1878," *Journal of Economic History*, 18 (June 1958), 161–175.

Handlin, Oscar. *Boston's Immigrants: A Study in Acculturation*, rev. ed. Cambridge, Harvard University Press, 1959.

Hazard, Blanche E. *The Organization of the Boot and Shoe Industry in Massachusetts before 1875.* Cambridge, Mass., Harvard University Press, 1921.

Hoover, Edgar M., Jr. *Location Theory and the Shoe and Leather Industries.* Cambridge, Harvard University Press, 1937.

Jensen, Merrill. *The New Nation.* New York, Alfred A. Knopf, 1950.

Kahl, Joseph A. *The American Class Structure.* New York, Reinhart, 1957.

Karson, Marc. *American Labor Unions and Politics, 1900–1918.* Carbondale, Southern Illinois University Press, 1958.

Katz, Michael B. *The Irony of Urban School Reform: Ideology and Style in Mid-Nineteenth Century Massachusetts.* U.S. Office of Education. Washington, D.C., 1966.

Knights, Peter R. *The Plain People of Boston, 1830–1860: A Study in City Growth.* New York, Oxford University Press, 1971.

Lane, Roger. *Policing the City: Boston 1822–1885.* Cambridge, Harvard University Press, 1967.

Laslett, J. H. M. *Labor and the Left: A Study of Socialist and Radical Influences in the American Labor Movement, 1881–1924.* New York, Basic Books, 1970.

——and S. M. Lipset, ed. *Failure of a Dream? Essays in the History of American Socialism.* New York, Anchor Press, 1974.

Laslett, Peter. *The World We Have Lost.* New York, Charles Scribner's Sons, 1965.

Lebergott, Stanley. *Manpower in Economic Growth: The American Record since 1800.* New York, McGraw-Hill, 1964.

Lescohier, Don. "The Knights of St. Crispin 1867–1874: A Study on Industrial Causes of Trade Unionism." *Bulletin of the University of Wisconsin,* no. 355. Madison, Wis., 1910.

Lichtheim, George. *A Short History of Socialism.* New York, Praeger, 1970.

Lipset, S. M., and Reinhard Bendix. *Social Mobility in Industrial Society.* Berkeley, University of California Press, 1959.

Main, Jackson T. *Social Structure of Revolutionary America.* Princeton, N.J., Princeton University Press, 1965.

Miller, Douglas T. *Jacksonian Aristocracy: Class and Democracy in New York 1830–1860.* New York, Oxford University Press, 1967.

Montgomery, David. *Beyond Equality: Labor and the Radical Republicans, 1862–1872.* New York, Alfred A. Knopf, 1967.

Moore, Barrington. *Social Origins of Dictatorship and Democracy: Lord and Peasant in the Making of the Modern World.* Boston, Beacon Press, 1966.

Morgan, Edmund S. *The Puritan Family: Essays on Religion and Domestic Relations in Seventeenth Century New England*, rev. ed. New York, Harper & Row, 1966.

Morris, Richard B. *Government and Labor in Early America*. New York, Columbia University Press, 1946.

Nettles, Curtis P. *The Money Supply of the American Colonies before 1720*. New York, A. M. Kelley, 1964.

Ollman, Bertell. *Alienation: Marx's Concept of Man in Capitalist Society*. Cambridge, Eng., Cambridge University Press, 1971.

Perlman, Marc. *Labor Union Theories in America*. Evanston, Row, Peterson & Company, 1958.

Perlman, Selig. *A Theory of the Labor Movement*. New York, The Macmillan Company, 1928.

Phillips, James D. *Salem and the Indies*. Boston, Houghton Mifflin, 1947.

Powderly, Terence V. *The Path I Trod*. New York, Columbia University Press, 1940.

Riessman, Leonard. *Class in American Society*. Glencoe, Free Press, 1959.

Rogoff, Natalie. *Recent Trends in Occupational Mobility*. Glencoe, Free Press, 1953.

Saxton, Alexander. *Indispensable Enemy: A Study of the Anti-Chinese Movement in California*. Berkeley, University of California Press, 1971.

Schlakman, Vera. *Economic History of a Factory Town, A Study of Chicopee, Massachusetts*. Smith College Studies in History, no. 20 (October 1934–July 1935).

Schlesinger, Arthur M. *The Colonial Merchants and the American Revolution*. New York, Atheneum edition, 1968.

Sennett, Richard, and Jonathan Cobb. *The Hidden Injuries of Class*. New York, Alfred A. Knopf, 1973.

Seybolt, Robert F. *Apprenticeship and Apprenticeship Education in Colonial New England and New York*. New York, Columbia University Press, 1917.

Shannon, David. *The Socialist Party of America: A History*. Chicago, Quadrangle Press, 1955.

Sharkey, Robert. *Money, Class, and Party: An Economic Study of the Civil War and Reconstruction*. Baltimore, The Johns Hopkins University Press, 1959.

Taylor, George R. *The Transportation Revolution 1815–1860*. New York, Holt, Rinehart, & Winston, 1962.

Thernstrom, Stephan. *Poverty and Progress: Social Mobility in a Nineteenth Century City*. Cambridge, Mass., Harvard University Press, 1964.

——*The Other Bostonians: Poverty and Progress in the American Me-*

tropolis 1880–1970. Cambridge, Mass., Harvard University Press, 1973.

Thompson, E. P. *The Making of the English Working Class.* New York, Random House, 1966.

Torrey, Bates. *The Shoe Industry of Weymouth.* South Weymouth, Mass., Weymouth Historical Society, 1933.

Tryon, Rolla M. *Household Manufacturers in the United States, 1640–1860.* Chicago, University of Chicago Press, 1917.

Ulman, Lloyd. *The Rise of the National Trade Union, The Development and Significance of its Structure, Governing Institutions and Economic Policies.* Cambridge, Mass., Harvard University Press, 1966.

Unger, Irwin. *The Greenback Era: A Social and Political History of American Finance, 1865–1879.* Princeton, N.J., Princeton University Press, 1964.

Unwin, George. *Industrial Organization in the Sixteenth and Seventeenth Centuries.* Oxford, Clarendon Press, 1904.

Ware, Caroline. *Early New England Cotton Manufacture: A Study in Industrial Beginnings.* Boston, Houghton Mifflin Company, 1931.

Ware, Norman. *The Labor Movement in the United States 1860–1895; A Study in Democracy.* New York, D. Appleton & Company, 1929.

Weinstein, James. *The Corporate Ideal in the Liberal State: 1900–1918.* Boston, Beacon Press, 1968.

Williams, Gwynn. *Artisans and Sans-Culottes: Popular Movements in France and Britain during the French Revolution.* New York, Norton Co., 1969.

Williams, William A. *The Great Evasion: An Essay on the Contemporary Relevance of Karl Marx.* Chicago, Quadrangle Press, 1964.

Wilson, Fred A. *Some Annals of Nahant, Massachusetts.* Boston, Old Corner Book Store, 1928.

Winks, William E. *Lives of Illustrious Shoemakers.* London, 1883.

Wrigley, E. A., ed. *An Introduction to English Historical Demography from the 16th to the 19th Century.* New York, Basic Books, 1966.

Young, E. Harold. *History of Pittsfield, New Hampshire.* Pittsfield, 1953.

NOTES

Acknowledgments

1. Paul Faler, "Cultural Aspects of the Industrial Revolution: Lynn, Massachusetts, Shoemakers and Industrial Morality, 1826–1860," *Labor History* (Summer 1974), pp. 367–394; "Workingmen, Mechanics, and Social Change: Lynn, Massachusetts, 1800–1860," unpub. diss. (Univ. of Wisconsin, 1971); Alan Dawley and Paul Faler, "Working Class Culture and Politics in the Industrial Revolution: Sources of Loyalism and Rebellion," *Journal of Social History* (June 1976), forthcoming.

Introduction: A Microcosm of the Industrial Revolution

1. The song appeared in the *Awl,* July 24, 1844, organ of the Lynn shoemakers.

2. Lynn *Reporter,* March 21, 1860.

3. "Storm the Fort" became "Hold the Fort," a popular union song in the twentieth century; see Edith Fowke and Joe Glazer, *Songs of Work and Freedom* (Garden City, N.Y., 1960), pp. 36–67.

4. C. Wright Mills, *The Marxists* (New York, Dell Publishing Co., 1962); William A. Williams, *The Great Evasion: An Essay on the Contemporary Relevance of Karl Marx* (Chicago, 1964); Eugene Genovese, *The Political Economy of Slavery* (New York, Vintage, 1965); Barrington Moore, *Social Origins of Dictatorship and Democracy: Lord and Peasant in the Making of the Modern World* (Boston, 1966); David Montgomery, *Beyond Equality: Labor and the Radical Republicans, 1862–1872* (New York, 1967); useful expositions on class analysis have been undertaken by T. B. Bottomore, *Classes in Modern Society* (New York, Vintage, 1966), and Paul Baran and E. J. Hobsbawm, "The Stages of Economic Growth," in *Kyklos,* 14 (1961), reprinted in *Western Civilization: Mainstream Readings and Radical Critiques,* ed. Jeffry Kaplow, (New York, Alfred A. Knopf, 1973), pp. 62–72; the classic application of class analysis to historical events is Karl Marx's study of the Revolution of 1848 in France, *The Eighteenth Brumaire of Louis Bonaparte* (New York, 1963); orig. pub. 1869.

5. E. P. Thompson, *The Making of the English Working Class* (New York, 1966), p. 11, preface.

6. Studies of the textile industry in the United States include Caroline Ware, *Early New England Cotton Manufacture: A Study in Industrial Beginnings* (Boston, 1931); Constance M. Green, *Holyoke, Massachusetts, A Case History of the Industrial Revolution in America* (New

Haven, Conn., 1939); Vera Schlakman, *Economic History of a Factory Town, A Study of Chicopee, Massachusetts,* Smith College Studies in History, no. 20 (October 1934–July 1935).

7. John R. Commons, "American Shoemakers, 1648–1895; A Sketch of Industrial Evolution," *Quarterly Journal of Economics,* 24 (November 1909), 39–84; the same article is in a 1964 reprint of his *Labor and Administration* (New York, 1913).

8. Herbert Gutman, "Class, Status, and Community Power in Nineteenth Century American Industrial Cities—Paterson, New Jersey: A Case Study," in *The Age of Industrialism in America,* ed. Frederick Jaher, (New York, 1968). The progenitor of sociological and historical community studies in this country and still the best effort of its kind is the work on Middletown by Robert and Helen Lynd, *Middletown* (New York, 1929), and *Middletown in Transition* (New York, 1937); these and other major community studies are lucidly reviewed in Maurice Stein, *The Eclipse of Community* (New York, 1960); two works which had a direct impact on the present study of Lynn are Oscar Handlin, *Boston's Immigrants* (Cambridge, Mass., 1959), and Stephan Thernstrom, *Poverty and Progress: Social Mobility in a Nineteenth Century City* (Cambridge, Mass., 1964.)

9. *Boston Transcript,* 1850, quoted in *Lynn, 100 Years a City* (Lynn, Backson and Philips, 1950), p. 4

10. Frederick Douglass, *Life and Times of Frederick Douglass* (London, Crowell-Collier Publishing Co., 1962), pp. 224–225, orig. pub. 1892.

11. T. W. Higginson, *Cheerful Yesterdays* (Boston, 1898), pp. 114–115.

Chapter 1. Entrepreneurs

1. J. H. St. John de Crevecoeur, *Letters from an American Farmer* (New York, E. P. Dutton & Co., Inc., 1957), p. 51; orig. pub. 1782.

2. Jackson T. Main, *Social Structure of Revolutionary America* (Princeton, N.J., 1965), pp. 41–43; U.S. Bureau of the Census, *Historical Statistics of the United States, Colonial Times to 1957* (Washington, D.C., 1960), pp. 9–14.

3. E. J. Hobsbawm, *The Age of Revolution, 1789–1848* (New York, New American Library, 1964), ch. 2, gives an excellent account of England's rise to economic supremacy.

4. Alonzo Lewis and James R. Newhall, *History of Lynn,* 2 vols. (Lynn, 1897), I, 96–97, 204–208, 211–221, 280; Bernard Bailyn, *The New England Merchants in the Seventeenth Century* (Cambridge, Mass., 1955), pp. 60–71.

5. The information on iron and ships is from Lawrence H. Gipson, *The Coming of the Revolution, 1763–1775* (New York, Harper, 1954), pp.

14, 15; Hamilton is reported by John C. Miller, *The Federalist Era* (New York, Harper & Row, 1960), p. 63.

6. James Madison, *The Federalist,* No. 10 (New York, 1939), Random House ed., p. 56.

7. Arthur M. Schlesinger, *The Colonial Merchants and the American Revolution* (New York, 1968), Atheneum ed., p. 65; Lewis and Newhall, *History,* I, 335.

8. Merrill Jensen, *The New Nation* (New York, 1950), pp. 185–187; the first view is in Lewis and Newhall, *History,* I, 520; the second view is in a letter from John B. Alley to Seth Bryant, March 14, 1891, in Seth Bryant, *Shoe and Leather Trade* (Boston, 1891), p. 6.

9. Jensen, *New Nation,* pp. 291–293, 297.

10. Lewis and Newhall, *History,* I, 521; Miller, *Federalist Era,* pp. 15–16; Trench Coxe, *A View of the United States of America in 1794* (Philadelphia, 1794), pp. 467, 121–122, 283. The historian of the shoe industry, Blanche Hazard, claims that Madison was opposed to the protection of shoes, but the evidence she gives is a general statement by Madison against unreasonable protection and does not necessarily apply to the specific legislation of 1789. She seems also to be unaware of the evidence in Lewis and Newhall. See Blanche Hazard, *The Organization of the Boot and Shoe Industry in Massachusetts before 1875* (Cambridge, Mass., 1921) p. 40n.

11. *The Diaries of George Washington: 1748–1799,* ed. John C. Fitzpatrick, 4 vols. (Boston, 1825), 40; Duc de La Rochefoucauld Liancourt, *Travels through the United States . . .* (London, 1799), p. 13; Jedediah Morse, "Lynn," *American Gazetteer* (Boston, 1810), no pagination. See Appendix A below for statistics.

12. Coxe, *View,* pp. 121–122, 300, 266.

13. Hazard, *Shoe Industry,* pp. 5–6, 28, 188–189; Lewis and Newhall, *History,* I, 349.

14. There were an estimated 400,000 pairs of shoes, compared to approximately 2,000,000 women and girls in the population of the United States in 1800.

15. This portrait of Lynn is a composite drawn from the Valuations of Lynn, 1771, Massachusetts Archives, vol. 133, and from maps and drawings in Lewis' and Newhall's *History.*

16. Allan Kulikoff, "The Progress of Inequality in Revolutionary Boston," *William and Mary Quarterly,* 28 (July 1971), 385.

17. Simeon Baldwin, *Life and Letters* (New Haven, The Tuttle, Morehouse and Taylor Co., Conn., 1918), p. 13.

18. For a discussion of the merchant takeover in early modern England, see George Unwin, *Industrial Organization in the Sixteenth and Seventeenth Centuries* (Oxford, 1904), passim, and pp. 62–63 for shoemakers; for American artisans and public regulation, see John R. Commons, "American Shoemakers," pp. 221, 225, 227–228.

19. Account books belonging to Amos F. Breed, 1763–1772, and to Nathaniel Tarbox, 1774–1795.

20. Lewis and Newhall, *History*, I, 328; U.S., Eighth Census, *Manufactures of the United States in 1860*, p. xix.

21. *News*, Sept. 3, 1847.

22. Bates Torrey, *The Shoe Industry of Weymouth* (South Weymouth, Mass., 1933), p. 17; Benjamin Hobart, *History of the Town of Abington* (Boston, 1866), pp. 151–152; James D. Phillips, *Salem and the Indies* (Boston, 1947), pp. 170–190.

23. Valuations of Lynn, 1771; letter from Sylvanus Hussey to Nicholas Brown & Co., Jan. 4, 1773, in Hazard, *Shoe Industry*, p. 36.

24. Haverhill Board of Trade, *Haverhill, Mass., an Industrial and Commercial Center* (Haverhill, 1889), p. 29; Hazard, *Shoe Industry*, p. 40; *News*, Sept. 3, 1849.

25. Richard Bushman, *From Puritan to Yankee: Character and the Social Order in Connecticut, 1690–1765* (Cambridge, Mass., 1967), p. 287.

26. Breed's letters are in Lewis and Newhall, *History*, I, 519–527.

27. Ibid., *History*, I, 519–527.

28. Ibid., *History*, I, 527.

29. Ellen M. Burrill, *Essex Trust Co.* (Lynn, 1914), pp. xii-xiv.

30. Ibid., pp. xii–xiii, lxii–lxiii.

31. Account books for 1798–1812 belonged to Jonathan Boyce, James Breed, Jr., and Israel Buffum.

32. See Appendix A for output statistics.

33. Nathan D. Chase, scrapbook, p. 10.

34. *Record*, Sept. 13, 1837.

35. Lynn scrapbooks, vol. 1, p. 47; Paul Faler, "Workingmen, Mechanics, and Social Change: Lynn, Massachusetts, 1800–1860," unpub. diss. (Univ. of Wisconsin, 1971), pp. 144–146; U.S., Eighth Census, Industrial Statistics of Lynn.

36. David N. Johnson, *Sketches of Lynn, or the Changes of Fifty Years* (Lynn, 1880), pp. 17–19.

37. Faler, "Workingmen," pp. 145–148; Burrill, *Essex*, p. lxv; *News*, Jan. 21, 1848.

38. For 1789, Coxe, *View*, p. 266; for 1832, Lewis McLane, "Documents Relative to the Manufactures in the United States," *House Doc.*, 22 Cong., 1 sess., no. 308, I, 224–237.

39. John B. Newhall, "Early Lewis, Broad, and Nahant Streets," *Lynn Historical Society Register for 1906* (Lynn, Mass., 1906), p. 80; payrolls in 1830 estimated from McLane, "Documents," pp. 224–237; payrolls in 1850 calculated from U.S., Seventh Census, Industrial Statistics of Lynn.

40. See Appendix A for statistics and citations.

41. Lemuel Shattuck, *Report of a General Plan . . .* (Boston, 1850), p. 509; this work incorporated a document entitled "Annual Report of the

Board of Health of Lynn," which was a reliable and comprehensive description of the city in 1850, intended as a model for future reports even though there was no such board; *News*, Nov. 29, 1855; *Reporter*, Nov. 21, 1863.

42. State census of industry published every ten years after 1845 provide the employment figures; see Appendix A for citations.

43. Commons, "American Shoemakers," pp. 246, 247; Don Lescohier, "The Knights of St. Crispin 1867–1874: A Study on Industrial Causes of of Trade Unionism," *Bulletin of the University of Wisconsin* (Madison, Wis., 1910), pp. 15–16.

44. *Record*, March 13, 1839; Bryant, *Shoe Trade*, pp. 25–26: Lewis and Newhall, *History*, I, 542–544.

45. George R. Taylor, *The Transportation Revolution 1815–1860* (New York, 1962), passim; Lee Benson, *The Concept of Jacksonian Democracy; New York as a Test Case* (Princeton, N. J., Princeton University Press, 1961), pp. 12–13.

46. Commons, "American Shoemakers," pp. 219–224.

47. Newhall's dates are recorded in Lewis and Newhall, *History*, I, 567–573.

48. Benjamin F. Newhall, untitled memoir, quoted in Lewis and Newhall, *History*, I, 568; all succeeding quotations of Newhall are taken from the same source, pp. 567–574.

49. Lewis and Newhall, pp. 567–568.

50. For the Methodists, William H. Meredith, *An Account of the 51st Anniversary of the Boston St. Methodist Episcopal Church and of Methodist Beginnings in Lynn, Mass.* (Lynn, 1904), pp. 15–20; William R. Clark, *Discourse on the Formation and Progress of the 1st Methodist Episcopal Church in Lynn* (Boston, 1859), p. 14; for the Congregationalists, *275th Anniversary of the First Church of Christ* (Lynn, 1907), pp. 43–44; for the Quaker schism, *Trial of Benjamin Shaw . . . for Riots . . .* (Salem, 1822), no pagination; for the Unitarians, George H. Martin, *The Unfolding of Religious Faith in Lynn* (Lynn, 1912), pp. 23–24.

51. For a discussion of early nineteenth-century forms of social control in a New England community, see Stephan Thernstrom, *Poverty and Progress*, pp. 34–42.

52. *Mirror*, Dec. 23, 1826, Jan. 6, 1827, Aug. 8, 1829.

53. Lewis and Newhall, p. 570.

54. Of the 132 manufacturers listed in the census of 1860, 81 had not been listed in the previous federal census; similarly, Faler has checked the city directories of 1841 and 1851 and found that 103 new men were listed in the latter year, approximately two-thirds of the total number in business; see Faler, "Workingmen," p. 133.

55. Lewis and Newhall, p. 570.

56. Two of the discussions of the theory of class and history that bear

on the present question are Bertell Ollman, *Alienation, Marx's Concept of Man in Capitalist Society* (Cambridge, Eng., 1971); and Paul Baran and E. J. Hobsbawm, "The Stages of Economic Growth," pp. 62–72.

57. Max Weber, *The Protestant Ethic and the Spirit of Capitalism* (New York, 1958), Scribner's ed., p. 55.

58. *Benjamin Franklin, the Autobiography and Other Writings*, ed. L. Jesse Lemisch (New York, New American Library, 1961), p. 187.

59. Franklin, *Franklin*, p. 186.

60. Lewis and Newhall, p. 571.

Chapter 2. Artisans

1. Johnson, *Sketches*, p. 31.

2. Johnson, *Sketches*, pp. 35, 32.

3. *Awl*, July 24, 1844.

4. Faler, "Workingmen," p. 72; Faler, ibid., p. 73, is also the source for the quote from the petition; a full statement of the concept of the producing classes can be found in the *Awl*, Jan. 11, 1845.

5. Johnson, *Sketches*, p. 337, recounts the conversation between father and son; Chase, Lynn scrapbook, vol. 11; ledger of an anonymous shoe manufacturer, 1830–31.

6. Johnson, *Sketches*, p. 64; Hazard, *Shoe Industry*, p. 95n.

7. Nehemiah Collins, account book, 1761–62; wills were examined by Howard K. Sanderson, *Lynn in the Revolution* (Boston, 1909), p. 28; further material on eighteenth-century shoemaking is in John P. Hall, "The Gentle Craft; A Narrative of Yankee Shoemakers," unpub. diss. (Columbia University, 1953), p. 62; Joseph Lye's diary is quoted in H. F. Tapley, "An Old New England Town as Seen by Joseph Lye, Cordwainer," *Register of the Lynn Historical Society*, 19 (1915), 36–54. Lye's daily life resembled the utopian existence outlined by Marx and Engels in *The German Ideology* where people would be free to "hunt in the morning, fish in the afternoon, rear cattle in the evening, criticize after dinner;" excerpted in T. B. Bottomore, ed., *Marx's Early Writings* (New York, McGraw-Hill, 1964), p. 23.

8. Hazard, *Shoe Industry*, pp. 17–19, 207–210; Bates Torrey, *The Shoe Industry of Weymouth*, pp. 15–17; Benjamin Hobart, *History of the Town of Abington* (Boston, 1866), pp. 151–152; Haverhill Board of Trade, *Haverhill, Massachusetts: An Industrial and Commercial Center* (Haverhill, 1889), p. 29. Hazard failed to understand the rural origin of a large part of the labor force, though she presented evidence that indicated the rural link. Taking her analytical scheme from Commons' idea of the evolutionary stages in the organization of production, she saw market production growing out of the stage of custom work, and, therefore, mistak-

enly viewed custom shoemakers as the ancestors of the labor force in manufacturing.

9. Lucy Larcom, "Hannah Binding Shoes," quoted in Johnson, *Sketches,* pp. 338–340; *Awl,* July 17, 1844; John G. Palfrey, *Statistics . . . of Industry* (Boston, 1846), pp. 8–38; Johnson, *Sketches,* is replete with "salt notes," pp. 41–46.

10. E. Harold Young, *History of Pittsfield, New Hampshire* (Pittsfield, 1953), p. 75; letter from Northwood, *Awl,* Sept. 13, 1845.

11. Ivory Hill, diary, 1854–1857, New Hampshire State Historical Society, Concord, N. H.

12. A summary of the number of men employed in Lynn in 1850 is in Shattuck, *Report,* pp. 504–505; in the 1830s the shoemaker proportion in the local work force was still greater, as shown in the occupational tables compiled by Faler, "Workingmen," p. 302; in contrast, a commercial city like Boston contained smaller proportions of artisans—about one-third of the total employed in 1850, according to Handlin, *Boston's Immigrants,* pp. 250–251.

13. Trempleau County, Wis.: Merle Curti, *The Making of an American Community: A Case Study of Democracy in a Frontier County* (Stanford, Calif., Stanford Univ. Press, 1959); Philadelphia: Sam Bass Warner, *The Private City: Philadelphia in Three Periods of Its Growth* (Philadelphia, Univ. of Pennsylvania Press, 1968); Stuart Blumin, "Mobility and Change in Ante-Bellum Philadelphia," in *Nineteenth Century Cities,* ed. Stephan Thernstrom and Richard Sennett (New Haven, Yale Univ. Press, 1969); Boston: Peter Knights, *The Plain People of Boston, 1830–1860: A Study in City Growth* (New York, 1971).

14. Johnson, *Sketches,* p. 7; Norman Ware, *The Industrial Worker 1840–1860: The Reaction of American Industrial Society to the Advance of the Industrial Revolution* (Chicago, Quadrangle Books, 1964); orig. pub. 1924.

15. Faler, "Workingmen," p. 313; Faler also found the following proportions of propertyless polls: 1837—56 percent; 1842—61 percent; 1849—56 percent; 1860—53 percent; a ratable poll was a male adult in full possession of his faculties.

16. U.S., Seventh Census, manuscripts for Lynn; a sample of every fourth shoemaker was taken; of the 519 in the sample, 112 owned real property. All of these were heads of households, and an additional 237 heads of households (including unattached single men) owned nothing.

17. In Pittsfield, N. H., 70 percent of the shoemaker households owned property in 1860 (78 of 112); in Georgetown, Mass., 43 percent owned real property in 1850 (87 of 209).

18. Johnson, *Sketches,* pp. 164–156.

19. Ibid., pp. 164.

20. Lewis and Newhall, *History,* I, 590.

21. Hall, "Gentle Craft," pp. 231–233; Hall seems to overestimate the difference between rural and urban wages, contending that Pittsfield earnings were half that in Lynn, but his conclusion ignored the material in the U.S., Seventh Census, Industrial Statistics for Lynn and Pittsfield; see also *Awl*, Sept. 13, 1845; *Reporter*, Feb. 28, 1863.

22. Conflicting viewpoints are collected in *The Frontier Thesis: Valid Interpretation of American History?* ed. Ray Billington (New York, Holt, Rinehart and Winston, 1966); the source of the quotation is an essay in this collection by Ellen von Nardroff, "The American Frontier as a Safety Valve: The Life, Death, Reincarnation, and Justification of a Theory," p. 57; the view that high productivity in agriculture promoted capital intensive techniques in industry is argued by H. J. Habakkuk, *British and American Technology in the Nineteenth Century: The Search for Labor Savings Inventions* (Cambridge, Eng., Cambridge University Press, 1962) chaps. 2, 3.

23. Roads, *The History and Traditions of Marblehead* (Boston, 1880), pp. 267, 276–279; Johnson, *Sketches*, p. 113; *Bay State*, March 8, 1860; the best general discussion of the topic is in Taylor, *Transportation Revolution*, p. 267.

24. Faler, "Workingmen," p. 309; concerning the 1851 fathers, 44 could be traced, of which 26 were manufacturers or merchants; Faler found similar patterns for 1851–1860.

25. Johnson, *Sketches*, pp. 102–103.

26. *Awl*, July 24, 1844.

27. Johnson, *Sketches*, p. 95.

28. *Mirror*, May 22, 1830.

29. Edward Pessen, "The Egalitarian Myth and the American Social Reality: Wealth, Mobility, and Equality in the 'Era of the Common Man,'" *American Historical Review*, 76 (1971), 989–1034.

30. *Record*, Jan. 1, Jan. 8, Jan. 15, Jan. 29, 1834; *Mirror*, Aug. 14, 1830; see also Faler, "Workingmen," pp. 396–397; Hall, "Gentle Craft," pp. 158–159.

31. Johnson, *Sketches*, pp. 157–158.

32. The *Awl* was sold regularly in several New England cities besides Lynn.

33. *Awl*, July 17, July 24, Nov. 9, 1844; the last statement was taken from an address to a convention of New England mechanics held in Boston Oct. 16–17, 1844, and attended by delegates from Lynn.

34. *Awl*, Nov. 9, 1844, Feb. 8, 1845.

35. Norman Ware made the idea of a conflict between reform and trade unionism a central theme of *The Industrial Worker*; the idea was carried to a ludicrous extreme by Daniel Bell, who, through a flaw in historical perception, dismissed anything but his idea of trade unionism as a "chi-

mera from the gaudy bag of utopian dreams," in *Marxian Socialism in the United States* (Princeton, N. J., 1967), p. 11.

36. *Awl*, July 24, 1844, May 25, 1845.

37. Rowland Berthoff, *An Unsettled People: Social Order and Disorder in American History* (New York, Harper and Row, 1971), chap. 10.

38. Interesting material on the rise of the professional politician is in Richard N. Current, *Daniel Webster and the Rise of National Conservatism* (Boston, Little, Brown and Company, 1955); Thurlow Weed, *Autobiography* (New York, 1840); David Donald, *Lincoln Reconsidered* (New York, Random House, 1956).

39. The Free Soil campaign generated intense political heat in Lynn, as reflected in the name of a new paper, *The Sizzler*. The paper was edited by a Quaker abolitionist and friend of Frederick Douglass named William Bassett and was devoted to "Free Soil, Free Speech, Free Labor, and Free Men."

40. *Awl*, Oct. 9, 1844.

41. Broadside, "Reasons and Facts Against the Pending Charter . . . ," April 15, 1850.

42. *News*, April 27, 1849, April 5, April 26, 1850.

43. *Awl*, July 24, Aug. 21, 1844, April 18, 1845; for a penetrating discussion of the Revolutionary traditions in Lynn, see Faler, "Workingmen," pp. 371–375.

44. Excellent comparative material on French and English artisans of the late eighteenth century is available in Gwynn A. Williams, *Artisans and Sans-Culottes: Popular Movements in France and Britain during the French Revolution* (New York, 1969), which summarizes the work of Richard Cobb, Albert Soboul, George Rude, and Edward Thompson.

45. See the work of Mark Hovell, *The Chartist Movement* (Manchester, Eng., Manchester University Press, 1966).

Chapter 3. Factories

1. Johnson, *Sketches*, pp. 146, 154, describes Lynn's growth in the 1830s; *Lynn Freeman*, March 5, March 12, May 21, 1842, provides information on the demand for a higher tariff.

2. Taylor, *Transportation Revolution*, pp. 286–287; Warner, *Abstract of the Census of Massachusetts, 1865* (Boston, 1867), pp. 291, 784–793; Palfrey, *Statistics, 1845*, pp. 373–377; Francis DeWitt, *Statistical Information Relating to Industry in Massachusetts . . . 1855* (Boston, 1856), pp. 634–643. The same statistical sources showed that Haverhill's shoe industry was experiencing the same problem of declining productivity in binding.

3. See Appendix A.

4. *Reporter*, Feb. 28, 1863.

5. *New Hampshire Statesman*, Dec. 4, 1858; *Reporter*, Nov. 21, 1863.

6. *Reporter*, Feb. 28, 1863.

7. Carroll D. Wright, *Census of Massachusetts, 1875* (Boston, 1876), for 1875, II, pp. 825, 827; *News*, ads. June 6, 1856, Feb. 10, 1854; *Reporter*, June 21, 1862, Oct. 7, 1865; Johnson, *Sketches*, p. 340.

8. U.S., Seventh Census, Statistics on Industry in Lynn, data on the firms of John Wooldredge and George Keene; Wright, *Census, 1875*, II, 39–41.

9. *Reporter*, Feb. 28, 1863.

10. U.S., Eighth Census, *Manufactures . . . 1860*, pp. lxxi-lxxii.

11. *Reporter*, Oct. 7, 1865.

12. *News*, Nov. 10, Nov. 16, Nov. 24, 1857, gave detailed reports on the meetings about the effects of the depression.

13. *News*, July 27, 1858, March 1, 1859.

14. The strike was given extensive coverage in the Lynn papers, especially the *Bay State*, a Democratic paper, and the *News*, usually Republican; it was also covered by the *Independent Democrat* of Concord, N. H. March 1, March 8, 1860; and the *New Hampshire Patriot*, Feb. 29, March 7, 1860, published in Concord; the strike was also reported in the eastern urban press, such as the *Boston Journal*, the *New York Illustrated News*, and *Frank Leslie's Illustrated Newspaper*. The estimate of 20,000 strikers was proposed by Philip Foner, *History of the Labor Movement in the United States* (New York, 1947), I, 240. George Taylor apparently followed Foner's account, in the *Transportation Revolution*, p. 284.

15. *News*, March 21, 1860.

16. *Bay State*, March 8, 1860, describes the women's march; Barbara Welter discusses "The Cult of True Womanhood, 1820–1860," in *The Underside of American History* (New York, Harcourt Brace Jovanovich, 1971), 2 vols., I, 205–228.

17. *Bay State*, April 5, 1860.

18. The "Cordwainers' Song" was printed in the March 21, 1860, *Reporter*, and reprinted a quarter century later in the *Lynn Saturday Union*, Sept. 26, 1885, in an issue commemorating the Great Strike.

19. *News*, Feb. 22, 1860; *Bay State*, April 12, 1860.

20. *Bay State*, April 12, 1860.

21. Ibid., April 12, 1860.

22. Ibid., March 8, 1860.

23. Ibid., March 8, 1860.

24. Ibid., March 8, 1860.

25. Ibid., March 8, 1860.

26. Police court proceedings are recounted in the *Bay State*, March 2, 1860; information on property ownership and birthplace of those arrested

is in the U.S. Eighth Census manuscripts: the five included one Lynn native, one Irish immigrant, two Canadian immigrants who were probably of Irish ancestry, and one who escaped notice in the records.

27. The gift of wood to the strikers was reported in the *Bay State*, April 12, 1860; Alley's contortions were depicted in the *News*, March 21, 1860.

28. Descriptions of the factory system appeared in the *Reporter*, Nov. 21, Feb. 28, 1863, Oct. 21, 1865, June 5, 1869; the quote is from the *Reporter*, Feb. 28, 1863.

29. Ibid., Nov. 21, 1863.

30. Ibid., Feb. 28, 1863.

31. Hazard, *Shoe Industry*, pp. 245–246; Johnson, *Sketches*, pp. 342–343.

32. Johnson, *Sketches*, p. 342.

33. Ibid., p. 341.

34. See Appendix A for the sources on overall employment and output; see Alan Dawley, "The Artisan Response," unpub. diss. (Harvard University, 1971), pp. 109–111, for a discussion of the changes in daily output. The factory average was 6 prs./worker/day, while the average in the 1840s was 2–3 prs./worker/day.

35. U.S., Eighth and Ninth Census manuscripts, Industrial Statistics on Lynn.

36. Price information for 1860 is based on calculations from the U.S., Eighth Census manuscripts, Industrial Statistics on Lynn; the 1865 price is from Warner, *Information*, p. 77; the 1870 price cannot be calculated from the census manuscripts, owing to incomplete returns; Lewis and Newhall, *History*, II, 39, estimate $1.60, while the *Reporter*, Jan. 14, 1871, indicated an average price of $2; *Reporter*, Nov. 14, 1866, describes the high turnover in shoe firms.

37. *Reporter*, Nov. 16, 1861, Dec. 23, 1865.

38. Clarence Hobbs, *Lynn and Surroundings* (Lynn, 1886), p. 71.

39. Johnson, *Sketches*, p. 16; *Reporter*, Feb. 28, 1863.

Chapter 4. The City

1. Barrington Moore, *Social Origins*, pp. 111, 155.

2. Johnson, *Sketches*, p. 355; G. W. Mudge, "Lynn," *Boot and Shoe Recorder*, Aug. 10, 1892; *Reporter*, March 17, 1877, reports a speech by Mudge on the history of the shoe and leather trades; Mudge's political writings appeared in the *News*, March 9, March 16, 1855; the *News*, Sept. 21, 1855, Nov. 11, 1856, covered the initial organization of the Republican party.

3. *News*, March 24, 1857; *Biographical Directory of the American Congress*, s.v. John B. Alley, p. 474; *News*, Sept. 21, 1855, Sept. 7, 1858.

4. Alley's wealth is from the U.S., Eighth Census manuscripts for Lynn; a list of eleven officers of the Board of Trade appeared in the *News*, March 24, 1857, and seven of them appeared in political notations over the next few years; all seven were Republicans.

5. J. B. Alley, *Principles and Purposes of the Republican Party*, pp. 3, 5, pamphlet based on a speech in the House of Representatives, April 30, 1860; another of Alley's speeches was also published as a Republican pamphlet, *Speech on the State of the Union in the House of Reps., Jan. 23, 1862*; his published writings include a study of the origins of the Civil War around the theme of a slave power conspiracy.

6. Abraham Lincoln, Letter to Horace Greeley, Aug. 22, 1862, reprinted in Don Fehrenbacher, ed., *Abraham Lincoln: A Documentary Portrait* (New York, New American Library, 1964), p. 193.

7. The best study of the prewar Republican party is Eric Foner, *Free Soil, Free Labor, Free Men* (London, Oxford Univ. Press, 1970); it is a brilliant exposition of the way the party's ideas struck a resonant cord among several northern social interests; see especially his Introduction and chap. 1.

8. *News*, March 14, 1860.

9. *Bay State*, March 8, 1860.

10. Edward P. Usher, *A Memorial Sketch of Roland Greene Usher 1823–1895* (Boston, 1895), pp. 30–35.

11. *Bay State*, Dec. 6, 1860; Hiram N. Breed, "Inaugural," *City Docs.*, 1861, p. 4; *News*, Jan. 23, June 16, 1961.

12. The story of these events was compiled from the *News*, Feb. 27, April 24, 1861, and the *Reporter*, Jan. 11, 1862, Dec. 12, Dec. 19, 1863.

13. Between 1840 and 1870 the voters elected men from a mixture of occupations to fill top local offices; there was still a mixture during the Republican sweep in the 1860s, but shoe manufacturers were more heavily represented than ever before: in 1865 they accounted for twelve of the thirty officials, while a typical prewar year saw about half that number; occupations of city officials were determined by checks in the city directories.

14. Rev. J. W. F. Barnes, quoted in the *Reporter*, Jan. 22, 1868.

15. For a discussion of the counterpart of "iron reform" in intellectual history, see George Fredrickson, *The Inner Civil War* (New York, Harper, 1965).

16. Mayor Peter M. Neal is described in the *Reporter*, Dec. 14, 1861; his campaign for police reform appeared in his inaugural addresses printed in the annual *City Documents* for 1862 and 1863; the long quote is from his 1864 inaugural, pp. 15–16.

17. "Petition," Market Street businessmen and residents, *Reporter*, April 18, 1863.

18. "Inaugural," *City Docs.*, 1866, p. 7.

19. Usher, *Usher*, p. 24.

20. Information on Barrett was compiled from U.S., Seventh Census manuscripts for Lynn, 75; *Reporter*, Oct. 1, 1864, Oct. 5, 1870; and city directories for the 1860s; his recommendations appeared in his "Annual Report," *City Docs.*, 1866, pp. 34–39.

21. Barrett, "Report," *City Docs.*, 1866, pp. 36, 34.

22. Expenditure is in the annual reports of the city marshal and the Committee on Accounts, 1860–1870; the size of the police force is in the city marshal's "Report," *City Docs.*, 1870, pp. 52–58.

23. City marshal, "Report," *City Docs.*, 1870, pp. 52–58.

24. D. N. Barrett, letter to the *Reporter*, May 7, 1866.

25. *Reporter*, Dec., 12, 1866.

26. *Reporter*, Dec. 7, Dec. 11, 1867.

27. Roger Lane, *Policing the City: Boston, 1822–1885* (Cambridge, Mass., 1967), chap. 3.

28. *News*, Sept. 26, 1860.

29. Chief engineer, "Report," *City Docs.*, 1863, pp. 37–43, and 1865, pp. 40–41; George Hood, "Inaugural," *City Docs.*, 1851, p. 7; *Transcript*, Feb. 22, 1873; *Reporter*, June 9, Nov. 24, 1866; Edwin Walden, "Inaugural," *City Docs.*, 1869, pp. 14–15.

30. Lewis and Newhall, *History*, II, 29–31; *Reporter*, Aug. 4, 1869.

31. *Reporter*, Aug. 18, Dec. 1, 1869, Dec. 10, Dec. 14, 1870; for an expanded discussion of the topic, see Dawley, "Artisan Response," pp. 269–271.

32. For prewar attitudes on poor relief, see Andrews Breed, "Inaugural," *City Docs.*, 1855, p. 7; Edward Davis, "Inaugural," *City Docs.*, 1859, pp. 13–14; W. F. Johnson, "Inaugural," *City Docs.*, 1858, p. 7; for the wartime attitude, see P. M. Neal, "Inaugural," *City Docs.*, 1861, pp. 12–13.

33. The postwar attitude toward poor relief was in the Committee of Accounts, "Report," *City Docs.*, 1866, pp. 20–21; *Reporter*, Feb. 5, Feb. 8, 1868, Dec. 25, 1869; Edwin Walden, "Inaugural," *City Docs.*, 1870., pp. 12–13.

34. City marshal, "Report," *City Docs.*, 1881, p. 11; Rev. Joseph Cook, *Outlines of Music Hall Lectures on Factory Reform* (Boston, 1871), p. 18.

35. Rev. J. W. Barnes, quoted in the *Reporter*, March 4, 1868; report of the Women's Union for Christian Work in the *Reporter*, Nov. 13, 1869; a boardinghouse with more than forty tenants appeared in the census for the first time in 1870; altogether the city directories listed twenty-six boardinghouses in 1871 and fifty-three in 1880.

36. *Reporter*, Feb. 4, 1871.

37. Cook, *Factory Reform*, pp. 3–19.

38. Cook, ibid., pp. 31–33.

39. Barnes, *Reporter*, March 4, 1868.

40. Cook, *Factory Reform*, pp. 20–28.

41. Cook, ibid., p. 43; *Reporter*, Feb. 4, Feb. 11, 1871.

42. Cook, quoted in the *Reporter*, March 29, 1871.

43. *Reporter*, March 1, July 29, 1871; W. F. Mitchell's diary quoted in the *Transcript*, Feb. 22, 1873.

44. According to a report in the *Transcript*, Feb. 6, 1875, the mission books showed an annual rate of $1400 spent from 1872 to 1875; other information is in the *Transcript*, Oct. 3, 1874, April 24, 1875, Feb. 22, 1873; the demise of the mission is traced in the *Transcript*, Feb. 6, 1875, and the *Reporter*, Sept. 30, 1876, Jan. 9, 1878.

45. *Reporter*, Nov. 14, 1868; *Transcript*, Oct. 12, 1872, April 10, June 5, 1880.

46. *Reporter*, Jan. 11, 1871; the controversy surrounding the Women's Union appeared in successive issues of the *Transcript*, March 23, April 5, April 12, 1873.

47. *Transcript*, Jan. 25, 1879.

48. *Transcript*, Oct. 12, Oct. 26, 1872, April 10, 1880; *Reporter*, Oct. 25, 1871, is the source of information on visitors to the Women's Union.

49. *Reporter*, Aug. 8, March 11, 1868; *Transcript*, June 15, 1872.

50. School Committee, "Report," *City Docs.*, 1874, p. 32; *Reporter*, Feb. 28, 1877; School Committee, "Report," *City Docs.*, 1869, pp. 34–35.

51. School Committee, "Report," *City Docs.*, 1868, pp. 4–7; School Committee, "Report," *City Docs.*, 1876, pp. 68–76; *Reporter*, Oct. 4, 1871.

52. School Committee, "Report," *City Docs.*, 1872, p. 11.

53. The oration was delivered by Edwin L. Sargent and was published in the *Reporter*, May 22, 1869. One significant school reform had already taken place before the factories—the founding of a high school amid controversy in 1850. Michael Katz, *The Irony of Urban School Reform: Ideology and Style in Mid-Nineteenth Century Massachusetts*, U.S. Office of Education (Washington, 1966), pp. 26–29, describes the high school as one of the innovations of emerging industrialism, which was resisted by the "working class," i.e., farmers, fishermen, laborers, and artisans. If we lay aside Katz's use of the term "working class," which he employs in a confused and unenlightening fashion, then the pattern he describes for Beverly, Mass., holds for Lynn, where people identified as mechanics led the opposition to the high school from 1847–1850.

54. Cook, *Factory Reform*, pp. 80–83.

55. *Transcript*, April 26, 1873; revivalism was noted in the *Reporter*, May 5, Oct. 13, 1877, Jan. 16, 1878.

56. Lewis Mumford displays an extraordinarily radiant architectural vision of social history in his works on urban history, *The City in History* (New York, Harcourt Brace and World, 1961), and *The Culture of Cities* (New York, Harcourt Brace and World, 1938); on a less ambitious level, see Sam Warner, *Streetcar Suburbs: The Process of Growth in Boston* (Cambridge, Mass., Harvard University Press, 1962); the lines of poetry are from Bertolt Brecht's "A Worker Reads History," in *Selected Poems*, trans. H. R. Hays, copyright 1947 by Bertolt Brecht and H. R. Hays. Reprinted by permission of Harcourt Brace Jovanovich, Inc.

57. Visual descriptions of Lynn are based on drawings, paintings, and photographs at the Lynn Historical Society.

58. Broadside, "Reasons and Facts Against the Pending Charter for a City . . . ," April 15, 1850.

59. High Rock was a favorite perch for observers to draw and photograph the town below; the sequence of observations beginning in 1849 and running until the early twentieth century is like time-lapse photography, revealing the city's changes in slow motion. These visual materials are at the Lynn Historical Society.

60. Lewis and Newhall, *History*, I, 591–592; *The City Hall of Lynn . . . 1867* (Lynn, 1869), pp. 1–2.

61. *City Hall*, pp. 35, 41.

62. *Reporter*, Aug. 14, 1869.

63. *City Hall*, pp. 80, 96.

64. Ibid., pp. 102.

65. Cyrus M. Tracy, "Poem of the Day," *City Hall*, p. 66.

66. *City Hall*, pp. 56, 57.

67. Ibid., pp. 80–81; *Reporter*, Nov. 25, 1865.

Chapter 5. Workers

1. The material on the "S." family was compiled from the Massachusetts Bureau of the Statistics of Labor, *Second Annual Report*, 1871, pp. 612–616.

2. *Ritual*, Knights of St. Crispin, no date or place of publication; a copy is in the Wisconsin Historical Society.

3. The description is based on photographs in the collection of the Lynn Historical Society.

4. Bureau of Labor, *Second Annual Report*, 1871, p. 614.

5. Johnson, *Sketches*, p. 20.

6. See Appendixes B and C for explanations of the methods in compiling Table 3; factory workers born in New Hampshire and Maine accounted for 22 of the 23 percentage points in the "New England" category.

7. The estimate that half the Massachusetts-born came from communi-

tïes outside Lynn is based on nativity statistics of all men over fourteen in Lynn in 1875; 57 percent were Massachusetts-born, and Lynn natives accounted for 31 of these percentage points, while persons born elsewhere in Massachusetts made up the remaining 26 points; the figures are from Wright, *Census, 1875,* I, 351.

8. The Northwood, N. H., census manuscripts showed the number of shoemakers increasing from 156 in 1850 to 225 in 1860 and declining to 152 in 1870. The manuscripts in nearby Pittsfield showed an identical pattern. These figures reveal a clear shift in the shoe work force from rural to urban centers, but they do not trace individual movement: only a costly and enormously time-consuming trace of tens of thousands of individuals in the census manuscripts of New England could demonstrate beyond statistical doubt the connections between rural residents and factory personnel. For the present study, neither funds nor time was available; however, it is very likely that such a name check would only add additional evidence to the pattern already established by other sources, all of which converge to support the conclusion that substantial numbers of outworkers migrated to Lynn factories.

9. The nativity of the Lynn population in 1875 is in Wright, *Census, 1875,* I, 351.

10. *Reporter*, Feb. 28, 1863; Cook, *Factory Reform*, pp. 18–19; city physician, "Report," *City Docs.*, 1866, p. 28.

11. Handlin, *Boston's Immigrants,* pp. 38, 53.

12. The census manuscripts are vivid indicators of the Irish influx into the city and their concentration in nearly all-Irish neighborhoods; though the Irish contributed less than one-fifth of the labor force in the local shoe industry in 1870 (see Table 3), there were three or four Irish names among the sixteen officers of the Crispin lodge in 1875, *Transcript*, Jan. 30, 1875, and one of the two Lynn delegates to the national convention in 1872 was clearly Irish, Knights of St. Crispin, *Proceedings* (New York, 1872), 23.

13. The increasing proportion of Canadian immigrants was recorded in successive census reports; for 1875: Wright *Census, 1875,* I, 275–276; for 1880: U.S., Tenth Census, I, 885; for 1885: Wright, *Census, 1885,* I, pt. 2, pp. 126–127. By 1885 there were 2049 Irish immigrants in Lynn and 1538 Canadians.

14. Wright, *Census, 1885,* I, pt. 2, pp. 128–129.

15. *Reporter*, March 11, Aug. 26, 1868, Oct. 25, 1871.

16. Bureau of Labor, *Annual Reports* for 1871, pp. 93–94, and 1873, pp. 304–306; monthly shoe output was compiled from the *Reporter* and the *Transcript*, 1868–1880.

17. U.S., Tenth Census, XX, 14. The quote applies to the state shoe industry as a whole; it was taken from information solicited by the Census Bureau among people familiar with the industry.

18. City marshal, "Reports," *City Docs.*, 1861, p. 40; 1875, pp. 1–3; and 1878, p. 16.

19. The graph was compiled from the city marshals' "Reports," *City Docs.*, 1857–1880.

20. Monthly lodgings 1871–1878 are reported in the city marshal's "Report," *City Docs.*, 1878, p. 13; production statistics for the first six months of 1872 and 1873 are in the *Reporter*, Jan. 17, 1874, and the remaining months are filled in from the *Transcript*, Aug. to Dec., 1873.

21. Ray Ginger, "Labor in a Massachusetts Cotton Mill, 1853–1860," *Business History Review*, 28 (March 1954), 67–91, makes the glaring mistake of concluding that the disappearance of a name from the payrolls of one textile corporation marked the disappearance of that person from the ranks of "permanent" factory employment. There were, of course, other mills, other industries, and other towns ready to rehire.

22. Thernstrom, *The Other Bostonians: Poverty and Progress in the American Metropolis, 1880–1970* (Cambridge, Mass., Harvard University Press, 1973), Tables 9.1, 9.2, pp. 222, 226, points out that high levels of migration were a consistent American pattern even before the Industrial Revolution, a fact which may have increased the elasticity of the labor supply, offset labor scarcity, and perhaps fostered industrialization. At any rate, the existence of laborers in the condition of movable goods in the marketplace is a precondition for successful industrialization.

23. John Commons, "American Shoemakers," pp. 39–84; Carl Bücher, *Industrial Evolution*, orig. pub., 1893, trans. into English in 1901, reprinted by A. M. Kelley in 1968; George Unwin, *Industrial Organization in the Sixteenth and Seventeenth Centuries*.

24. Commons, "American Shoemakers," pp. 73–74.

25. Lescohier, "Knights of St. Crispin," pp. 19–24; John Commons, et al., *History of Labour in the United States* (New York, 1966), II, 78, orig. pub. in 1918; Hazard, *Shoe Industry*, pp. 144–156; A. E. Galster, *The Labor Movement in the Shoe Industry with Special Reference to Philadelphia* (New York, 1924), passim; Norman Ware, *The Labor Movement in the United States 1860–1865; A Study in Democracy* (New York, D. Appleton & Company, 1929), p. 20; David Montgomery has seen through the green hands theory and has, indeed, departed from the entire Commons' approach to nineteenth-century labor history in *Beyond Equality*, p. 154, and passim; so has Gregory Kealey, "Artisans Respond to Industrialism: Shoemakers, Shoe Factories and the KOSC in Toronto," *Historical Papers* (1973), pp. 137–157.

26. John P. Hall, "The Knights of St. Crispin in Massachusetts, 1869–1978," *Journal of Economic History*, 18 (June 1958), 161–165.

27. The information on Crispin occupations incorporates a correction for the census error in listing ward 4 occupations; see Appendix C for an explanation of the ward 4 factor. The raw data from the manuscripts

showed 491 "works in shoe factory," 475 ordinary shoemakers, 3 cutters, and 13 in miscellaneous categories. To correct for the error, a factor of 263 was shifted from the nonfactory to the factory category, so that there were 754 factory Crispins in a total of 982 for whom there was occupational information. This proportion of three-quarters is a slight understatement of the true proportion of factory workers, since it was not possible to correct the ward 4 error for Crispins who had been present in 1860.

28. The estimate of one-half of the factory employees enrolled in the KOSC is based on the known minimum of 750 factory workers in Unity Lodge in 1870, plus an estimate of 400–500 in Mutual Lodge, which would total about half the 2345 factory workers in the city.

29. These figures are not samples, but direct total population counts.

30. *Little Giant,* Jan. 15, 1870; Galster, *The Labor Movement in the Shoe Industry*, pp. 105–108; E. F. Wetherell, *After the Battle, or a Lesson from the Lynn Strike* (Lynn, 1903), passim.

31. See Table 4 for figures on property holdings.

32. *Reporter,* Jan. 30, 1878, compares wages of different operations and shows lasting somewhere in the middle.

33. Tabulations for birthplace and length of residence in Lynn based on U.S. Eighth and Ninth Census manuscripts for Lynn, 1860 and 1870.

34. Lescohier, "Knights of St. Crispin," pp. 19–24.

Chapter 6. The Poor and the Less Poor

1. Concerning wealth, the richest man in 1860 was Republican congressman John B. Alley, who was worth a quarter of a million dollars, according to the property listings in the census manuscripts. Ten years later the richest man was Simon Bubier, shoe manufacturer and Republican mayor, who was listed at half a million. Concerning poverty, the 1860 census listed 1518 propertyless shoeworkers (nearly all of whom lacked sufficient income), while the 1870 census listed 2680 propertyless shoeworkers.

2. The first quote is from an editorial defending the factory system in the *Transcript,* Dec. 20, 1879; the second is from an anonymous critic in Mass. Bureau of Labor, *Fourth Annual Report*, 1873, p. 306.

3. Carroll Wright's "The Factory as an Element in Civilization," orig. pub. in the *Journal of Social Science*, 16 (December 1882), 101–126, can be found more conveniently located in Sigmund Diamond, ed., *The Nation Transformed* (New York, George Braziller, 1963), pp. 42–54; Wendell Phillips' view was presented in a Dec. 7, 1871, speech and pub. in John Swinton, *Striking for Life* (New York, 1894), which has been reprinted

4. See the section on "Moral Police" in Chap. 4 for the controversial views of the Rev. Mr. Cook.

5. Andrew Carnegie, "Wealth," orig. pub. in 1889 and reprinted in *The*

Gospel of Wealth, ed. E. C. Kirkland (Cambridge, Mass., Harvard University Press, 1962).

6. Apparently, $500 was the rock-bottom price for a new house at mid-century; the extensive survey of Lynn published in Lemuel Shattuck, *Report of a General Plan . . . ,* p. 509, said workers' homes cost from $500 to $1200; Edgar W. Martin, *The Standard of Living in 1860* (Chicago, Univ. of Chicago Press, 1942), p. 423, cites plans from Godey's *Lady Book* for a 2-story, 6-room cottage costing $550.

7. *Transcript,* Jan. 3, Jan. 10, 1880.

8. See Appendix B for a detailed description of research methods and Appendix C for a description of a correction of an error in the raw data from 1870.

9. The number of propertyless shoemakers increased from 1512 to 2680; the number with a competence increased from 644 to 783. See Appendix A, Table 8, for the increase in resident male employment from 2569 to 3737.

10. This process of gradual accumulation is carefully dissected in Stephan Thernstrom's *Poverty and Progress,* pp. 136, 160–163.

11. The gain in 139 propertied shoemakers was exceeded by a gain of 182 manufacturers between 1860 and 1870. The long quote is from the same Bureau of Labor testimony that is quoted at the beginning of the chapter, *Fourth Annual Report,* 1873, p. 306.

12. Ibid., *Seventh Annual Report,* 1876, pp. 123–124.

13. Ibid., *Sixth Annual Report,* 1875, pp. 240–252, contained results of an income survey which put the shoemaker average at $536, but this survey was less extensive than the one taken in 1876, so its results have been discounted.

14. U.S., Eighth Census manuscripts, Lynn Statistics of Industry.

15. Mass. Bureau of Labor, *Sixth Annual Report,* 1875, pp. 446–449.

16. U.S. Census Bureau, *Historical Stastistics of the U.S.: Colonial Times to 1957* (Washington D.C., 1960), p. 127.

17. Bureau of Labor, *Seventh Annual Report,* 1876, pp. 123–124, gives figures for Essex County, and, as in the case of male shoeworkers, these have been used for women shoeworkers in Lynn; the income information for 1850 is in Shattuck, *Report,* p. 509.

18. Wright, *Census, 1875,* II, 391, 611.

19. Statistics on family and marital status for 1870 are an actual count from the U.S., Ninth Census manuscripts; statistics for 1850 based on a sample population of one quarter of the male shoeworkers listed in the by Greenwood Press (Westport, Conn., 1970), p. 390.
U.S., Seventh Census manuscripts.

20. See Appendix B for a discussion of research methods used in compiling Table 5. Thernstrom has presented a highly useful set of occupa-

tional categories for historical researchers in *Other Bostonians,* Appendix B, pp. 289–302, though a few of his occupations could just as reasonably be listed elsewhere: e.g., foremen and self-employed artisans could be listed as skilled blue-collar workers, rather than as low white-collar, which is what Thernstrom has done. Aside from these minor differences, the categories "manual" and "nonmanual" in Table 5 duplicate Thernstrom's division between "blue collar" and "white collar."

21. The numbers of people in manual occupations outside shoemaking are taken from an occupational census of Lynn performed in 1875 and published in Wright, *Census, 1875,* II, 500. For purposes of comparison, it is assumed that occupational totals in 1875 are similar to the totals in 1870 because the depression would have prevented any marked increase in the number employed.

22. The numbers in nonmanual occupations are taken by direct count from the census manuscripts of 1870. The numerical totals are: 96 ex-shoemakers among 395 manufacturers; 78 among 600 shopkeepers; 68 among 508 clerical workers; 13 among 172 professionals and officials.

23. The 1880 figure of 20 percent shoemaker mobility into nonmanual occupations may overstate the actual percentage, since it is based on the city directory of 1880 rather than the census, and since city directories normally had a bias toward the people in more secure jobs, which would favor nonmanual over manual occupations.

24. To obtain an estimate of the number of ordinary shoemakers who went into nonmanual occupations, two groups of extraordinary shoe-makers must be set aside: cutters and those with nonmanual fathers. Among the 257 ex-shoemaker recruits to nonmanual occupations in 1870, 76 were cutters and at least 41 had nonmanual fathers. Since many cutters had nonmanual fathers, these groups overlap. If we estimate that 20 shoe-makers with nonmanual fathers were cutters, then the size of the ordinary shoemaker group is $257 - (76 + 41 - 20) = 160$. Thus 160 ordinary shoemakers among 1626 shoemakers studied made the jump from manual to nonmanual occupations.

25. The city directories for 1860 and 1871 list a slight increase of shoe manufacturers (from 177 to 196) but an enormous gain in the number of accessory manufacturers (28–139).

26. For explorations of the factors affecting social mobility see Joseph Kahl, *The American Class Structure* (New York, 1957), pp. 253–262; Natalie Rogoff, *Recent Trends in Occupational Mobility* (Glencoe, Ill., 1953), pp. 31–32.

27. The estimate of the amount of mobility was arrived at as follows: of the 978 individuals who remained from 1860 to 1880, 569 of them ended as shoemakers, and of these, 482 were also shoemakers in 1870. Thus it would appear from the census that about half the original group

were permanent shoemakers. However, if the city directories had been used for the intercensus years, they would have shown a number of cases where a shoemaker entered another occupation but returned to shoemaking within a few years. Consequently, the number of permanent shoemakers would have declined to less than one-half.

What about the size of the group of permanent manual laborers? Beginning at nearly 100 percent (a tiny few sons of shoemakers in 1860 were in nonmanual jobs, reducing the percentage below 100), the percentage declined to 83 percent in 1870 and declined slightly to 78 percent in 1880 (see Table 5). Thus the overwhelming majority of shoemakers appear to have remained manual workers. However, once again the appearance of long-run stability masks a great deal of temporary mobility. Some of the temporary mobility was recorded by the census, but it was only the tip of the iceberg, since many people who left manual occupations and returned in a year or two were not recorded as mobile in the census.

To calculate the minimum amount of shoemaker mobility to nonmanual occupations, we begin with a base of about one-fifth over the twenty years. Second, we add the group revealed by the census who became nonmanual but returned to a manual occupation by 1880, increasing the number of men with nonmanual experience from 200 to 259. Third, we add the group of mobile individuals not measured by the census; that would, no doubt, increase the total to more than 300. All in all, comparing this to the 978 men remaining in 1880 yields a result of about one-third. (Since this percentage was reached in twenty years, the lifetime mobility for shoemakers and their sons would be somewhat higher.)

Thus it is worth reemphasizing two divergent points: (1) the great majority of manual workers made no permanent move into nonmanual occupations; (2) a substantial minority experienced mobility, often temporary, into nonmanual occupations.

For comparative material, see Thernstrom, *Other Bostonians,* pp. 74–75, 110; S. M. Lipset and R. Bendix, *Social Mobility in Industrial Society* (Berkeley, Calif., 1959), pp. 25–26, Table 2.1.

Chapter 7. Militants

1. Several histories of the American labor movement emphasize militancy: Louis Adamic, *Dynamite* (Gloucester, Mass., Peter Smith, 1963), rev. ed., orig. pub. 1934; R. O. Boyer and H. M. Morais, *Labor's Untold Story* (New York, United Electrical, Radio, and Machine Workers of America, 1955); Jeremy Brecher, *Strike!* (San Francisco, Straight Arrow Books, 1972); Sidney Lens, *The Labor Wars* (New York, Doubleday and Co., 1973); Samuel Yellen, *American Labor Struggles* (New York, Monad Press, 1974), orig. pub. 1936.

2. The most significant exceptions are southern sharecroppers and first generation peasant immigrants.

3. Montgomery, *Beyond Equality*, p. 14, calculates the number of paid-up Crispins in Massachusetts at 8,400, based on the income of the Grand Lodge, a figure which contrasts sharply with the 40,000 claimed by Crispin spokesmen.

4. In the nation, the U.S., Ninth Census, III, 591, listed 160,000 male boot and shoemakers; subtracting an estimated 60,000 cobblers, the remaining 100,000 shoeworkers in manufacturing were the potential Crispin pool; that was also about the size of the pool reported in the U.S., Tenth Census, II, 9, which tallied 104,021 shoemakers in manufacturing. One student of the Crispins has pared down national membership claims to a reasonable estimate of 50,000, or half the shoemakers in manufacturing and about one-third of the total in the country—see Lescohier, "Knights of St. Crispin," p. 8.

5. Not all the men in the Unity Lodge dues book were enrolled at the same time, but the peak membership came between 1870 and 1872, and it stood well over 1000 shoemakers of all types; combining this with the several hundred members of KOSC Mutual Lodge, the total was very likely half or more of the 3737 male shoemakers in the city. The dues book of Unity Lodge is incorporated in the Lasters' Protective Union dues book and is in Harvard's Baker Library.

6. Montgomery, *Beyond Equality*, p. 140.

7. I am indebted to David Montgomery for highlighting this fact.

8. Bureau of Labor, *Second Annual Report*, 1871, p. 615.

9. *Transcript*, Aug. 17, 1872.

10. *Reporter*, July 31, Dec. 20, 1869, Sept. 2, 1871; Eleanor Flexnor, *Century of Struggle* (New York, Atheneum, 1970), p. 140.

11. The basic works of the Wisconsin School on shoemakers have been discussed in the section of "Who Were the Knights of St. Crispin?" in Chap. 5.

12. The same is true of the Knights of Labor, which was seen in Massachusetts as a revival of Crispinism; Frank Foster, "Shoemakers in the Movement," *The Labor Movement: The Problem of Today*, ed. George E. McNeill (Boston, 1887), p. 212.

13. "American Shoemakers," passim.

14. Commons, *History of Labour*, I, 6; David Saposs continues the Commons' theme in the first two chapters of the same volume, especially pp. 28–30.

15. Commons, "American Shoemakers," reprinted in his *Labor and Administration*, p. 259.

16. Commons, *Myself* (New York, The Macmillan Co., 1934), p. 169;

I am indebted to Phillip Singerman for this reference and for insight into the political nature of Commons' work. In an unpublished paper "John R. Commons: Application of the Pragmatic Method," 1972, Singerman argues that Commons' proposals for resolving strife would tend to "stabilize the society and reinforce the power and privilege of certain groups." For a more developed version of this interpretation of the Progressive movement, see James Weinstein, *The Corporate Ideal in the Liberal State: 1900–1918* (Boston, 1968), p. xiii, and passim. The best exposition of the Progressive effort at conservative reform written by a Progressive is Herbert Croly's *The Promise of American Life,* orig. pub. 1909, repub. by E. P. Dutton (New York, 1963), especially pp. 131, 357–368, 385–398.

17. Commons, "Economists and Class Partnership," *Labor and Administration,* pp. 51–70; the quotes are on pp. 67 and 59.

18. James Madison, *The Federalist,* No. 10 (New York, Random House, 1937), p. 56.

19. Commons, *Labor and Administration,* pp. 20–22, chap. 5; Morton White, *Social Thought in America: The Revolt against Formalism* (Boston, Beacon Press, 1947), provides a useful analysis of the Progressive mind.

20. Commons' reform activities are revealed in his *Labor and Administration,* chaps. 13, 21, and 23.

21. Testimony of L. C. Legro, treasurer of the Lynn Crispin local, and of two other anonymous shoeworkers in the Bureau of Labor, *Second Annual Report,* 1871, pp. 95–98.

22. Bureau of Labor, *Second Annual Report,* 1871, pp. 95–98; Bureau of Labor, *Eighth Annual Report,* 1877, p. 30.

23. Montgomery, *Beyond Equality,* pp. 143–144, describes the method of posting wage rates.

24. *Transcript,* Aug. 10, Aug. 17, 1872.

25. Bureau of Labor, *Eighth Annual Report,* 1877, p. 40; Transcript Aug. 24, 1872.

26. *Transcript,* Jan. 20. 1875; *Reporter,* Jan. 1, Jan. 15, Jan. 19, Feb. 2, April 12, 1876.

27. An excellent monograph on the strikes of 1877 is Robert Bruce, *1877: Year of Violence* (Indianapolis, Bobbs-Merrill, 1959); *Reporter,* July 25, 1877; *Vindicator,* Dec. 27, Dec. 29, 1877.

28. *Reporter,* Jan. 9, Jan. 16, Feb. 2, Feb. 13, Feb. 16, 1878.

29. *Reporter,* Feb. 2, Feb. 16, 1878

30. Letter in the *Reporter,* March 6, 1878.

31. The phrase "underpaid labor aristocrat" was coined by David Montgomery; it accords well with the figures on lasters' incomes in Essex County, reported by the Bureau of Labor, *Seventh Annual Report,* 1876,

pp. 123–124, which puts it at $436; this was only slightly above the $420 median for all Essex county shoemakers and well below what a skilled hand workman might well expect to earn.

32. J. H. M. Laslett, *Labor and the Left: A Study of Socialist and Radical Influences in the American Labor Movement, 1881–1924* (New York, Basic Books, 1970), pp. 55–56; 646 members of the LPU were recorded in a dues book from 1878 to 1882, which is now in Harvard's Baker Library; some of the names overlapped with the Crispin Unity Lodge, whose members were enrolled in the same book; the *Knight of Labor* claimed 1200 LPU members; the founding of the LPU under Crispin auspices is mentioned in the *Reporter*, March 9, 1878, and the preamble to the Lasters' constitution was virtually identical to the Crispins'; *Knight of Labor*, Aug. 22, 1885, praised the LPU.

33. The membership claims are made in the *Knight of Labor*, June 25, July 11, Aug. 22, 1885; the labor force for 1885 is estimated from data in the U.S., Tenth Census, 1880, XVIII, 249, which showed 12,420 men and women in Lynn's labor force, and the U.S., Eleventh Census, 1890, V, 315, which showed over 20,000, p. 318.

34. *Knight of Labor*, July 18, July 25, Aug. 1, 1885, May 1, 1886.

35. *Knight of Labor*, Sept. 5, 1885; the Irish influence is indicated in Terence Powderly's *The Path I Trod* (New York, 1940), and in Wright, *Census, 1885*, I, pt. 2, pp. 128–129. It is interesting that Big Bill Haywood of the IWW got his "first lessons in unionism" from an Irish Knight; see Haywood's *Autobiography* (New York, International Publishers, 1929), 1969 ed., pp. 30–31.

36. *Knight of Labor*, June 5, June 12, Aug. 29, 1885.

37. *Knight of Labor*, June 12, 1880; *Item*, March 26, April 5, 1886.

38. The only run of the *Awl*, 1844–1845, is at the Lynn Historical Society, as are a few scattered copies of the *Little Giant*, 1870; the *Vindicator*, 1878, and the *Knight of Labor*, 1885–1886, are at the Lynn Public Library; no copies of the *New England Mechanic* have survived.

39. Norman Ware displays a respect for the democratic sensibilities of the Knights of Labor but criticizes them as being full of hot air, calling Powderly a "wind-bag" in *Labor Movement*, p. xvi; Gerald Grob goes further into the clouds of imaginative nonsense to dismiss the National Labor Union and the Knights of Labor as anachronisms "vainly struggling to hold back the onrushing tide" of industrialism; see Grob, *Workers and Utopia: A Study of Ideological Conflict in the American Labor Movement* (Evanston, Northwestern University Press, 1961), p. 188.

Chapter 8. Politicians

1. See the section on "The Great Strike" in chap. 3 for background information.

2. See "The Politics of Capital" in chap. 4 for a discussion of the election of 1860.

3. Hiram N. Breed, quoted in the *Reporter*, Jan. 11, 1862; S. P. Cummings, quoted in the *Transcript*, Aug. 3, 1872; *Knight of Labor*, Aug. 8, 1885.

4. This theme is also developed in "The Politics of Capital" and "The Mark of Business Rule" in chap. 4.

5. The Crispin influence in the Labor Reform movement is succinctly described by Montgomery, *Beyond Equality*, pp. 369–370; state election returns can be found in the *Reporter*, Sept. 1, 1869, Nov. 12, 1870.

6. Biographical information on Sanderson is in the *Reporter*, Dec. 14, 1878.

7. Montgomery, *Beyond Equality*, offers convincing documentation for the overlap of the two spheres of labor activity in the 1860s and 1870s; see especially his discussion of the National Labor Union, pp. 176, 194–195; two writers in the Commons' tradition who helped create this false dichotomy are John Andrews, in Commons, et al., *History of Labour*, II, 157, and Gerald Grob, *Workers and Utopia*, p. 31. Commons himself was less inclined to emphasize this distinction and, instead, often pointed to the political activities of trade unionists in seeking protective legislation; cf. Commons, "American Shoemakers," in *Labor and Administration*, p. 259.

8. The resolutions were published in the *Reporter*, Oct. 27, 1869.

9. *Reporter*, Oct. 27, Sept. 1, 1869; *Proceedings of the International Grand Lodge of the Knights of St. Crispin*, Third Annual Convention, 1870, pp. 23–24.

10. Benjamin F. Butler, *Butler's Book* (Boston, 1892), pp. 967, 922; see Irwin Unger, *The Greenback Era: A Social and Political History of American Finance, 1865–1879* (Princeton, N.J., 1964), pp. 378–380, for a discussion of the national Greenback-Labor movement.

11. These events are described in the *Reporter*, Feb. 13, 1878.

12. Sanderson's role in the strike of 1878 was mentioned in the *Vindicator*, Feb. 23, 1878; the subsequent election campaign was covered in the December 1878 issues of the *Transcript*; the vote count was not printed until the next year, *Transcript*, Dec. 13, 1879.

13. *Transcript*, Jan. 11. 1879.

14. The controversy over the anniversary celebration appeared in the *Transcript*, June 21, 1879; the quote is from the issue of June 28, 1879.

15. *Transcript*, Jan. 25, 1879.

16. For a discussion of George Hood and the controversy over the adoption of a city charter see "The Tree of Liberty" in chap. 2; the thoughts of a Workingman on elections were in the *Reporter*, Sept. 4, 1878.

17. Proceedings of the national convention of the Knights of St. Cris-

pin, 1878, are excerpted in Lescohier, "The Knights of St. Crispin," pp. 58–59; P. Foner, *History of the Labor Movement,* I, 486, claims that labor voters did not necessarily agree with the anticommunist statements sometimes issued by local Greenback-Labor clubs.

18. The class position of Workingmen's candidates is analyzed later in this chapter in "Politics as a Safety Valve."

19. *Reporter,* May 8, 1878.

20. This fatuous flirtation with Protestant clergymen is described in the *Reporter,* Jan. 16, 1878.

21. Homeownership is discussed in chap. 6, "Wealth and Poverty"; the tax rate and the vote count are in the *Transcript,* Nov. 29, Dec. 6, Dec. 13, 1879. Apart from the solid reelection victory of the Workingmen (2936 to 1932) amid charges that the city was being run "Tammany-style," the election of 1879 was historically significant because women got the vote for the first time; however, they did not get a whole vote, because they were excluded from the general election and only allowed to participate in the balloting for school committee.

22. Lovering's career information comes from the *Biographical Directory of the American Congress, 1774–1961* (Washington, D.C., 1961), p. 1237, and Henry Fenno, *Our Police* (Lynn, 1895), p 84; Fenno's book covered important segments of Lynn's political history, as well as the police department.

23. *Knight of Labor,* Nov. 21, 1885; membership claims reached a peak of 10,000 in the *Knight,* July 11 and Aug. 22, 1885; even discounting half, the remaining 5,000 would about equal the number of people who normally voted in local elections; *Knight of Labor,* Dec. 18, 1885, reported the victory.

24. Ibid., Dec. 12, 1885.

25. Friedrich Engels, *The Condition of the Working Class in England,* preface to the American edition of 1887, reprinted by Stanford University Press, ed. W. O. Henderson and W. H. Chaloner (Stanford, Calif., 1958), pp. 354, 355–358.

26. *Transcript,* Dec. 13, 1889; Fenno, *Our Police,* p. 94.

27. Fenno, *Our Police,* 132; *Transcript,* Dec. 5, Dec. 12, 1890.

28. Fenno, *Our Police,* 97, 132.

29. *Weekly Times,* Nov. 6, 1896.

30. *Knight of Labor,* Oct. 9, 1886.

31. Ibid., May 29, June 5, 1886.

32. Independent Labor party: *Transcript,* Dec. 13, 1889; People's party: *Transcript,* Nov. 11, Dec. 15, 1892, Dec. 14, 1894; Socialist Labor party: *Transcript,* Dec. 14, 1894; Social Democracy (Socialist party): *Evening News,* Nov. 7, 1900.

33. The relation between socialism and the labor movement in the shoe industry is covered in detail by Henry Bedford, *Socialism and the Workers*

in Massachusetts 1886–1912 (Amherst, Mass., University of Massachusetts Press, 1966), in J. H. M. Laslett, *Labor and the Left,* esp. pp. 56–66. Although Laslett's analytical approach produced far more insight than Bedford's narrative, his chapter on "DeLeonite Socialism and the Irish Shoe Workers of New England" suffers from two faults: (1) he overstates the Irish and understates the Yankee influence in the industry; and (2) since he had to rely on the Commons writers, particularly Hazard and Lescohier, for his information on the economic history of the shoe industry, and since they are poor sources on the impact of the factory system and the Knights of St. Crispin, Laslett is incorrect about the timing and the consequences, of the conversion to factory methods. Factories swept through the industry in the decade before the depression of the 1870s, yet socialist influences appeared 15 to 20 years later. Therefore he is wrong in asserting that socialism was the direct response of artisans to the factory system. The first generation of ex-artisan factory workers protested vehemently, but their protests through the Knights of St. Crispin and the Knights of Labor did not take a socialist form. The Boot and Shoe Workers Union, formed in 1894, was a socialist organization, but it represented something other than the immediate response of skilled workers to the experience of proletarianization; it represented a new group of factory workers who had gone beyond the artisan radicalism of the first factory generation to a deeper analysis of the political, not just the economic, sources of their deteriorating condition. Still, despite Laslett's faults, his work on the subject is far better than the writings of the Commons' school and should be consulted for its wealth of information and thought-provoking analysis.

34. Haverhill is covered in Bedford, *Socialism and the Workers,* chap. 3, and Laslett, *Labor and the Left,* p. 74; Brockton is covered in Bedford, chap. 4; Lynn is covered in Laslett, pp. 70, 82–84; see also the rather spotty study of the *Labor Movement in the Shoe Industry* by A. E. Galster.

35. Laslett, ibid., p. 83.

36. The term "ex-worker" is my own counterpart of Robert Dahl's excessively florid "ex-plebes." The transition in Lynn politics from business to ex-worker leadership paralleled the same process described by Dahl in his study of New Haven, though it occurred slightly earlier in Lynn (1880s rather than the 1890s); Dahl, *Who Governs: Democracy and Power in an American City* (New Haven, Conn., Yale Press, 1961), pp. 25–51.

37. Sanderson's capsule biography is in the *Reporter,* Dec. 14, 1878.

38. The biographies were compiled by Fenno, *Our Police,* pp. 84, 111.

39. The occupational pattern of the city council in 1885 did not differ substantially from the pattern in 1886, 1880, or 1878, though it differed greatly from the city council's elected in the 1860s when shoe manufacturers were much more in evidence; for example, in 1865, twelve of the thirty members were shoe manufacturers.

40. David Lockwood's study of *The Blackcoated Worker* (London, Allen and Unwin, 1958), pp. 208–13, squeezes class analysis into the too narrow confines of one social stratum in an effort to explain the consciousness of clerks; it would be an exercise in futility to follow the suggestion of this otherwise excellent study and try to explain the mentality of every social stratum and substratum in terms of class position.

41. Mass. Bureau of Labor, *Second Annual Report,* 1871, pp. 600–618; see Table 4 for the citations on property holdings.

42. Lipset and Bendix, *Social Mobility in Industrial Society,* pp. 76–77, chap. 3, passim.

43. *Poverty and Progress,* pp. 269, 270, 160.

44. Ibid, p. 181; in his recent work on Boston, Thernstrom has grown considerably more cautious about the link between mobility and consensus, recognizing that "nothing like an adequate basis for testing it is available at the present time"; *Other Bostonians,* p. 258.

Conclusion: Equal Rights and Beyond

1. Berthoff, *An Unsettled People,* Pt. One, approaches colonial history from the point of view of the limits on wealth.

2. Eugene Genovese has written extensively on this subject; see his *Political Economy of Slavery* (New York, Vintage, 1965), *The World the Slaveholders Made* (New York, Pantheon, 1969), and *Roll, Jordan, Roll* (New York, Pantheon, 1974).

3. Peter Laslett employs the concept of a "one-class" society in *The World We Have Lost* (New York, Charles Scribner's Sons, 1965); although his contention that property distinctions were not among the fundamental facts of English society in 1700 is unconvincing and the "one-class" concept is unenlightening, he offers a superlative exposition of the preindustrial household.

4. This interpretation harks back to the Progressive historians' view of the Civil War as an event causally linked to the rise of industrial capitalism; see Charles and Mary Beard, *The Rise of American Civilization* (New York, Macmillan Co., 1930); however, two corollaries of the Progressive interpretation are *not* being advanced here: (1) there is little justification for describing the Civil War as a decisive cause of industrialization—see the debate over this issue in Ralph Andreono, ed., *Economic Impact of the American Civil War* (Cambridge, Mass., Schenkman Publishing Co., 1967); (2) there is no necessary link between the immediate economic aims of Northern industrialists and the outbreak of war in 1861, a point Moore makes in chap. 3 of *Social Origins.*

5. The following Massachusetts communities showed less labor activism than Lynn; Chicopee: Schlakman, *Economic History of a Factory*

Town; Holyoke: Green, *Holyoke*; Newburyport: Thernstrom, *Poverty and Progress*; Springfield: Michael Frisch, *Town into City: Springfield, Massachusetts, and the Meaning of Community 1840–1880* (Cambridge, Mass., 1972).

6. Towns where labor's influence equaled Lynn are discussed by Gutman, "Industrial Workers Struggle for Power"; Gerd Korman, *Industrialization, Immigrants, Americanizers* (Madison, State Historical Society of Wisconsin, 1967), a study of Milwaukee; Henry David, *The Haymarket Affair* (New York, Russell and Russell, 1958), 2nd ed., gives a glimpse of labor's influence in late nineteenth-century Chicago.

7. "Industrial Workers Struggle for Power," passim. For a thought-provoking comparison between Lynn and Fall River, see John Cumbler, "Continuity and Disruption: Working Class Community in Lynn and Fall River, 1880–1950," unpub. diss. (Univ. of Michigan, 1974), and by the same author, "Labor, Capital, and Community: The Struggle for Power," *Labor History*, 15 (Summer 1974), 395–415.

8. David Potter, *People of Plenty* (Chicago, Univ. of Chicago Press, 1954); Ellen von Nardroff, "The American Frontier as a Safety Valve," in *The Frontier Thesis: Valid Interpretation of American History?* ed. Ray Billington (New York, 1966), pp. 51–62; Fred Shannon's criticism of Turner, "A Post-Mortem on the Labor-Safety-Valve Theory," is in the same volume, pp. 41–50; Thernstrom, *Poverty and Progress*.

9. The argument is put forth by Thernstrom in "Working Class Social Mobility in Industrial America," a paper delivered at the Anglo-American Colloquium of the Society of Labor History, June 1968; it is also available as "Socialism and Social Mobility," in *Failure of a Dream? Essays in the History of American Socialism*, Peter Laslett and S. M. Lipset, eds. (New York, 1974), pp. 509–525.

10. Between 1860 and 1870, 47 percent of all shoeworkers and their sons over ten disappeared from Lynn (1357 of 2877).

11. See Big Bill Haywood's *Autobiography*, and William Z. Foster, *American Trade Unionism* (New York, International Publishers, 1947), chap. 1.

12. Merle Curti, *The Making of an American Community* (Stanford, Calif., 1959).

13. Many of the results of mobility studies are summarized by Thernstrom, *Other Bostonians*, pp. 232–261.

14. The debate opened with Lipset's and Bendix's *Social Mobility in Industrial Society*, pp. 11–75, which was answered by Thernstrom, *Poverty and Progress*, pp.181–182; Lipset and Thernstrom continued the discussion in *Failure of a Dream?* ed. Lipset and Laslett, pp. 509–552.

15. Gompers, *Seventy Years of Life and Labor: An Autobiography*, p. 383.

16. Bell, *Marxian Socialism*, p. 5; see also the concluding chapter of

Marc Karson, *American Labor Unions and Politics, 1900–1918* (Carbondale, Ill., 1958).

17. Grob, *Workers and Utopia,* pp. 188–189.

18. Perlman, *Theory of the Labor Movement* (New York, 1928), passim.

INDEX

Industrial Workers of the World, 183, 214, 231
Inequality, 3, 5, 54–55, 61; and factory system, 133–134; and mobility, 167; and radicalism, 241. *See also* Equality
International Workingmen's Association, 175
Irish: in Democratic party, 208; in labor movement, 137–138, 190, 232; in Newburyport, Mass., 218
Iron-clad oath, 173, 187

Jacksonian democracy, 236
Johnson, David N., 51, 52, 53, 135; on factory system, 93, 96
Journeymen Cordwainer's Society, *see* Mutual Benefit Society of Journeymen Cordwainers

Knight of Labor, 189, 190, 191, 195, 205, 227
Knights of Labor: decline, 208; influence in politics, 206; in Lynn, 176, 189–193; in shoe industry, 212; and radicalism, 210–211
Knights of St. Crispin, 114, 129–130, 175–178, 227; condemns violence, 200; membership, 145–147; militancy, 184; and police, 202; in politics, 195, 197–198; 203; Unity Lodge, 175

Labor: "aristocracy," 186; division of, 27, 29, 92–93; migration, 135–137, 142; productivity, 75, 77, 92, 93, 94, 224; recruitment, 74–75, 134–139
Labor movement: among artisans, 62–63; after Civil War, 238–239; and class consciousness, 233–234; Female Society of Lynn, 62; Ladies Association of Binders and Stitchers (1860), 88; Ladies Stitching Association (1880s), 189; Lynn Mechanics Association (1859–1860), 79, 88, 177; and social mobility, 216; Working Women's Associates (1871), 178. *See also* Knights of Labor; Knights of St. Crispin
Labor Reform party, 196–198
LaFollette, Robert, 18
Larcom, Lucy, 47

La Rochefoucauld, Duc de, 15
Lasters, 189, 212, 213
Legro, L. C., 185
Lescohier, Don, 144, 147, 180
Lewis, Alonzo, 22, 23, 82
Liberalism, 183, 184
Liberty Tree, *see* Equal Rights
Lincoln, Abraham, 68
Lipset, Seymour M., 217, 218
Little Giant, 191
Living standards: artisans, 51–55; debate over, 149–159; determinants of, 156, 159; living wage, 159, 177; "opulence," 168, 172; "poverty," 167, 168–170; "prosperity," 167, 170–171; "subsistence," 167, 170. *See also* Income
Lockout, 186
Lovering, Henry B., 199, 205
Ludlow massacre, 181
Lye, Joseph, 46–47
Lynn, Mass: description of, 8, 16–17, 123–125; as microcosm of Industrial Revolution, 8; as microcosm of labor history, 176; population, 29, 53. *See also* Equal rights; Labor movement; Shoe manufacturing; Strikes

Madison, James, 13, 14, 22, 26, 183
Manufacturing, 12–13. *See also* Shoe manufacturing
Marblehead, Mass., 29, 47
Martineau, Harriet, 27
Marx, Karl, 4, 58, 181
Massachusetts Bureau of Statistics of Labor, 129, 134, 139, 156, 217
Mechanization: McKay stitcher, 92–93; rhythm of production, 93–94; sewing machine, 76–77, 78, 92. *See also* Factory
Mercantilism, 13
Militancy, 174, 194
Mills, C. Wright, 4
Minimum wage, 157
Mitchell, W. F., 117–119
Moore, Barrington, 4, 98
Montgomery, David, 4, 175, 197
Morocco Finishers, 189
Mudge, George W., 99
Mutual Benefit Society of Journeymen Cordwainers, 2, 62, 177

Socialist party, 212, 213
Society for the Promotion of Industry, Frugality, and Temperance, 36
"Storm the Fort," 3, 193
Strikes, 173; and Knights of St. Crispin, 185; strikebreaking, 187–188; of women, 62; in 1835, 62; in 1844, 64; the Great Strike of 1860, 2, 78–79, 102–103, 130, 177, 194, 227; in 1870, 184–185; in 1872, 186; in 1878, 187, 199–200, 204–205; in 1880s, 206; in 1890, 208

Tarbox, Nathaniel, 19
Tariff, 14–15
Taylor, George R., 31, 80
Temperance, 36–37
"Ten-footers," 17, 42, 135
Textile industry, 29, 73, 228–229
Thernstrom, Stephan, 218, 219, 230
Thompson, Edward P., 4
Tobin, James, 212
Tocqueville, Alexis de, 11, 67
Trade unions, see Labor movement; Knights of Labor; Knights of St. Crispin; Strikes
True Womanhood, 179
Turner, Frederick J., 54, 217, 230

Unemployment, see Floating population; Living standards
United Shoeworkers of America, 213
U.S. Commission on Industrial Relations, 183
Unwin, George, 143
Urbanization, 97–128, passim; architecture and social values, 122–128; and contradictions of capitalism, 97; fire department, 111; and industrialization, 98; political changes, 69; poor relief, 112–113; social reform, 119–120
Usher, Roland G., 103, 106–107, 109, 127

Vindicator, 191
Violence: in strike of 1860, 85–88; in strike of 1878, 187, 188, 200

Wage slavery, 158
Ware, Norman, 51, 144
Washington, George, 15, 16
Wealth: property ownership, 51–52, 149, 153. *See also* Living standards
Williams, William A., 4
Wilson, Henry, 160
Wisconsin, 183
"Wisconsin school," 65, 197
Women: in Lynn, 75, 78, 228; migratory workers, 114; in the strike of 1860, 81–83; textile operatives, 229. *See also* Feminism
Women's Union for Christian Work, 168
Working class: attitude toward social mobility, 216–217; cultural life, 190; discontent, 194; in Europe and the U.S., compared, 237; labor market, 225; political ideas, 237. *See also* Class; Class consciousness; Class conflict; Labor; Labor movement; Shoemakers
Workingmen's party (1860), 102, 103; (1878–1890), 195, 199–207, 208, 209, 215, 227
Wright, Carroll, 150

Yankees, 190, 219, 232
Yellow-dog contract, 173

HARVARD STUDIES IN URBAN HISTORY